AF235283

SOVIET ARTILLERY TRACTORS
OF WORLD WAR II

To Elizabeth

SOVIET ARTILLERY TRACTORS OF WORLD WAR II

James Kinnear

OSPREY PUBLISHING
Bloomsbury Publishing Plc
Kemp House, Chawley Park, Cumnor Hill, Oxford OX2 9PH, UK
Bloomsbury Publishing Ireland Limited,
29 Earlsfort Terrace, Dublin 2, Ireland
1385 Broadway, 5th Floor, New York, NY 10018, USA
E-mail: info@ospreypublishing.com
www.ospreypublishing.com

OSPREY is a trademark of Osprey Publishing Ltd

First published in Great Britain in 2026

A catalogue record for this book is available from the British Library

ISBN: HB 9781472872005;
eBook 9781472871978;
ePDF 9781472871985;
XML 9781472871992

26 27 28 29 30 10 9 8 7 6 5 4 3 2 1

Cover, page design and layout by Stewart Larking
Index by Alan Rutter
Printed by Repro India Ltd

Front cover: (top) A Voroshilovets towing a 280mm Br-5 tracked heavy artillery piece without disassembly into separate carriage and barrel loads. (Author's collection) (bottom) A restored to running condition Komintern artillery tractor at the Motors of War museum, Moscow. (Author's collection)
Back cover: (top–bottom) Production series (M-1937) Komsomolets artillery tractors towing 45mm M-1932 anti-tank guns through Red Square, 1940. (Author's collection) STZ-5 tractors towing 76.2mm M-1939 USV Divisional guns through Red Square, 1940. (Author's collection) The STZ-5 BM-13 in Novomoskovsk. (Author's collection) A column of captured STZ-3 and KhTZ-3 tractors in Finnish service. (Esa Muikku)
Author photograph: Author's collection.

ACKNOWLEDGEMENTS
The author would like to acknowledge the kind assistance of the owners and staff of the Museum of Russian Military History, Padikovo and the Shamansky Workshops, Mytischi, both in the Moscow region, and the Motors of War Museum in Moscow for allowing unrestricted access to restored tractors in their respective collections (and for the tea and biscuits). Thanks also go individually to Andrey Aksenov, Mikhail Baryatinsky, John Ham, Alexsei Kreshin, Alexander Morzhitsky, Esa Muikku, Felix Oganesyan, Ivan Paderin, Yuri Pasholok, Andrey Puzanov, Yevgenny Shamansky, Mikhail Svirin and Igor Zheltov for their kind assistance with material and technical clarifications. The author would also like to acknowledge the dedicated French researcher on Soviet vehicles Alain Dupouy, whose avant-garde books provided inspiration for my own interests. A man whose humanity and humour while visiting our home in Moscow many years ago will always be remembered. And with special thanks as always to my wife Elena for her translation and for her endless patience.

PICTURE CREDITS
All pictures, including those on the cover, are from the author's collections unless otherwise noted. In particular, the author would like to express his appreciation to Andrey Aksenov, John Ham, Alexei Kreshin, Alexander Koshchavtsev, Viktor Kulikov, Alexander Morzhitsky, Esa Muikku, Yuri Pasholok, Pastvu.com, Yevgeny Shamansky (Shamansky Workshops), SA-Kuva (Finnish State Archives), Mikhail Svirin, Museum of Russian Military History, Padikovo, Ilya Pereyaslavtsev, Jochen Vollert and Igor Zheltov. Artworks are by Andrey Aksenov and are credited where they appear.

RGAEh – Russian State Economic Archive (РГАЭ).
RGAKF – Russian State Archive of Cinematic and Photographic Documentation (РГАКФ).
RGVA – Russian State Military Archive (РГВА).
TsaMO RF – Central Archives of the Ministry of Defence of the Russian Federation (ЦАМО РФ).
TsGAKFF – Central State Archive of Cinematic and Photographic Documentation (ЦГАКФФ).

CONTENTS

AUTHOR'S NOTES

RUSSIAN DEFINITION OF TRACTOR AND TYAGACH

There is a subtle difference between Tractor (Трактор) and Tyagach (Тягач) in Russian terminology. A 'tractor' (traktor obshego naznachenya – general-purpose tractor) is primarily an agricultural or industrial tractor with a seat for the driver and the ability to mount attachments, but no passenger compartment or load platform. By contrast, a 'tyagach' (sometimes described as transportny-traktor-tyagach – transport tractor-artillery tractor) is designed specifically for towing artillery, and for ammunition transport purposes. A tractor could (as with the S-60, S-65, STZ/KhTZ-3) also be used as a tyagach, with such agricultural tractors being drafted into military service in large numbers in 1941. A purpose-designed tyagach with crew cab and load area (such as the STZ-5, Komintern or Voroshilovets), also described in Russian as a 'transportny-tyagach' (transport tractor) or 'gruzovoi' (transport or load) tractor, was by definition never intended for use in more utilitarian agricultural or civil engineering roles. An artillery tractor (tyagach) was intended for moving artillery (with crews and ammunition) in front line or nearby locations, while other tractors such as the S-60 and S-65 were intended primarily for moving heavier artillery further from the front line. Albeit, as the photographs in this book recount, in time of total war all such peacetime definitions were replaced by utilizing any tractor type available for any role it was powerful enough to perform.

TRACTOR DESIGNATIONS

The designation of Soviet artillery tractors varies according to source. Design bureau designations such as STZ-NATI 1TA (SKhTZ-NATI 1TA) were usually abbreviated by the production plant (to STZ-3 and KhTZ-3 in the case of the STZ-NATI 1TA) but the full STZ-NATI 1TA designation rather than the shortened plant designation continued to be used in the operator manuals and by the Red Army, perhaps reflecting the agricultural origins of the tractor. The STZ-5 2TV was however generally known in Red Army service by the shortened STZ-5 plant designation. The ChTZ-built Stalinets-60 and Stalinets-65 were likewise in official documentation referred to by their full designation, with the abbreviated S-60 and S-65 being used in service and in later historical documentation. Abbreviated names are used in the text of this book for brevity and economy of text.

PLACE NAMES

The tractors described in this book were produced in the Russian and Ukrainian Soviet Socialist Republics of the former Soviet Union, with the Soviet names of cities used throughout the book being historically correct for the time period described. Cities in Ukraine are also referred to by their Soviet wartime names rather than those adopted post-independence in 1991, hence Kharkov (Kharkiv), Odessa (Odesa), etc.

STATISTICAL DATA

Where available, data has been taken from original Red Army and manufacturing plant records, and other official documents such as acceptance trials. Though there are minor conflations even in official data, the original data available today is remarkable compared to only a few years ago.

SOVIET TRACTOR PRODUCTION PLANTS

- Altaisky Traktorny Zavod (ATZ) (Алтайский Тракторный Завод – АТЗ), Rubtsovsk: SKhTZ-3 (ATZ-3).
- Chelyabinsky Traktorny Zavod (ChTZ) (Челябинский Тракторный Завод – ЧТЗ) (1932–41): Stalinets-60, Stalinets-65, Stalinets-2.
- Gorkovsky Avtomobilny Zavod (GAZ) (Горьковский Автомобильный Завод – ГАЗ): Komsomolets, GAZ-60, GAZ-20, GAZ-22 prototypes.
- Kharkovsky Tractorny Zavod (KhTZ) (Харьковский Тракторный Завод – ХТЗ): SKhTZ-15/30 (KhTZ-1), KhTZ-3.
- Kharkovsky Parovozostroitelny Zavod (KhPZ) (Харьковский Паровозостроительный Завод – ХПЗ): Kommunar, Komintern, Voroshilovets, AT-42 (re-named Plant No. 183 from 1936).
- Stalingradsky Traktorny Zavod (STZ) (Сталинградский Тракторный Завод – СТЗ): SKhTZ-15/30 (STZ-1), STZ-3, STZ-5.
- Yaroslavsky Avtomobilny Zavod (YaAZ) (Ярославский Автомобильный Завод – ЯАЗ) – Yaroslavl Automobile (Truck) Plant (YaAZ): Ya-11, Ya-12, Ya-13, Ya-14.
- Plant No. 37, Moscow: T-20 Komsomolets.
- Plant No. 178, Leningrad: T-26T, T-26T2.
- Plant No. 183, Kharkov: See KhPZ.

INTRODUCTION

A line-up of Red Army artillery tractors restored by the Shamansky Workshops in Mytischi and located at the Motors of War Museum in Moscow.

As the Soviet Union rapidly industrialized in the 1930s in accordance with a series of state Five-Year Plans, mechanization of the Red Army (RKKA) was undertaken in parallel, with a particular emphasis on mechanizing Red Army artillery units. From a standing start a decade prior, the Soviet Union had by the mid-1930s become the world leader in tractor production, assembling both wheeled and tracked tractors in massive quantities. The great majority of tracked tractors were used in agriculture and civil engineering, but the same designs were also employed with minor modifications by the Red Army. Specialized military transport tractors, some being armoured and others unarmoured but with a load area for crews and ammunition, also began to appear at this time, but in limited quantities compared to their civil counterparts.

The experience gained in the production of ostensibly civil tractors in the 1930s would within the decade prove invaluable to the Red Army and the Soviet Union, when in 1941 the huge available park of 'civil' tractors was drafted into Red Army service to compensate for the massive losses of specialized military tractors in the first months of the war. The experience gained in producing tracked tractors was also invaluable in that plants such as STZ in Stalingrad and ChTZ in Chelyabinsk, set up as tractor plants, were able later to convert to tank production, having much of the heavy machine tooling and engineering expertise to do so. Soviet tractors were mundane though essential artillery transport vehicles, but the industry that developed them would become strategically significant in the very survival of the Soviet state. Most of the tractor types that scattered the battlefields of 1941 would for their part also be those that would tow heavy artillery all the way to Berlin in 1945.

The history of ostensibly civil (tractor) and military (tyagach) artillery tractor development in the Soviet Union is both intermixed and nuanced. The first mass produced tracked tractors such as the STZ-NATI 1TA (STZ-3/KhTZ-3)* and the much larger Stalinets-60 and Stalinets-65 were designed as general purpose tractors for use in agriculture, civil engineering and by the Red Army. The development of specialized artillery tractors with a fully enclosed crew cab and load area for ammunition such as the Komintern and STZ-5 occurred slightly later than the 'civil' developments, but production was small in scale compared to the vast production numbers used in agriculture and to a lesser extent in civil engineering.

At the outbreak of war in 1941, the Red Army had almost 45,000 military tractors in service, of which approximately 50 per cent were serving with artillery units. Of these, only 45 per cent were specialized artillery tractors ('tyagachi')† such as the Komsomolets, Komintern, Voroshilovets, STZ-5 and S-2, the balance being ostensibly civil 'narodnokhozyaistvennie' (i.e. agricultural) types such as the STZ-NATI 1TA (SKhTZ-NATI), Stalinets-60 and Stalinets-65. At the outbreak of war, there were approximately 6,700 Komsomolets, 1,600 Komintern and 500 Voroshilovets specialized artillery tractors in service with the Red Army.

Tracked tractors of all types were used not only to tow artillery pieces, but also to transport ammunition trailers, gun crews and general cargo. In the early war years of 1941–42 specialist military and drafted civil tracked tractors were in great demand, exacerbated by reduced production output as former tractor plants were evacuated or converted to more urgent tank production. With the huge losses of equipment including artillery tractors suffered by the Red Army in the late summer and autumn of 1941, civil, primarily 'agricultural' tractors

* The STZ-NATI, collaboratively developed between NATI tractor design institute and STZ engineers, was later designated STZ-NATI 1TA and generically as SKhTZ-NATI when later assembled at STZ and KhTZ as the STZ-3 and KhTZ-3 respectively.

† The plural of 'tyagach' is 'tyagachi'; similarly, 'bronetraktor' becomes 'bronetraktori' and 'povozka' becomes 'povozki'.

were drafted into military service in large numbers, where they served alongside the rapidly decreasing numbers of specialized military tractors due to combat attrition. Despite the loss of production facilities during the most difficult early months of the war, as of 1 September 1942 there nevertheless remained 19,879 tracked artillery tractors in Red Army service. This combination of specialized military and ostensibly civil tractors would continue to serve the Red Army until the end of the war. Although they played a critical role in the war and indeed its final outcome, these unassuming workhorses have historically been neglected as a matter for serious study both in their country (today two countries) of origin and abroad. This is the story of these utilitarian machines that provided mechanization of the Red Army's artillery forces throughout the war and that played a major but largely unnoticed role in the ultimate Soviet victory as they were used to tow the Red Army 'God of War' from the gates of Moscow in 1941 to the centre of Berlin in 1945.

The de-classification of much Soviet wartime era material in recent years and subsequent research using original Red Army and manufacturing plant archives has led to a much more complete and accurate understanding of Soviet tank and armoured vehicle development during the 1941–45 'Great Patriotic War'. By contrast, the subject of Red Army artillery tractors has to date not been widely researched, and in the case of artillery tractors some of the historical documentation was lost during the war. Much of the history of Red Army artillery tractors remains to be written.

This book is based entirely on original Russian sources as a guide to the artillery tractors which moved Soviet artillery before and throughout the war on the Eastern Front. For the first time in English the history of Red Army artillery tractors is presented from the Soviet perspective, detailing the machines, their development, their operational use and the industrial capacity that produced them. Where available, technical data from original documents has been used in preference to other Soviet/Russian secondary sources.

RED ARMY LOSSES IN PERSPECTIVE

The majority of early wartime photographs of Red Army artillery tractors published abroad were taken by Axis rather than Red Army forces, portraying tractors destroyed in combat or captured machines in Wehrmacht and Axis forces service. While accurately recording the massive combat losses in material and manpower suffered by the Red Army in the early months of the war, this historical record was also the result of large scale use of German photography on the battlefield during Operation *Barbarossa*, an officially encouraged policy for home front domestic propaganda purposes.

Many Wehrmacht soldiers carried cameras and duly recorded the exploits of the Axis forces on the Russian Front, hence the vast archives of private photographs in circulation as a permanent record today. By contrast, the majority of photography in the Red Army was by official embedded photographers rather than serving soldiers, a marked contrast between the forces which is reflected in the photographic archives of 1941–42 available today. The Red Army was also in defensive mode in the early months of the war, losing personnel, material and ground, hence the limited recording of events for posterity. This would change as the war progressed; hence the extensive coverage of destroyed Red Army equipment in 1941 would be replaced by a historical record of the Red Army on the offensive in the months to come. Another factor consistent throughout the war was that photography in the Red Army was generally more orientated towards personnel than equipment. Such nuances are important when reviewing photographs as presented in history books on the Eastern Front. The Wehrmacht and Axis photographs taken in 1941 give the impression that vast amounts of Red Army equipment, artillery tractors included, had been destroyed during these months, but as Red Army records show, although losses were on a massive scale, they were far from the total destruction that Axis forces photography undertaken in 1941 – and until recently the only accessible historical public record – would suggest. As the war situation on the Eastern Front changed, so did that photographic historical record. By 1945, the prevailing photographic record is of the Red Army armoured 'steamroller' steadily moving westward. That record included Red Army tractors towing Soviet artillery into Axis Europe, with a surprising number of slow but steady stalwart tractors from the immediate pre-war era still providing stellar service at the time of Soviet victory in the war, as recorded for posterity by Red Army photographers.

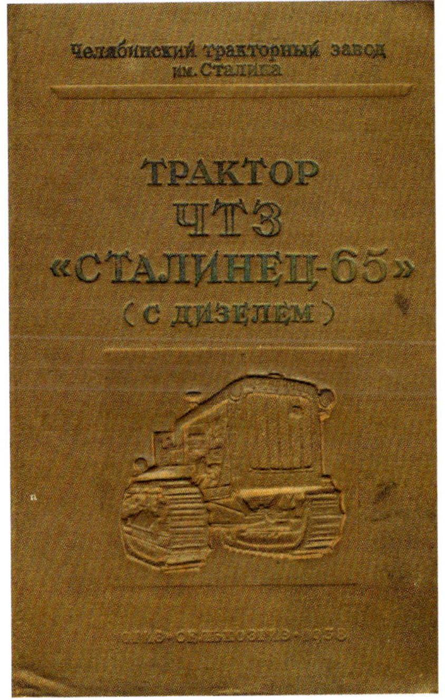

TOP S-60 Operator's Manual

ABOVE S-65 Operator's Manual

CHAPTER 1

INDUSTRIALIZATION AND EARLY SOVIET TRACTOR DEVELOPMENT

At the time of the October Revolution in 1917, as the internal combustion engine began to replace the centuries-old tradition of using the noble and intelligent horse for the transport of military loads, Imperial Russia had substantial manufacturing capability in some specific military weapons, particularly artillery, but the country was not significantly industrialized, trailing behind the United States, Great Britain and Europe industrially, and also with regard to mechanization of the armed forces. In 1912, there were 32.8 million horses in Imperial Russia, and horses remained the standard means of transport for light and medium artillery in the Imperial Russian Army, as was common worldwide at the time. This number would remain constant for some years, but would drop dramatically from nearly 30 million in 1928 to under 15 million by 1933, due to a combination of the mechanization of agriculture, famine in the southern regions of the Soviet Union, and the mechanization of civil and Red Army transport previously undertaken by the horse.

An Allis-Chalmers tractor at an Imperial Russian Army Officer Training Academy in 1916.

Red Army mechanization remained in its infancy, however. Imperial Russia had built armoured cars on imported chassis during World War I, and made use of imported vehicles including tracked tractors, but by comparison with other world powers the development and mass production of heavy vehicles including tractors for civil and military purposes occurred slightly later, dating from the end of the second decade of the 20th century. But when the country did belatedly industrialize, it would do so on a massive scale. As regards tractors specifically, the total Soviet tractor park was in 1928 some 27,000 vehicles. By 1932, that number had grown exponentially to 148,000 tractors. By 1936 the Soviet Union had become the largest manufacturer of tractors in the world.

The production and deployment of tracked vehicles as artillery tractors in the Red Army increased exponentially in the 1930s in parallel with civil tractor production, but the story goes back to long before World War I when Imperial Russia began to build significantly larger calibre artillery that required mechanical transport. The future development of indigenous vehicles for the Imperial Russian Army had already been formalized at the very beginning of the 20th century, with wheeled and half-track armoured vehicles, general purpose transport vehicles including tracked tractors and half-track designs such as those developed by Kégresse,* and specialist vehicles such as aerosans all being tested and often adopted by the army of Tsar Nicholas II.

The Russo-Balt plant (Russko-Baltisky Vagonny Zavod – RBVZ) founded in Riga in 1869 was at the forefront of light, half-track and armoured vehicle development in the first decade of the 20th century, having begun the series production of light passenger vehicles in 1909, with the Russo-Balt name becoming synonymous with such production before moving on to heavier vehicle types. A few months later, the 1st Reserve Vehicle Regiment was formed in 1910 in St Petersburg, and in 1911–12 it undertook operational trials with various imported trucks and chassis with a view to selecting the best foreign design principles for military service and for mass production in Russia. The interest in foreign tracked tractors was also established before World War I, with the first foreign tracked tractor manufacturer to have its tracked designs tested for potential Soviet production being the American company Holt (renamed Caterpillar in 1925). Tracked tractor testing was undertaken ostensibly for agricultural use by the General Directorate for Agriculture (GUZiZ) in 1913 in Kiev, with Holt winning a gold medal at the International Automobile Transport Exhibition held in St Petersburg the same year. In the immediate pre-war era, foreign heavy tractor designs favoured by Imperial Russia included Holt, Hornsby, Lombard and Ruston.

At the outbreak of World War I, the Imperial Russian Army had 711 military transport vehicles of various types, of which 418 were light passenger vehicles, the balance being trucks and tractors. During the war, further mechanization of the army added 3,562 light vehicles and 475 trucks, representing the first steps towards a mechanized army that would soon be equipped entirely with indigenously produced vehicles, including tracked artillery tractors.

During World War I, the Imperial Russian Army employed several tracked artillery vehicle types, with Holt and Allis-Chalmers half-track tractors being used to tow heavy artillery. Plans were made in 1916 to import American, British and French designs with a view to establishing local assembly, and early in 1917 decisions were already being made by the Military Industrial Committee (VPK) and ministries of agriculture and war with plans to develop the capability to produce 4,000 foreign sourced and indigenous tractors and tracked tractors annually.

In order to formalize transport vehicle development in the Soviet Union a centralized institute (Scientific Automobile Laboratory – NAL) was set up in

* The Frenchman Adolphe Kégresse (1879–1943) was in charge of Tsar Nicholas II's motorized transportation, but was also influential in developing half-track designs later extensively tested by the NAMI/NATI tractor design institute as the Soviet Union developed its own indigenous all-terrain transport vehicles.

October 1918 to develop mechanized transport for both civil and military use, which was renamed NAMI (Scientific Automobile Institute) in 1920. In 1931 it was again re-designated as NATI (Scientific Automobile and Tractor Institute) reflecting the priority of tractor and truck rather than automobile production. NATI would be central to almost all tractor development in the Soviet Union, with designs usually being developed and prototyped at NATI in collaboration with designers at the plants that would later be charged with undertaking series production.

Immediately after the Russian Revolution, the Obukhov (later Bolshevik) plant was on 16 December 1917 given an order to assemble several Holt-75 tractors and to prepare to produce a further 500 'large' (Holt-75) and 500 'small' (Holt-40) tractors. This requirement was on 11 February 1918 modified to the production of 220 larger Holt-75 tractors for the Main Artillery Directorate of the Red Army (GAU KA) and 130 for 'narodnogo khozaistva' or domestic/agricultural use. At the beginning of 1918 the Obukhov plant in Petrograd* began preparations for the series production of wheel-tracked tractors based on imported models, but this plan was also curtailed due to the Russian Civil War and a decision to potentially evacuate manufacturing plants from Petrograd, with a plan to import a further 2,000 Holt tractors also lost in the chaos of the time. Assembly of the first three Holt-75 tractors was completed at the Obukhov plant in October 1919, against a production expectation of 200 tractors, with 25 planned for GAU, of which they received precisely three by the end of the civil war. Achieving 'series' production proved to be difficult. Approximately 50 Holt-75 tractors were nevertheless ultimately assembled locally over the years 1920–25 in a process of 'import replacement'. The Red Army continued to utilize their three tractors, one in Leningrad Military District and two in the 4th Artillery Division. The drive behind the requirement for such heavy tracked tractors was the development of special purpose heavy artillery (TAON) units within the Imperial Russian Army, with six heavy artillery brigades formed which required powerful transport tractors.

In 1919, the Central Committee of the Communist Party of the Soviet Union (TsK KPSS) founded a special State Commission on Tractor Construction to investigate the mechanization of Red Army artillery and the production of tracked tractors for that purpose. In a procedure that would be

* The Obukhov plant was founded in 1854 as a steel plant, and from 1860 became one of the two principal manufacturers of artillery in Imperial Russia, the other being the Motovilikha plant located in Perm. The Obukhov plant was also known as the State Armaments Plant, with the acronym GOZ, and was renamed as the Bolshevik plant in 1922. St Petersburg was renamed Petrograd in October 1914 and again renamed Leningrad from January 1924.

later repeated for all manner of requirements, including tanks, trucks, artillery tractors and much else, procurement specialists were sent abroad to contract for foreign wheeled and tracked tractor types, and the means to mass produce them in the emerging Soviet state. In 1921, the TsK issued a resolution entitled *About the Red Army*, which detailed the need to grow the operational-tactical capability of the Red Army, specifically to exponentially increase the level of 'motorization and mechanization' for which purpose the country would need to rapidly industrialize. The need to manufacture tractors was dictated primarily by the huge loss to agriculture during World War I and the following civil war of working animals including horses and oxen and the loss of an already small number of tractors imported into Russia, coupled with the upcoming collectivization of Soviet agriculture.

On 7 August 1922, at a general ministry meeting under the tutelage of the Tractor Commission, Artillery Committee Decision No. 1219 reviewed the difficulties being experienced with tractor assembly at the Obukhov plant, with the decision to produce only one tractor type: the Holt-75; an order was placed to build 200, of which 25 were for the Red Army for use as artillery tractors. There was however still a need for a 'fast' artillery tractor, hence the smaller Holt-40 (Holt 5-ton), which had seen service in World War I and prototypes of which had arrived in Russia in 1922, was also considered for series manufacture in Russia. The Holt-40 tractor would be modified and merged with design elements of the similar American 'Kleytrak' (Cletrac-Cleveland) tractor, being produced at the Obukhov (now renamed Bolshevik)* plant from 1924 to 1930 as the 'Bolshevik' tractor. The plant also produced a limited number of the smaller and less powerful GOZ tracked tractor, colloquially called the 'Malyutka' (little one), the GOZ first being demonstrated on 22 November 1923.

The production of Holt-40 and much larger Holt-75 tractors was on a limited scale, but gave Soviet industry the vital experience necessary to produce tracked tractors and, not entirely unrelated, tanks. Two years later, in 1923, Gosplan, the Soviet central planning organization, issued a strategic directive regarding the mechanization of Soviet agriculture. The Tractor Commission investigated the merits of (steel) wheeled versus tracked tractors in the climatic specifics of Soviet agriculture, and concluded that tracked chassis overall had 1.5x the tractive effort of wheeled types in most soil conditions, including ploughed wet

* On 4 November 1922, by resolution of the Petrosovet (Petrograd Council) the Obukhov foundry was renamed as the (somewhat all-encompassing) Petrograd State Armaments, Optical and Steel Foundry Plant 'Bolshevik'. Two years later via the Opytny Konstruktorsko-Mekhanichesky Otdel (Experimental Design Mechanical Department – OKMO) organization founded within the plant, work began on tank development in Leningrad.

A captured Bullock-Lombard tractor on display in Red Square, Moscow, in the summer of 1920.

soil specific to late season vegetable rather than grain growing (the former often bogged down wheeled tractors). Tracked tractors were a specific of Soviet industrialization, in that the harsh climate and not least the wet 'Rasputitsa' (bad roads) season(s), required tractors capable of operating on very soft and muddy ground, whether military or civil. Somewhat counter-intuitively, tracked tractors were also determined to be overall more fuel efficient relative to tractive effort. This extensive technical review would lead directly to the purchase and evaluation of the German Hanomag WD-50 tracked tractor for agricultural and civil engineering applications, and also by the Red Army as an artillery tractor. The development of Soviet tracked tractors for military use was directly linked to civil production and development long before civil tractors were drafted into military service in 1941.

In the 1920s the Soviet Union purchased for evaluation and potential indigenous mass production a range of foreign wheeled and tracked tractor types, from both small and large companies, including Fordson, Hanomag, Holt, John Deere, Titan and others. Military developments were at the time a secondary consideration to the mechanization of agriculture, with Vladimir Ilyich Lenin having in March 1919 at the 8th Meeting of the Supreme Soviet put forward a plan for said mechanization of agriculture via the Supreme Soviet of Narodnogo Khozaistva (Supreme Council of the National Economy – VSNKh), which was responsible for the national economy (agriculture). A critical conclusion from the meeting was that the Soviet Union had neither the technical experience nor the time to develop indigenous tractors to mass production, but had the technical skills to industrialize based on the best available technology sourced from abroad. Accordingly, having evaluated the designs of several foreign manufacturers, the decision was taken to purchase six Fordson 20hp kerosene fuel tractors from the United States for evaluation trials, on the basis that they were modern (the Fordson was a 'monocoque' tractor without a separate chassis), simple in construction and sufficiently rugged for Soviet operating conditions. The wheeled Fordson design was concluded to be most appropriate for mass production for Soviet agricultural purposes in local manufacturing and climate conditions. It was further concluded that only the Krasny Putilovets (Putilov) plant in Petrograd had the capacity and existing engineering experience to produce the Fordson in the vast numbers envisaged for Soviet agriculture. An agreement was thereby concluded with Fordson for the licence-production of 50,000 tractors in the Soviet Union. The first batch of Fordson-Putilovets tractors left the production line in Leningrad on 1 October 1924, during which year only 74 tractors were produced as the plant geared up for mass production, the plant producing 49,568 Fordson-Putilovets such tractors from 1924 to 1932. The Kolomensk plant in Bryansk meantime from 1923 began production of the 'Kolomenets' two-cylinder wheeled agricultural tractor, while wheeled tractors were also developed and produced at several other Soviet plants, with manufacturers including Karlik and Zaporozhets. The numbers produced were however moderate by later standards. An armoured artillery tractor version of the Fordson-Putilovets tractor with machine-gun defensive armament was developed to prototype stage, but was not developed further as the armour weight severely limited the tractor's towing capability.

With domestic tractor production established, 1,505 tractors were also imported from abroad in 1923–24, rising to 7,300 tractors imported in 1924–25 and 11,725 in 1925–26. Russian factories had by 1 October 1925 also built 600 indigenous tractors. The local production plan for 1925–26 was to produce 900 FP (Fordson-Putilovets), 250 Kolomenets, 300 Zaporozhets, 100 Karlik, 100 Bolshevik and 150 Kommunar tractors,* with the import plan for 1926–27 being for 17,500 tractors to be purchased from the United States and other countries. The ambitious Gosplan requirement, as put forward by the Central Committee of the All-Union Communist Party (Bolshevik) (TsK VKP(b)) – specifically by F.Ye. Dzherzhinsky – was to build an industry capable of producing 220,000 tractors annually.†

The Soviet Union in 1921 had meantime tested for manufacture the aforementioned American Cletrac-Cleveland 'Kleytrak' Model-40, powered by a four-cylinder Widely 29hp engine, which became one of the first small tracked

* Kolomenets tractors were produced in Bryansk, Zaporozhets tractors in Kichkasse and Karlik tractors in Baronske.

† Dzerzhinsky was from 1922 Director of the aforementioned Supreme Soviet of the National Economy, but better known abroad as also being the head of the Checka, and later OGPU secret police organizations.

tractors used in civil roles – and also by the emerging Red Army. The Bolshevik plant meantime in 1924 produced the first Soviet prototype of the 'Bolshevik' tracked tractor based on Holt and Cletrac-Cleveland design principles, the tractor later entering small scale series production.

With regard to larger and more powerful tractors, one of several types of tracked tractor procured abroad with a view to domestic series production was the Hanomag WD-50, of which a prototype purchased from Germany arrived in the Soviet Union in May 1922. The prototype (known as the G-50 (Ganomag-50) or VD-50 in Russian) was evaluated and the design significantly reworked at the Kharkov Steam Locomotive Plant (KhPZ) to adapt the machine for local production and operational norms. The result was the 'Kommunar' tracked tractor, assembled in Kharkov initially with a 50hp engine running on ligroin fuel, and later with more powerful petrol engines. The need to establish an additional tractor assembly plant (KhTZ) in Kharkov in the vast agricultural region of Ukraine had also been established soon after the formation of the Soviet Union, concurrently with decisions on the need for an assembly plant for wheeled and tracked tractors in Stalingrad and for heavy tracked tractors in Chelyabinsk. The KhPZ plant in Kharkov had existing heavy engineering experience of building steam locomotives and latterly tanks and the city was thereby well positioned to undertake the additional production. The Soviet Union meantime continued to import Holt (Caterpillar) tracked tractors, culminating in the production a few years later of a modified Caterpillar-Sixty (60) design in the Soviet Union as the Stalinets-60 (S-60). Meantime, in accordance with Letter No. 926s addressed to the heads of GAU, military construction, military technology, and other departments, contracts were on 22 June 1924 placed with several other tractor manufacturers. A total of 228 Clayton and 282 Ruston tractors were delivered from Great Britain together with 90 Lombard tractors and a further 112 Clayton tractors from the United States.

The testing and redesign of imported tracked tractors for domestic Soviet production was not done in isolation, but was rather one aspect of industrializing the country and mechanizing agriculture, transport and not least the Red Army. In 1917, long before the series production of tracked tractors had become established, work had started on a new automobile plant in Moscow, AMO (Later ZiS/ZiL), to which three Lombard tractors were delivered for repair as the plant geared up for the production of transport trucks. AMO in November 1924 produced the first pre-series batch of ten AMO-F-15 trucks, a Soviet modification of the Italian FIAT-15-ter; mass production ensued the following year, with the plant within a few years developing the indigenous ZiS-5 truck design. By the mid-1920s the fledgling Soviet Union was industrializing at a pace not seen since Ford had begun conveyer production of the Ford Model T in the United States. The country needed vastly increased truck, tractor and tank production capacity, to be achieved by the building of entirely new and newly equipped assembly facilities.

A watershed moment in the industrial development of transport vehicles in the Soviet Union was the 14th Congress for Industrialization of the USSR held in 1925; this set forth plans to build vast new tractor plants, with Dzherzhinsky personally emphasizing the need to simultaneously train and build a skilled workforce for such vast production increases. The lack of sufficient skilled workers was at the time the main reason for delayed series production of the Kommunar tracked tractor.

The decision to build the country's first tractor plant in Stalingrad was made in 1926 by the above noted VSNKh, with construction of the new Stalingrad Tractor Plant (Stalingradsky Traktorny Zavod – STZ) being started on 12 June 1926. The STZ was founded in 1927 and the first STZ-1 wheeled agricultural tractor, based on the American McCormic tractor and powered by a 30hp engine, left the assembly line in June 1930. The STZ was followed by the Chelyabinsk Tractor Plant (Chelyabinsky Traktorny Zavod – ChTZ) in 1930 and the Kharkov Tractor Plant (Kharkovsky Traktorny Zavod –KhTZ) in 1931. All of these plants were equipped with production tooling and technology from the United States, with American contractors present on site during the plant building and machine tooling installation stages. In the years ahead, STZ would produce the SKhTZ-15/30 (STZ-1), STZ-NATI 1TA (STZ-3) and STZ-NATI 2TV (STZ-5), ChTZ would produce the Stalinets-60, Stalinets-65 and Stalinets-2, KhTZ would also assemble the SKhTZ-15/30 (KhTZ-1) and the STZ-NATI 1TA (KhTZ-3), while the existing Kharkov Steam Locomotive Plant (KhPZ – Plant No. 183 from 1936) would alongside tank production assemble the Kommunar, Komintern and Voroshilovets tractors. In May 1925, a TsK resolution committed to the redevelopment of the AMO truck plant in Moscow to enable the production of 25,000 trucks annually, and to the building of a new assembly facility in Nizhny Novgorod (later Gorky) with a planned annual output of 100,000 light vehicles and trucks. The GAZ plant, also built with American assistance and production tooling, would concentrate on light vehicle and truck (including half-track) production in the pre-war era, but would also later produce a small batch of Komsomolets artillery tractors.

The 16th Party Congress held in April 1929 introduced the first Soviet Five-Year Plan (1929–33), with an industrial emphasis on heavy engineering and military production development. One of many critical decisions taken was to build an entirely new heavy tracked tractor plant at Chelyabinsk, as noted above, later to be known as Chelyabinsk Tractor Plant (ChTZ). The Soviet

Union again evaluated several foreign tractor types for local mass production, and selected the American Caterpillar 'Sixty' to be built in Chelyabinsk. The Soviet version, significantly modified to accommodate the specifics of Soviet manufacturing, operational use and available fuel types, was to be designated Stalinets-60 (S-60)* with a planned production run of 40,000 tractors. As the Red Army had no specialized artillery tractors at the time, the ostensibly 'civil' S-60 design was employed for artillery tractor purposes. Tractors such as the Komintern designed specifically for military purposes would follow some years later. In December 1929, the TsK meantime issued a resolution which widened the Red Army mechanization and motorization programme initiated in 1921, forming mechanized brigades consisting of 220 tanks and 56 armoured cars, with mechanized corps to be equipped with 490 tanks and 215 armoured cars. Supporting units, including artillery, were to be similarly enlarged and mechanized.

On 17 June 1930, the wheeled SKhTZ-15/30, based on the American McCormick-Deering International-15/30 design, and designated STZ-1 by the plant, rolled off the assembly line of the Stalingrad Tractor Plant (STZ). The first 50 pre-series STZ-1 tractors were delivered in 1930, with production ramping up massively to 17,536 tractors produced in 1931. Construction of the new KhTZ tractor plant at Kharkov began in January 1930, with the first SKhTZ-15/30 tractor leaving the production line on 1 October 1931; a total of 977 SKhTZ-15/30 (KhTZ-1) tractors were produced in 1931, rising rapidly to 16,333 delivered in 1932. Production rose exponentially at both plants thereafter, with peak production being in 1934, during which year STZ and KhTZ delivered 40,299 and 40,377 tractors respectively. Production continued at both plants until 1937 when the SKhTZ-15/30 was replaced by the tracked STZ-NATI 1TA, also generically known as the SKhTZ-3. In 1932, a new experimental design bureau (KEhO) was formed at STZ under the direction of engineer V.G. Stankevich, with the new design team at STZ working with NATI in Moscow and their colleagues at KhTZ in Kharkov to develop a new tracked tractor to replace the wheeled STZ-1/KhTZ-1, primarily for use in agriculture, but also as a light artillery tractor. Two tractor types were developed from a common design, one principally intended as an agricultural tractor and the other as a high speed (road) transport tractor. These would be developed into mass production as the STZ-NATI 1TA (SKhTZ-3/STZ-3/KhTZ-3) and STZ-NATI 2TV (STZ-5) respectively, both of which would be widely employed as artillery tractors during

* The Stalinets-60 and Stalinets-65 were in the manuals always referred to by their full name, which was sometimes abbreviated in service. Over time the abbreviated form has become the norm, but the full form is more correct.

World War II. The mass production of tracked tractors for the mechanization of Soviet agriculture began with the start of STZ-NATI 1TA series production at STZ on 1 July 1937, with a modified version from the following year also being produced at KhTZ in Kharkov. The STZ-NATI or STZ-NATI 1TA in its STZ and KhTZ versions would become the most mass produced of Soviet tracked agricultural tractors, and would also be employed in significant numbers by the Red Army as an artillery tractor for medium artillery and anti-aircraft guns.

The First Five-Year Plan established at the 16th Party Congress in April 1929 had included the founding of new tractor production facilities at ChTZ in Chelyabinsk and KhTZ in Kharkov in addition to STZ at Stalingrad as founded in 1927. The Second Five-Year Plan (1933–37) involved the establishment of some 4,500 large scale production workshops throughout the Soviet Union, including expansion of the huge integrated plants such as ChTZ with large foundry facilities, and developing the plants at Kharkov and Stalingrad which would be integral to the industrial output that would mechanize the Red Army, and within a decade would also provide the ability to endure a war for the very survival of the state. Production of the ligroin (kerosene) powered S-60 tractor began at ChTZ in Chelyabinsk in 1933, with the first batch of S-60 tractors leaving the production line on 1 June 1933. A total of 68,997* Stalinets-60 tractors were assembled before the S-60 was replaced in production by the S-65 in 1937. The diesel powered S-65 production replacement was produced from 1937 to 1941, with 37,626 of these tractors built.

MANUFACTURING AND FUEL STANDARDIZATION

The concept of standardization was reviewed concurrently with the start of wheeled tractor series production in the Soviet Union, a key component of which was the requirement to standardize fuel between tractor types and between civil and military applications. On 15 November 1930, the TsK VKP(b) reviewed the fuel standardization with a view to rapid development of engines running on 'tyazholoye toplivo' – heavy fuel (i.e. diesel). Even before the ligroin powered S-60 had entered series production in 1933, work had been undertaken on the development of a diesel powered variant. With series production of wheeled tractors underway and the tracked S-60 being prepared for mass production, a resolution of the Council of People's Commissars of the Soviet Union (SNK SSSR) dated 15 May 1932 required the import and testing of a range of 'heavy fuel' engines. Two years later, testing was duly undertaken

* 69,621 per some original Russian sources.

The Krasny Peterburg armoured tractor based on a Holt chassis, Moscow region, 1920.

from 15 June to 1 November 1934, on 58 truck and tractor engines obtained from 20 manufacturers from ten countries, only four of which were indigenous Soviet designs. Foreign supplied engines including from Bofors, Caterpillar, Kemper and National were tested on a range of ChTZ, GAZ, KhTZ, YagAZ (YaG) and ZiS truck and tractor chassis, alongside a version of the S-60 designated TsOM, with the results reviewed from 16 November 1934. The state Auto-Tractor Industry Directorate (GUATP) had earlier established that the Soviet Union required a tractor park of 500,000 tractors of all types, which would require the refining of greatly increased volumes of kerosene and ligroin, while the development of indigenous Soviet diesel engines continued apace. With production of the Bolshevik and Kommunar tracked tractors based on US and German designs established, and the decision to produce the Caterpillar 'Sixty' in the Soviet Union at ChTZ taken, work continued on the selection of engines and fuel types for such tractors produced on a massive scale. Meantime, with the ligroin fuel S-60 now in production at ChTZ, the plant in collaboration with NATI developed the M-13 diesel engine as work continued to determine whether diesel or fuel oil was more appropriate for tracked tractors than petrol. This work ultimately resulted in the M-17 diesel engine being selected for the later Stalinets-65, which entered production in 1937.

CHAPTER 2

MASS PRODUCTION, WAR AND EVACUATION

Soviet tractor development was an integral element of transport vehicle development more generally in the 1930s. The massive and widely dispersed industrial capacity built up in the Soviet automotive industry in the 1930s, which incorporated 'doubler' plant capacity and contingency planning, would in the dark years of 1941–42 play a major role in the survival of the Soviet Union. Secondary vehicle production, a classification which included tracked artillery tractors, would in those years be secondary to tank and armoured vehicle production, but the latent capacity within automotive plants would later in the war also play a critical role in increasing tracked artillery tractor production for the war effort.

A Holt tractor at the Obukhov plant in Petrograd, September 1922.

Light vehicle, truck and tractor production was a major priority within the first Five-Year Plan (1929–33), with plans unveiled to establish modern light vehicle and truck production in Moscow, Gorky and Yaroslavl with a total annual production target of 200,000 vehicles. A contract for the establishment of a new factory in the Soviet Union, with American technical assistance and initial component supply, was signed with the Ford Motor Company, with the Nizhny Novgorod Automobile Plant (NAZ) being established in the city of Nizhny Novgorod. The plant was completed in late 1931, and the first pre-series batch of ten NAZ-AA 4x2 trucks was delivered on 29 January 1932, with series production commencing on 1 April 1932. The NAZ designation was modified to GAZ in 1933 with the change of the city name to Gorky. The older YaG (YaGAZ) plant established in Yaroslavl in the early 1920s to produce heavy trucks and engines would later also play a major role as engine supplier and latterly in the production of tracked artillery tractors.

The TsK paid great attention to Soviet industrial development, and in particular to 'auto-tractor' (i.e. truck and tractor) production. One of the critical decisions with regard to the future industrialization of the country made in the spring of 1929 was construction of the aforementioned ChTZ tractor plant at Chelyabinsk beyond the Ural mountains. Tractor assembly was however not the entire story. The related SNK SSSR resolution indicated that ChTZ would act as a 'doubler' plant for tank production in the event of war, as would become its role a decade later. As the ChTZ plant was being completed, a proposal to

Bolshevik tractors parade on 25 Oktyabr Prospekt, Leningrad, mid-1920s.

assemble the obsolescent T-18 tank there was rejected on 6 January 1930, with similar plans for the T-12 and T-19 also duly rejected on 20 March the same year. The decision taken was that in peacetime the T-12 (factually now its T-24 replacement) would be produced at KhPZ in Kharkov where it was designed. These plans were ultimately shelved when the T-24 did not enter full series production, with medium tank (future T-28) production being assigned to Leningrad. As regards the tracked tractors to be built at Chelyabinsk, the 'Kleytrak-40' (Cleveland Tractor Co.) and Holt (Caterpillar) 'Sixty' (Caterpillar 60) were reviewed, with the decision ultimately being taken to produce a localized variant of the heavier Caterpillar-60 at Chelyabinsk as the Stalinets-60 (S-60). Series production of the S-60 tracked tractor began at ChTZ in Chelyabinsk in 1933 with the S-60 replaced in production by the diesel powered S-65 in 1937. The decision to establish tractor production at Chelyabinsk would however within a few years be a critical element in the survival of the country as heavy tank production was evacuated from Leningrad to Chelyabinsk in the autumn of 1941. While the plant was still in the design stage, work had in February 1930 also begun on establishing the Chelyabinsk Prototype Tractor Plant (Opitny Zavod Traktorstroya), which as Plant No. 100 NKTP (People's Commissariat of Heavy (i.e. tank) Production) would in the future also become synonymous with heavy tank production.

In November 1929, the TsK had also taken the decision to build a second plant in Kharkov for tracked tractor production, distinct from the existing Kharkov Steam Locomotive Plant (KhPZ – from 1936 Plant No. 183) which was at the time developing the T-24 manoeuvre tank, and would later produce the T-34 medium tank. The new Kharkov Tractor Plant (KhTZ) was to initially assemble the same NATI Moscow institute developed wheeled agricultural tractors as STZ in Stalingrad, namely the SKhTZ-15/30 (KhTZ-1) before later starting SKhTZ-NATI* (KhTZ-3) tracked tractor production.

Returning to the 'doubler' plant theme, as ChTZ began series production of the S-60 in 1933, the Military Mobilization Command (VMU) of Gosplan, per Resolution No. 11-10/50s (s – secret) dated 21 March 1933 and Resolution No. 10/85ss (ss – top secret) dated 19 April, instructed ChTZ to prepare for contingency production of the T-28 medium tank at a rate of 100 tanks per month in the event of major war. The overall state priority was to build several heavy industry assembly plants, but what was to be manufactured in these facilities was subject to constantly revised provisions. That ChTZ could convert from tracked tractor to tank production, as would occur in 1941, was 'baked in' at the outset.

The realization of TsK efforts to industrialize the country started in preceding years would materialize in the early to mid-1930s. From their respective production start-ups in 1930–31 until 1937, STZ and KhTZ combined would produce 397,000 SKhTZ-15/30 wheeled tractors under their respective plant designations. Both plants would in 1937 start production of the tracked STZ-NATI 1TA tractor as the STZ-3 and KhTZ-3 respectively, taken into service by the Red Army as an artillery and general purpose tractor, with concurrent development of the STZ-5 'high speed' transport tractor as a dedicated artillery tractor. The KhPZ tank plant had from 1934 meantime slowly started assembly of the Komintern artillery tractor, using the chassis of the now abandoned T-24 tank, followed in 1939 by the more powerful tank-engine powered Voroshilovets. Plant No. 37 in Moscow in 1937 meantime began series production of the Komsomolets armoured tractor for moving anti-tank guns in front line positions.

* SKhTZ-NATI is a combined generic designation. The original design was the STZ-NATI (STZ-NATI 1TA) which was produced at STZ and KhTZ under respective STZ-3 and KhTZ-3 plant designations, with differing cabs and other details.

Kommunar tractor assembly at KhPZ in Kharkov.

The exponential increase in tracked tractor production in the Soviet Union mirrored that of vehicle (particularly truck) production during the same years. The mass production of transport vehicles ramped up significantly in the years from 1932 to 1940. In 1930, Soviet annual production of all vehicle types was approximately 4,000 vehicles. By 1935 it was 95,000. In 1938, still a time of primarily civil orientated production, the Soviet Union produced 211,114 vehicles of all types. This output would dramatically decrease with the outbreak of war. During the years of the Soviet Great Patriotic War, from 22 June 1941 to 9 May 1945, total Soviet domestic vehicle production was only 205,000 vehicles due to priority being switched to tank and other heavy armaments production. Following the disruptions of late 1941, Soviet production for the total year 1942 had dropped to 32,300 vehicles, at a time when the country had suffered massive combat losses during the initial months of the war, with tractor production being reduced even more severely due to evacuation and higher priority tank production priorities. By 1944, annual production had increased again to 57,400 vehicles as Soviet domestic production recovered from plant evacuation, re-establishment in new locations and other priorities. The provision of Lend-Lease vehicles to the Soviet Union greatly assisted the mobility of the Red Army during the war years, a fact that has always been acknowledged in full by the Soviet

Union and later Russian Federation; 401,000 Lend-Lease vehicles of all types were supplied during the war, primarily by the United States, Great Britain and Canada, with the United States also providing several tracked artillery tractor types. The development, production and deployment of Red Army tracked artillery tractors was closely aligned with that of military transport vehicles more generally, with artillery tractors being essential to the Red Army war effort.

I.V. Stalin took a personal interest in artillery tractor development. On 16 May 1935, accompanied by TsK VKP(b) leadership including M.I. Kalinin, A.A. Zhdanov, L.M. Kaganovich and G.K. Ordzhonikidze, Stalin visited the NATI test polygon to review trials of the STZ-NATI and KhTZ prototypes. On 18 July, STZ, KhTZ and NATI workers received thanks from the Central Committee for their work on the STZ-NATI, as announced in the Soviet newspaper *Pravda*.

At the end of the 1930s, the Red Army defined four types of artillery tractor for future development, namely three tractor types orientated towards towing anti-tank, divisional and corps level guns respectively, and a fourth specialized high power tractor type (such as the future Voroshilovets) intended for towing high power (and weight) strategic reserve artillery, with a secondary role of tank and armoured vehicle recovery.

Krasny Putilovets (Fordson Putilovets) tractors on parade in Leningrad in 1929.

By this time the mechanization of Red Army artillery units was becoming established, though it remained behind Statute* requirements. The distribution of artillery tractors in 1938 in the three Military Districts shown below is indicative of the relatively small numbers of specialized tractors in Red Army service in the months immediately prior to the Soviet–Finnish Winter War of 1939–40 compared to the S-60 and S-65, with the significant Red Army artillery presence in the Far East of the country also being of note.

Military District	Moscow (MVO)	Leningrad (LVO)	ZaBaikal (ZabVO)
Pioner	47	2	-
Komsomolets	64	93	54
Kommunar	178	271	171
Komintern	192	132	71
S-60	391	438	328
S-65	42	269	118

In 1939, Red Army artillery tractors would be engaged in combat on both the eastern and western borders of the Soviet Union, being engaged against Japanese forces in the Khalkin Gol battles from May to September of that year, followed immediately thereafter by the Soviet–Finnish Winter War fought from December 1939 until March 1940.

In 1940, years of experimental development on diesel engines had meantime resulted in the BD-2 entering series production at Kharkov as the V-2 diesel engine, initially installed in the T-34 (and Leningrad KV) tanks and the Voroshilovets artillery tractor. The same year, the M-40 diesel engine, also adapted from an aviation engine design, was being prepared for series production at the Leningrad Kirov Plant (Leningradsky Kirovsky Zavod – LKZ) in Leningrad and KhTZ in Kharkov, the latter having built the first ten pre-series engines by June 1941. Further work was curtailed due to the new engine being considered insufficiently resolved to initiate full scale mass production, with further work concentrating on existing proven designs. On 26 November 1940, Commissar V.A. Malyshev of the Ministry of Medium Machine (i.e. tank) Building (NKSM) sent to TsK VKP(b) a report concerning the potential to establish STZ as a 'doubler' plant for V-2 tank (and artillery tractor) engine production, however such plans were not completed at STZ. Some months later, now in a state of war, the State Defence Committee (GKO) in July 1941 considered the assembly of T-60 light tanks at GAZ and KhTZ, also as 'doubler' plants, with the new production demands on GAZ taking priority over the assembly of Komsomolets

* Soviet 'Statutes' or 'norms' refer to the quantity of equipment that per State requirements should be within any given military unit when at full combat strength.

tractors, construction of which was never fully established at GAZ due to more urgent wartime priorities.

The table below shows the status of artillery tractors in Red Army service as of 1 January 1941:

	Statute Tractor Park	In artillery units	Repair (medium)	Repair (capital)	Out of service
Kommunar	94	504	71	198	269
Komintern	6,891	1,017	164	87	251
Voroshilovets	733	228	23	15	38
STZ-3 (KhTZ-3)	384	3,658	504	348	852
STZ-5	5,478	2,839	251	55	306
Komsomolets	2,810	4,401	506	337	843
S-60	44	1,631	206	343	549
S-65	3,068	7,170	677	320	997
Note: 951 S-2 tractors should also have also been in service per Soviet Statutes, but none were in operational service on this date.					

Meantime, as of 1 July 1940, there were 112,005 tracked tractors in service in the Soviet agricultural sector, of which 53,576 were the S-60, 14,642 were the S-65 and 5,452 were gas generator (solid fuel powered) tractors. This represented a huge strategic reserve, the significance of which would soon come into its own.

WAR AND CHANGED PRIORITIES

Red Army experience in the Soviet–Finnish Winter War of 1939–40, particularly the heavy losses of artillery tractors in the Karelian Isthmus, resulted in a change in philosophy with regard to the mechanization of artillery. Soviet losses during the short war were primarily due to becoming trapped in light forests and on forest roads, without the ability to disperse under fire, rather than to losses from enemy tanks, of which the Finns possessed relatively few. Tractors, particularly the Komsomolets, were thereafter prioritized for towing heavier artillery than designed, while the movement of 45mm anti-tank guns reverted to the horse. Anti-tank guns were also not so useful where fixed emplacements and fortifications were a more typical target. While Komsomolets tractors continued to perform front line operations, T-37A reconnaissance tanks and T-27 tankettes were relegated to use as armoured artillery tractors for anti-tank guns in rear areas, a somewhat paradoxical but practical solution to events on the ground.

The summer of 1941 would engulf the Soviet Union in total war, with the demarcation between military and civil (primarily agricultural) tractors being blurred as civil tractors were drafted into Red Army service to replace the relatively few available specialized military tractors destroyed in the first weeks of combat. The Red Army on 1 January 1941 had, among other types, some 4,401 Komsomolets armoured artillery tractors in service, together with

ABOVE An STZ-15/30 (STZ-1) tractor during military evaluation.

3,658 SKhTZ-NATI 1TA (STZ-3/KhTZ-3) tractors and 7,170 powerful but slow S-65 'Stalinets' tractors. At the time of the outbreak of war in June 1941, the overall Red Army tractor park consisted of approximately 44,900 tractors, of which some 65 per cent were basically civil types also used by the Red Army, namely the SKhTZ-NATI 1TA (KhTZ-3/STZ-3), and Stalinets-60 and Stalinets-65. For context, there were in 1941 some 121,200 tracked tractors in agricultural service available to be drafted into military service.

The KhTZ tractor plant in Kharkov was clearly in a not dissimilar 'line of business' to the nearby No. 183 and No. 75 plants with their official military plant designators, and the question thereby arises why KhTZ was not drawn into military tractor production earlier. In the months prior to the outbreak of war, KhTZ had been considered as the centre for T-50 light tank production, which would require a new dedicated workshop and additional machine tooling, but this would still not resolve issues related to V-4 engine production for the T-50 at Plant No. 75. In accordance with a state resolution dated 5 July 1941, the decision was made to evacuate Kharkov Engine Plant No. 75 and send the machine tooling and workers to ChTZ for use in tank assembly at Chelyabinsk. Only days later, on 13 July 1941, GKO Resolution No. 124 was issued, allocating the machine tooling destined for the planned workshop at KhTZ in Kharkov to STZ in Stalingrad. The existing KhTZ production tooling was soon thereafter evacuated to STZ and to Plant No. 264 NKTP, in order to produce the T-60 small tank in what was a rapid moving logistical and manufacturing puzzle.

With the outbreak of war and the massive losses that followed, all distinctions between civilian and military were blurred, and any available vehicle was pressed into service in any role as required. At the outbreak of war on 22 June 1941, the Red Army possessed, as noted, approximately 44,900 artillery tractors, of which only 15 per cent were specialized transport-tractor types intended for long-haul road marches such as the STZ-5, Komintern and Voroshilovets; while, relative to the number of artillery pieces in service, artillery units faced a shortage of all tractor types even before war broke out. In the western border regions of the Belorussian and Ukrainian republics that absorbed the initial brunt of Operation *Barbarossa*, the 6th Anti-Tank Artillery Brigade in the Western Special Military District had, for instance, only 21 per cent of its paper Statute fulfilment of transport vehicles and artillery tractors at the outbreak of war, while the 8th Brigade had precisely three tractors in service. In June 1941, most units had an average of 20.5 per cent of paper Statute norms available and in serviceable condition. Of the approximately 44,900 tractors in Red Army service, only around 30 per cent were specialized military types, including 4,401 armoured Komsomolets tractors used primarily for towing anti-tank guns, and 1,581 Komintern and 470 Voroshilovets tractors. There were approximately 1,488 older Kommunar tractors in service, but the vast majority were mechanically worn from prolonged service and only 504 were listed as serviceable, with the overwhelming majority of serviceable artillery tractors being the S-60 and S-65 types (10,603 and 5,559 respectively) and the lighter STZ-3/KhTZ-3 (an estimated total of 14,600 in service).

LEFT ChTZ-60 (Stalinets-60) tractors on the assembly line at ChTZ in Chelyabinsk.

ChTZ-65 (Stalinets-65) tractors during assembly at ChTZ.

СТАЛИНЕЦ
ЧТЗ
ДИЗЕЛЬ

The first weeks of the war were disastrous for the Red Army in terms of manpower and material losses, with artillery units and their essential artillery tractors being no exception. In the first two weeks of the war, the 3rd, 6th, 8th, 13th, 14th and 17th Mechanized Corps were decimated together with almost all their equipment including artillery tractors, while another ten mechanized corps lost a substantial volume of manpower and equipment. The front line rapidly moved east, devastating the Belorussian and Ukrainian republics, with the Red Army conceding ground in order to muster forces deeper within Soviet territory. Soviet 45mm anti-tank guns were more than capable of defeating the majority of Wehrmacht armour such as the Pz.Kpfw.II, the Czechoslovakian origin Pz.Kpfw. 38(t) and even the Pz.Kpfw.III; but the lack of mechanized transportation allowing rapid redeployment or retreat caused the loss of much towed artillery during the Blitzkrieg phase of the 1941–45 war. The severe lack of artillery tractors led to their being used primarily to transport heavier artillery pieces, with the transport of light artillery, particularly 45mm anti-tank guns and regimental artillery, being entrusted (as in the Wehrmacht and other armies at the time) to the ever-dependable horse, as had occurred in the fighting against Finland in the winter of 1939–40.

The severe loss of artillery tractors in the opening months of the war was made up by the mobilization of approximately 30,000 civil tractors. Soviet industry delivered 9,100 tracked tractors to the Red Army in 1941, and a further 3,400 in 1942, with an additional 600 civil tractors mobilized for the Red Army in 1942. The output of new tractors and mobilization of the civil tractor park resulted in the Red Army possessing 39,900 artillery tractors in September 1942,* only 5,000 or so fewer than in June 1941 despite the heavy attrition, attesting to the time-tested adage that the outcome of major wars is as much dictated by logistics and production capacity as it is by front line fighting.

In the opening months of the war, the Komsomolets armoured light tractor was used primarily to tow anti-tank guns in frontal areas; the STZ-3 and STZ-5 were used for towing medium calibre artillery; and the S-60, S-65 and the relatively small number of Komintern tractors were used to tow heavy artillery, particularly tracked pieces such as the 203mm B-4 howitzer.

The specifics of German Blitzkrieg war were particularly difficult for Soviet artillery units, in that heavy artillery towed by slow-moving tractors such as the S-60 and S-65 was not well dispositioned to rapid redeployment, with road speeds of 7km/h, reducing to 2–4km/h across terrain. In the early months it was not uncommon for Red Army artillery units to lose all of their material during

* On 1 September 1942, the Red Army had 9,464 S-60 and 10,415 S-65 tractors in service, still nearly half the total Red Army tractor park. The number of S-65 tractors in service in September 1942 was almost the same as in June 1941; the number of S-60 tractors having significantly increased due to mobilization.

The S-60/S-65 ChTZ (ChKZ) assembly workshop converted to KV-1 tank production.

The SKhTZ-NATI 1TA, produced at STZ in Stalingrad as the STZ-3.

combat engagements. The Komsomolets suffered disproportionate losses in that its role as an anti-tank gun tractor necessitated it operating within a few hundred metres of enemy forces. The exact overall losses are not known, but it is estimated that from June to December 1941 the Red Army lost more than 50 per cent of its entire artillery tractor park in combat. Four years later, however, the surviving slow and ponderous tractors such as the S-60 and S-65, joined by more modern wartime tractors, would tow the same heavy artillery pieces at a lumbering pace all the way to Berlin.

PLANT EVACUATION

The production of Komsomolets tractors was shut down at Plant No. 37 NKTP in Moscow in the autumn of 1941 as the plant prepared for evacuation to Sverdlovsk within the UZTM (Urals Heavy Machine Building Plant, also called Uralmash) structure, being henceforth reorientated on tank and self-propelled gun (SAU) production. NKSM, which included Plant No. 40 and GAZ, remained responsible for light tank production.

The first tractor plant to be threatened by the Axis advance in the summer of 1941 was KhTZ in Kharkov. As Axis forces closed on Kharkov, the machine tooling located in the Kharkov tank and tractor plants was in the autumn of 1941 evacuated by rail beyond the Ural mountains, with some tooling also sent to Stalingrad. The machine tooling from Plant No. 183, which was in 1941 producing the T-34 tank and the Voroshilovets tractor, was evacuated primarily to Nizhny Tagil. The KhTZ tractor plant was from October 1941 evacuated even further, to Rubtsovsk in the Altai region some 3,000km east of Moscow, where it was re-established as the newly built Altai Tractor Plant (Altaisky Traktorny Zavod – ATZ). The decision to establish the ATZ plant in Rubtsovsk was made by a TsK VKP(b) i SM SSSR (Central Committee and Council of Ministers) resolution dated 18 November 1941, which provided for the evacuation of tracked tractor production and repair tooling from KhTZ, the Odessa Agricultural Machine Building Plant (OZSM) and from STZ in Stalingrad. The first workshop was completed at ATZ in December 1941, with the first train loads of evacuated tooling arriving in January 1942 in the depths of Russian winter. Additional machine tooling for the near identical STZ-NATI 1TA as produced as the STZ-3 at STZ in Stalingrad was also later evacuated to Rubtsovsk. The first kerosene powered ATZ-built ASKhTZ-NATI (formerly SKhTZ-3) tractor was completed in Rubtsovsk on 24 August 1942, with initial production being on a limited basis over the next months as series production at the plant was established, the 1,000th tractor being completed in December 1943. Full scale production on an exponential scale commenced in 1944.

The LKZ (Kirov) plant in Leningrad, producing the KV heavy tank, was meantime relocated in the autumn of 1941 to Chelyabinsk, where ChTZ, then producing the S-65 and S-2 tractors, would terminate tractor production in lieu of higher priority KV-1 heavy tank production. ChTZ (in full the Chelyabinsk Tractor Plant in the name of Stalin) was renamed ChKZ (the Chelyabinsk Kirovsk Plant NKTP) from 6 October 1941. The plant would resume tracked tractor production only in the immediate post-war era. During the war, ChKZ produced 18,000 tanks, approximately 48,500 engines and a vast quantity of ammunition.

From the autumn of 1941, STZ in Stalingrad was the only remaining Soviet plant still series producing artillery tractors, in the form of the STZ-5, assembly of which continued until Stalingrad and its factories were overrun the following autumn. Thereafter, for the duration of the war only the Ya-12 was series manufactured in quantity, in Yaroslavl, with production transferred at the end of the war to Plant No. 40 in Mytischi.

Evacuation of the ZiS plant in Moscow also began in late October 1941, with machine tooling evacuated by rail to Ulyanovsk in the Volga region, to Miass in the Urals region, and also to Chelyabinsk and Shadrinsk. The operation involved 7,708 rail flat cars and box wagons loaded with 12,800 individual pieces of machine tooling; production was resumed at Miass within four months. The relocation resulted in ZiS-22 half-track production being terminated, with a significant delay before it would later re-enter production as the ZiS-42, and later still as the ZiS-42M.

ZiS-5 production was re-established at the Ulyanovsk Automobile Plant (Ulyanovsk Avtomobilny Zavod – UAZ) in May 1942, with the vehicles being designated ZiS-5 or more correctly UlZiS-5. Meantime in Miass, the UralZiS (UralAZ) plant began production of ZiS-5 engines and gearboxes in April 1942, followed by stamped components for ZiS and other vehicles from June the same year. After Axis forces were held in the outskirts of Moscow some machine tooling was relocated back to Moscow, with ZiS restarting limited production in the original location from June 1942. At Miass, mass production of complete ZiS-5V (UralZiS-5V) trucks began in 1944, with series production of the ZiS-42M half-track starting in July that year.

GAZ, located in Gorky (today Nizhny Novgorod) 440km east of Moscow, was not directly affected by the national plant evacuation plan undertaken from the autumn of 1941. The change in production priorities to a wide variety of military equipment, including T-60 and later T-70 tanks, the SU-76 SAU, BA-64 armoured cars, parts for other plants and vehicle and aviation engines to name but a small cross-section of manufacture, inevitably affected production of lesser priority vehicles such as the GAZ-60 half-track. The Komsomolets tractor was also produced at GAZ in limited pre-series production numbers.

As the front line moved westward later in the war, tracked tractor production was re-established at KhTZ in Kharkov and STZ in Stalingrad in 1944, with production continuing at these plants until 1949.

CHAPTER 3

TRACKED UNIVERSAL TRACTORS

The origin of tracked artillery tractors in the Red Army service began with a decree signed by V.I. Lenin in 1921, *About Agricultural Machine Building*, which required the Soviet Union to develop an industry capable of the mass production of wheeled and tracked tractors, primarily for civil (agricultural) purposes but also for military applications. To expedite the process, foreign tractor designs were, as previously noted, obtained from several countries, with the first tractors modified for use as locally assembled tracked artillery tractors in the Soviet Union being sourced from Holt in the United States and Hanomag in Germany. The Soviet Union acquired existing and proven foreign designs, adopted the best features and adapted them for the specifics of Soviet industry capability, road, ground and weather conditions. This process of foreign technology acquisition and adaptation was initially applied to trucks and tractors, but would later also be applied to tank manufacture. The first series production indigenous tracked tractors used by the Red Army for towing artillery were the Bolshevik and the Kommunar, adapted respectively from Holt and Hanomag designs.

A Bolshevik tractor during factory trials, Leningrad, 19 June 1925.

BOLSHEVIK

With the end of the Russian Civil War and a return to stability, the American Holt-40 (40hp) tracked tractor was in 1922 reviewed in the Soviet Union for potential civil and military applications, with Order No. 64 dated 8 July 1922 authorizing the purchase of a small number for evaluation and potential domestic production.

Bolshevik tractors on display in Red Square, Moscow, 1 May 1930. Photographer: O. Baranov.

The original Holt-40 was redesigned at the Obukhov plant in Petrograd in collaboration with the NAMI motor vehicle institute, which had overall responsibility for the evaluation of all new vehicle types, domestic and foreign, to suit local assembly capability, with the first domestically assembled Bolshevik tracked tractor being completed at the now renamed Bolshevik plant in August 1924. The first Soviet prototype, originally referred to colloquially as the Russky-Holt rather than the Bolshevik, was extensively tested under the auspices of D.K. Karelsky at NAMI. Following successful trials the tractor was accepted for production at the Bolshevik plant, being assembled in small annual batches, with ongoing changes to the design. By 3 August 1925 a total of 51 Bolshevik tractors had been assembled, in four separate series (1st Series – 18, 2nd Series – 12, 3rd Series – 15, 4th Series – six), with further small batches of 10–20 tractors built annually thereafter until production ceased in 1930.

The Bolshevik, produced from 1924 to 1930, was powered by a four-cylinder petrol engine developing 40hp coupled to a three-speed gearbox, providing the tractor with a maximum towing speed of 11km/h. The tractor was relatively powerful for its time, and was used by the Red Army to tow medium artillery and anti-aircraft guns and in tank and engineering units. In 1930, Bolshevik tractors were recorded in Red Army records as serving in the 9th, 110th, 120th and other artillery regiments and in the 3rd Tank and 127th Motor Rifle Regiments. It is worth noting the thoroughness of Red Army record keeping. As of 14 January 1930, the 3rd Tank Regiment recorded three Kommunar and

Bolshevik tractors on parade in Red Square in the late 1920s. The tractors were built in small batches, with detail changes in each batch.

13 Bolshevik tractors still in serviceable condition, with the Bolshevik tractors having individual odometer readings of 463–2,040km and engine working hours also duly noted by individual tractor serial number. A small number of Bolshevik tractors were operationally deployed in the Soviet Far East against Japanese forces.

KOMMUNAR

The decree *About Agricultural Machine Building* signed by Lenin in 1921 in part required the Kharkov Steam Locomotive Plant (KhPZ), which had produced its first agricultural tractor in 1909, to develop a new tracked tractor, primarily for agricultural and civil engineering purposes. As was to become a Soviet norm, with foreign designs acquired for evaluation and potential series production in the Soviet Union, at least one example of the German Hanomag WD-50 was purchased from Germany for such purposes, arriving in the country in May 1922. The smaller Hanomag WD-25 was in 1922 also tested but not accepted for civil and military service.

The Kommunar was the first tracked tractor to enter series production at KhPZ; it was a Soviet redesign of the Hanomag WD-50 prototype, significantly modified to better suit domestic manufacturing and operational conditions. Modification of the design was under the direction of K.I. Marin, with other engineers involved in developing the tractor for production being D.F. Bobrov, B.N. Voronkov, N.G. Zubarev, D.M. Ivanov and V.M. Krichevsky, names that would become a constant in Soviet artillery tractor design. The Kommunar was built of heavier gauge steel than the original, and was in consequence both more rigid and heavier. The increased use of cast iron parts and the conversion to kerosene fuel for use in Soviet operating conditions had added significant weight, while the four-cylinder four-stroke engines were also heavier than the German original. Various engine options were considered, including kerosene and petrol, with the early series production Kommunar 9G running on kerosene but started by a small petrol engine. Petrol was far more expensive than kerosene in the Soviet Union of the 1920s, hence the engine options depended on intended use – and whether civil or military. Available petrol was also low octane and provided less power output relative to kerosene powered engines, such that the original kerosene powered 9G ('Ganomag-50' or G-50) though nominally rated at 50hp actually developed 35–38hp in Soviet operating conditions.*

* The Kommunar was produced in several main series, with a number of sub-variants. The kerosene powered 9G (G-50, 9G-35/50) was followed by the 9GU (G-75) with a 75hp petrol engine, the 9EU 'fast tractor' and finally the 3-90 with a 90hp petrol engine.

ABOVE A photograph of the Kommunar tractor from the 50 Years of the NII-21 Institute official album.

Assembly of the Kommunar 9G began at KhPZ in April 1924, with the first tractor completed on 1 May 1924. The ostensibly agricultural Kommunar 9G was also tested for military service and was the same year delivered to the Red Army for use in towing artillery pieces that were too heavy for horse transport, the Kommunar, together with the Bolshevik, becoming the first Soviet domestic series production tracked artillery tractors used for such purposes.

The Kommunar was approved for series production after endurance tests conducted for the Red Army in the second half of 1924. The original intent was to rapidly grow output with a target to build 1,200 Kommunar tractors in 1925. By the end of 1924 only 12 Kommunar 9G tractors had actually been completed at KhPZ, however, with a further 20 by April 1925, at which point the 'hand built' production was halted in order to reorganize for mass production, which involved converting a rail wagon workshop, installing new machine tooling and not least gathering together the required skilled workers. Production restarted in 1925, with 62 built that year and 98 the following year. Intended as a universal tractor for civil or military use, six tractors from the first production batch were sent to GVTU, the Soviet Military Technical Command, for long term evaluation trials for service in the Red Army. The trials were successful, and the Kommunar was formally accepted into Red Army service in 1926 as the 9G.* Production increased to 103 tractors in 1927, rising to 273 in 1929 and remaining at a similar level until 1930, in which year 714 tractors were produced, directly related to the tractor being increasingly used by the Red Amy as an artillery tractor.

ABOVE An early Soviet-era drawing of the Kommunar tractor.

The 9G Kommunar as known in Red Army service was the first mass production tracked tractor employed as an artillery tractor in the Red Army. It was not ideal, being slow, with a front mounted engine, open cab with only a convex steel roof for weather protection and no cargo area – being designed as a tractor rather than a tyagach (artillery tractor). But it was the tractor which gave the Red Army its first widespread experience of mechanized artillery transportation. The Kommunar was also important in providing essential experience in mass production, which was at the same plant also being concurrently applied to the BT fast tank series, and would in time be applied to production of the T-34 medium tank.

OPPOSITE Kommunar tractors on parade in the Ukrainian Soviet Socialist Republic, draped in KhPZ banners.

* 9G: 9 – 9-tonne tractor weight, G – alternatively gusenichny (tracked) or 'Ganomag' – as pronounced in Russian.

ХПЗ

A Kommunar 9G during a 1920s parade, identification aided by '9Г' (9G) being helpfully painted on the side.

Kommunar tractors towing 203mm B-4 tracked howitzers await a Red Square parade in Moscow. (Sergei Popsuevich)

The power outputs of the three main production series of the Kommunar tractor are conflated in some sources, in part due to the horsepower rating depending on the fuel being used. The original 9G was evaluated and formally accepted for Red Army service when many tractors were already in operational service, with ongoing testing of new variants, of which there were many, as they were developed.

To match the increasing weight of Soviet artillery pieces, a more powerful variant, the Kommunar 9GU (U – Usovershenstvovanny – improved) was later introduced, powered by a petrol engine developing 75hp, which could tow heavy artillery at 7km/h, a speed considered adequate in the 1920s, with the 9GU being used in greater numbers by the Red Army. The 9G and 9GU versions

Kommunar tractors towing 76.2mm M-1915 anti-aircraft guns during a parade in the city of Vladimir.

were produced at KhPZ until 1930, when they were both replaced by the modernized 3-90 (Kommunar 3rd Model, 90hp). The 3-90 had a much-increased artillery towing speed of 15km/h on made roads; the later 3-90 was widely used in the Red Army as the preferred 'military' variant of the tractor, with a nominal towing capacity of 6,000kg.

The Kommunar was produced in three (four) distinct main production variants, namely the 9G (9G-35/50, G-50) which had a four-cylinder engine developing 50hp at 840rpm running on kerosene (61hp running on petrol), with a maximum towing speed of 7km/h (850 built 1924–30); the aforementioned 9GU (G-75, G-U) with a petrol engine developing 75hp on '2nd Sort' (Grade 2) petrol, a towing capacity of 12,000kg and a speed of 9km/h (1,100 built); the 9EU model with a petrol engine developing 75hp, a towing capacity of 11,300kg and a speed of 9km/h; and the final Kommunar 3-90 tractor, powered by a Type 3-90 engine developing 90hp. The Kommunar 3-90, also known as the T3-90 and as the 'New Kommunar', had for the time a remarkable towing speed of 14km/h with a reduced 6,000–9,000kg load. The total production run varies in different original sources, but the number 3,499 is from original archives, which also detail annual production.*

* There were many sub-variants and small production batches of the Kommunar tractor, including the 9A, 9B, 9V, 9G, 9D, 9DU, 9EU, 9ZU, 3-90, 9IU and 9PU. The Red Army had, for example, four 9A tractors in service. The 3-90 was the final variant built to military specification primarily for the Red Army.

Kommunar tractors towing 76.2mm M-1915/28 (9K) anti-aircraft guns through Red Square, Moscow, 7 November 1932. Photographer: O. Baranov.

The Red Army regularly tested new Kommunar variants during the 1930s as they were developed. The 3-90 variant, developed specifically as a 'fast' tractor for the Red Army, was the most commonly used model in the 1930s. The 9GU was generally used for RVGK (Reserve of the Supreme Command) reserve artillery systems. The 9EU, with a lower towing capacity but slightly higher road speed, was primarily used for anti-aircraft guns. With the outbreak of war, Kommunar tractors were used for all towing purposes as available.

The Kommunar was originally designed as a multi-purpose agricultural and industrial tractor, but with the ability to tow artillery being fundamental to its development. In Soviet-era terminology the Kommunar was a tracked tractor rather than a purpose designed artillery tyagach, albeit towing heavy artillery was one of its primary roles. A distinctive feature of the Kommunar was the rear mounted cylindrical fuel tank. The production variants had differences in their running gear, radiator and cooling system and other components. The Kommunar featured a rivetted chassis and hull mounted on running gear consisting of six road wheels and three return rollers, with a front mounted drive sprocket and rear idler, all protected by a large dirt shield. The original Kommunar 9G was intended to tow artillery up to 6,000kg in travel order, with a maximum speed of 16km/h – typical column march speed – but the tractor could at slower speed tow the heaviest of Soviet artillery pieces. The Kommunar could tow two Br-10 'povozka' trailers with tracked heavy artillery piece barrels.

A total of between 3,499 and 3,650 (sources differ) Kommunar tractors were built at KhPZ in Kharkov from 1924 to 1935, according to most sources, including 850 9G 50hp models, 1,100 9GU 90hp and 1,700 3-90 90hp models.

Production of the 3-90 continued to 1935, when series production of the Komintern, the first purpose designed artillery tyagach, was fully established at KhPZ, with approximately 2,000 Kommunar tractors built to 1931 and approximately 1,500 built from 1932 to 1935, the latter being the 3-90 'fast tractor' type built to military specification for the Red Army.

Per most sources there were four main production models:

9G	50hp at 850rpm	built 1924-30	50hp	16km/h, towed load 6,000kg
9GU	75hp at 1,100rpm	built to 1930	75hp	9km/h towed load 12,000kg
9EU	75hp at 1,100rpm	built to 1930	75hp	11km/h towed load 9,000kg
3-90	90hp at 1,250rpm	built 1930-35	90hp	14km/h, towed load 6,000kg

The Kommunar was widely used in the Red Army of the 1920s and 1930s for towing artillery, with the majority of Kommunar production in the second half of the 1920s going to the Red Army. The tractor was paraded on Moscow's Red Square towing the 203mm B-4 tracked howitzer (operationally towed in split carriage and barrel loads by two tractors) and the 76mm M-1915 and latterly M-1915/28 anti-aircraft gun. On 15 March 1938, the Red Army had 1,815 serviceable Kommunar tractors remaining in service, and by 1941 most Kommunar tractors were already at the end of their operational service life. Although being gradually replaced by more modern tractors such as the

Kommunar tractors towing 203mm B-4 tracked howitzers during a November parade on Red Square, Moscow.

TOP A typical scene in the late summer of 1941. An abandoned Kommunar tractor and 76.2mm M-1931 (3K) anti-aircraft gun.

ABOVE Kommunar tractors at a Wehrmacht field storage and maintenance facility.

Komintern and Voroshilovets specifically designed as tyagachi (artillery tractors) with enclosed cabs and rear cargo load areas, the Kommunar remained in use due to the overall deficit of specialist tractors.

A total of 1,488 Kommunar tractors of all types were recorded as in Red Army service on 1 January 1941, which included tractors awaiting capital repair or being scrapped, with 504 in service with Red Army artillery units as of June 1941. The largest deployment of 146 Kommunar tractors was in the Kiev Military District, with 105 in the Odessa Military District, 40 in the Leningrad Military District and smaller numbers in other districts. The majority of Kommunar tractors in service with the Red Army at the outbreak of war were destroyed within the first weeks of the conflict, but the number in Red Army service actually increased after the outbreak of war as civil tractors were drafted into service. Red Army records show that as many as 257 Kommunar tractors remained in Red Army service as of 1 September 1942. Many tractors were used in rear areas, on airfields for towing heavier aircraft and snow clearing, and in military plants, hence they survived the onslaught of 1941 due to their locations, with a small number surviving the war. The Wehrmacht captured and used some examples, but they were not standardized in service or given a German foreign vehicle identification designation. A Kommunar tractor survived at the NII-21 museum at Bronnitsy as late as 1967 before it was scrapped along with other exhibits.

The Kommunar tractor chassis was used for the SU-2 SAU and air-defence vehicle prototypes and as the basis for a tracked trenching machine. The BNV (initially named after the designer B.N. Voronkov) was developed in 1930–32 as a potential replacement for the Kommunar, being ultimately developed into the series production Komintern artillery tractor.

STZ-NATI 1TA (STZ-NATI) (SKhTZ-NATI) (STZ-3/KhTZ-3)

The STZ-NATI 1TA (in production also known as the SKhTZ-NATI/SKhTZ-3/STZ-3/KhTZ-3) was the first entirely indigenous Soviet tracked tractor design, developed by a combined team of NATI and STZ engineers under the direction of chief designer V.G. Stankevich. Soviet tractor designers were very much enthused by the tanks, tankettes and small tractors developed by the British company Vickers-Armstrong, and developed several indigenous designs based on the best design features of Carden-Loyd prototypes as evaluated in the Soviet Union. In 1931, the Soviet Union tested a Vickers Carden-Loyd tracked transport tractor, and the following year it developed two tractors based on the best principles of the British design, one primarily for agricultural use and a high speed tractor-transporter load carrier variant intended principally for the Red Army.

The STZ-3/KhTZ-3 production variants of the SKhTZ-NATI 1TA were not designed specifically as military tractors, but from the outset such a use was envisaged. This STZ-6 military tractor prototype has the rubber rimmed wheels and road track of the STZ-5.

The base variant for the new tractor design was the STZ-NATI 1TA (SKhTZ-NATI),* developed at NATI in Moscow in collaboration with designers from STZ as a general purpose tracked tractor for agricultural and military use, to be built at STZ in Stalingrad, with a civil agricultural variant to be built at KhTZ in Kharkov and a reconfigured transport tractor (tyagach) artillery tractor to be also built at STZ. In due course these tractors would become better known by their respective manufacturing plant designations – STZ-3, KhTZ-3 and STZ-5. The STZ-NATI 1TA used in its design experience gained in the Komsomolets Type A and Type B prototypes

* The generic term SKhTZ-NATI is often used to describe two slightly different tractors, originally developed at NATI as a single design, the STZ-NATI or STZ-NATI 1TA, with the generic combined SKhTZ-NATI designation appearing later, as did the shortened designations used by the STZ and KhTZ assembly plants.

(A) An early STZ-3 at the STZ plant. Note the open cab compared to the similar KhTZ-3 variant.
(B) An injured Red Army soldier assisted by a Finnish soldier passes an STZ-3 abandoned during fighting in Finland. The Geneva Convention was strictly observed by both sides during the Winter and Continuation Wars. (SA-Kuva)
(C) An abandoned KhTZ-3 towing a 122mm M-1910/30 howitzer abandoned during the 1939–40 Soviet–Finnish Winter War.
(D) An STZ-3 being driven by a Finnish soldier, Sommee, 2 September 1941. (SA Kuva)

(E) This rear view of a KhTZ-3 and 152mm M-1909/30 howitzer abandoned in Finland shows the more substantial full cab arrangement of the KhTZ-3.
(F) Finnish forces attempting to start an abandoned KhTZ-3. (SA-Kuva)
(G) An abandoned KhTZ-3 and 76.2mm M-1931 (3-K) anti-aircraft gun, Rautalahti, 21 August 1941. (SA-Kuva)
(H) An STZ-3 in Finnish service towing a GAZ-AAA.
(I) An STZ-3 in Finnish service. (SA-Kuva)

ABOVE A destroyed STZ-3 located at Porlampi, near Sommee, after the Battle of Porlampi, 5 September 1941. (SA-Kuva)
RIGHT A burned out STZ-3 lost during fighting in Finland.
BELOW A KhTZ-3 abandoned in a typical Finnish forest, Omeliasta itään, 26 July 1941. (SA-Kuva)

A column of captured STZ-3 and KhTZ-3 tractors in Finnish service, summer 1942 or 1943. (Esa Muikku)

A KhTZ-3 disembarking from a train, Finland, summer 1942 or 1943. The Finnish number plate SA-17124 is black lettering on a greenish yellow base. The original KhTZ radiator has been replaced with an STZ type. (Esa Muikku)

and the STZ-3-A-50 developed in May 1933 (a Soviet iteration of the British Carden-Loyd military tractor), with the STZ-NATI 1TA (in production the STZ-3, KhTZ-3) and STZ-NATI 2TV (the production STZ-5) being developed concurrently with maximum commonality of components.

Two prototypes were developed at NATI in Moscow in collaboration with engineers at STZ in Stalingrad and latterly KhTZ in Kharkov with a view to series production of the STZ-NATI 1TA tracked tractor design at both plants, with production of the related STZ-NATI 2TV transport tractor model designed specifically for military application to be undertaken only at STZ. Both tractors used the same engine, running gear and suspension, the latter consisting of two

TOP RIGHT KhTZ-3 tractors towing 152mm M-1909/30 howitzers during a parade in Kishinyev, Bessarabia, 1940.

ABOVE A KhTZ-3 during trials with a 152mm M-10 howitzer.

pairs of bogie wheels, with rear drive sprocket, front idler and two return rollers, but with different layout, gearboxes, road wheels, return rollers and tracks, reflecting their specific applications. The STZ-NATI 1TA (sometimes also generically designated SKhTZ-3 and more specifically as STZ-3 as produced at STZ and KhTZ-3 as later produced at KhTZ) was developed as a tracked light tractor, set between the wheeled SKhTZ-15/30 and the large and powerful Stalinets-60, ostensibly a civil tracked tractor with front mounted engine and a rear mounted cab, designed for agricultural and civil engineering applications. The STZ-NATI 2TV (STZ-5 as designated at STZ), was meanwhile specifically designed as a transport tractor or artillery tractor with a forward control cab and rear cargo area for crew and ammunition.

The STZ-NATI 1TA was initially designed by a design group (known as a Design Bureau – KB) consisting of 30 engineers from NATI and the STZ KB under the overall direction of V.Ya. Slominsky, with the intent to also series produce the tractor at KhTZ in Kharkov. A special KB was assembled at STZ with a combination of NATI and STZ design engineers. The STZ team was overall headed by V.G. Stankevich, with other designers including V.A. Kargopolov (engine development), I.I. Drong, G.F. Matyukov, N.O. Sitkovsky and G.V. Sokolov. Three prototypes of the new STZ-NATI 1TA were extensively evaluated; the first trials of the STZ-NATI 1TA ostensibly agricultural tractor

A KhTZ-3 tractor with full cab working in the delivery yard at the STZ plant in 1942.

and the STZ-NATI 2TV (STZ-5) transport tractor (tyagach) were undertaken concurrently in 1935, with subsequent trials of both tractor types for Red Army service also took place concurrently at the Scientific Experimental Auto and Tank Test Range (NIABP) polygon at Kubinka the following year. The two STZ-NATI versions later competitively tested at Kubinka in 1936 were designated as the STZ-NATI (agricultural) and STZ-NATI (tyagach), with almost identical test results.

The STZ-NATI 1TA was approved for production by L.M. Kaganovich on 10 December 1935 following a demonstration to the Soviet leadership including I.V. Stalin, G.K. Ordzhonikidze, M.I. Kalinin and A.A. Zhdanov at which Stalin personally inspected several vehicle types, including the STZ-NATI 1TA and STZ-NATI 2TV.

The 1MA engine used in all versions of the tractor (also referred to as 1MV during trials at Kubinka in 1936) was a kerosene engine nominally developing 52hp, with the option of running on kerosene or 2nd Sort petrol – essentially a multi-fuel engine, but with significant fuel consumption. With the STZ-3 and KhTZ-3 in series production, STZ again considered the use of a diesel engine, the 1MD, to replace the 1MA kerosene unit, but again the diesel engine was considered not sufficiently developed for series production. Kharkov also developed a diesel powered version of the KhTZ-3, designated KhTZ-4, but this tractor did not enter series production.

Although the STZ-NATI 1TA (SKhTZ-3/STZ-3/KhTZ-3) tractors produced at STZ and KhTZ were generally similar in appearance, they had distinct design features beyond the radiator badge, particularly different cabs. The semi-open cab on the STZ-3 had a sloping windshield frame, but without glass fitted, and

ABOVE ASKhTZ-3 (ATZ-3) tractors produced by the Altai Tractor Plant at Rubtsovsk Station, 1944. Note the cab and ATZ (rather than KhTZ or STZ) radiator badge.

ABOVE RIGHT STZ-3 cab interior detail. This tractor, as displayed at an Oldtimer exhibition at the Crocus City complex, was restored by the Shamansky Workshops in Mytischi.

RIGHT The running gear of the same STZ-3 tractor.

open sides with sheet metal shielding on the lower section only, while the KhTZ-3 had a more square-set enclosed cab with vertical windscreen and full height cab side panels with windows on the cab sides. There were differences in fuel tank arrangements and even fuel filler caps, with current restorers in the Russian Federation surprised as to the wide variety of components produced when all production originated from the same NATI base drawings, as each plant adapted production in accordance with local supply chains. The STZ-3 variant produced for military service at STZ was fitted with track guards with curved rear sections and had standard military tools attached to the tractor, which was not a feature of tractors produced at KhTZ. The tow hook on tractors produced specifically for military use was provided with spring shock absorption. In 1936, a new small pitch lighter 'road' track was made available, which was generally fitted to the STZ-5, but could also be fitted to the STZ/KhTZ-3, as was the case with the KhT-16 armoured tractor conversions.

Preparation for STZ-NATI 1TA tractor production began at STZ, with the first 25 pre-series SKhTZ-NATI 1TA (STZ-3) tractors being delivered on

1 May 1936, with full series production starting in 1937, while the STZ-5 transport tractor was concurrently prepared for production. In 1938, Stankevich and other KEhO lead design engineers were arrested during the Stalin purges, with Stankevich subsequently released in 1940, thereafter being reassigned to Moscow to work on 'Katyusha' rocket launcher developments. The KEhO design department at STZ was thereafter split into two departments, both under the direction of M.M. Romanov, a graduate of the Novocherkassk Aviation Institute, and working respectively on agricultural (STZ-NATI 1TA) and military (STZ-5 2TV) developments.

The reasoning behind establishing additional production of the STZ-NATI 1TA at KhTZ in Kharkov was not just based on increasing overall production. KhTZ production and the KhTZ-3 version produced at the plant were intended to deliver tractors for use primarily in Soviet agriculture, but from a strategic perspective the STZ-NATI 1TA was also produced at KhTZ as a 'doubler' plant such that in the event of war KhTZ could increase tractor assembly while STZ could correspondingly reduce tractor production and revert to increased tank production. The STZ-3 variant produced at STZ in Stalingrad was intended primarily for military service, while the KhTZ-3 variant produced at KhTZ in Kharkov was intended primarily for agricultural and civil engineering use. The STZ-NATI 1TA (STZ-3/KhTZ-3) was essentially an agricultural tractor also used by the Red Army, but with an intended additional military role having been integral to its design. In the event of mobilization, both tractor types would be used by the Red Army; and the Red Army did in fact use both types in the 1939–40 Soviet–Finnish Winter War, with additional civil tractors pressed into military service from the summer of 1941.

On 21 October 1937, the senior military representative at STZ, Dvurechensky, wrote to the director of STZ and the head of the 6th Directorate of the Main Auto-Tank Command of the Red Army (GABTU) with regard to ten early production STZ-NATI 1TA tractors in operational service with the Auto-Armoured-Tank Command of the Red Army (ABTU RKKA), detailing a list of defects to be resolved in future production. From 15 to 30 November 1937 an STZ-3 (actually a KhTZ-3) tractor was tested at 12th Corps Artillery Regiment towing the 107mm M-1910/30 field gun and the 152mm M-1909/30 howitzer, achieving, for the time, an acceptable column speed of 8km/h (the same speed as the S-60/65 with heavier corps artillery).

Production of the first pre-series machines began in 1937 at STZ and KhTZ, with full series production commencing in 1938. The first STZ-NATI was completed at STZ on 11 July 1937, with production following at KhTZ from 17 September the same year. The KhTZ-3 was in series production in Kharkov from 1938 until the late summer of 1941, with the STZ-3 built in Stalingrad

ОЛИЗА МЕДИ

An STZ-3 at the Urals Military Glory Museum at Verkhnyaya Pyshma, Ekaterinburg. (John Ham)

An STZ-3 driver's controls, from an original Operator's Manual.

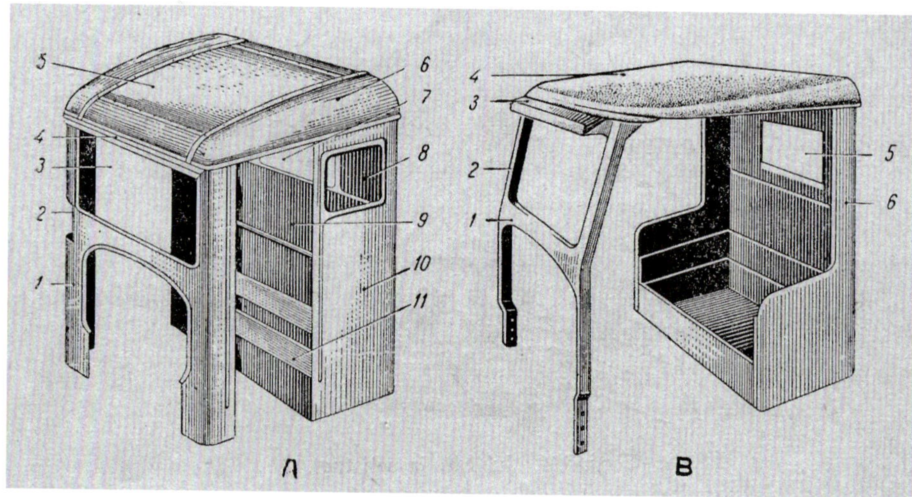

TOP RIGHT The KhTZ (left) and STZ (right) cabs from the same Operator's Manual.

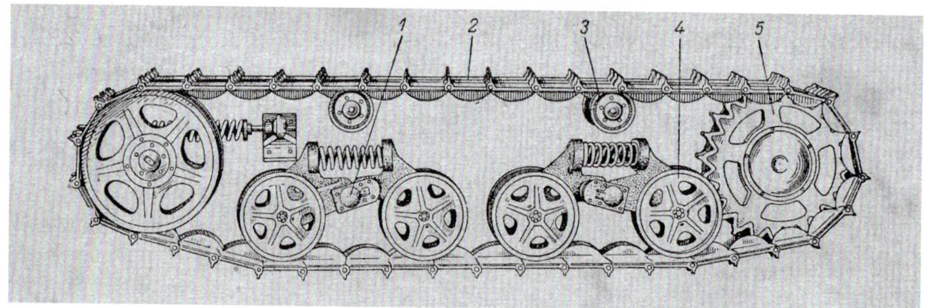

CENTRE RIGHT SKhTZ-NATI 1TA (KhTZ-3/STZ-3) running gear, with all-steel road wheels and 'agricultural' track.

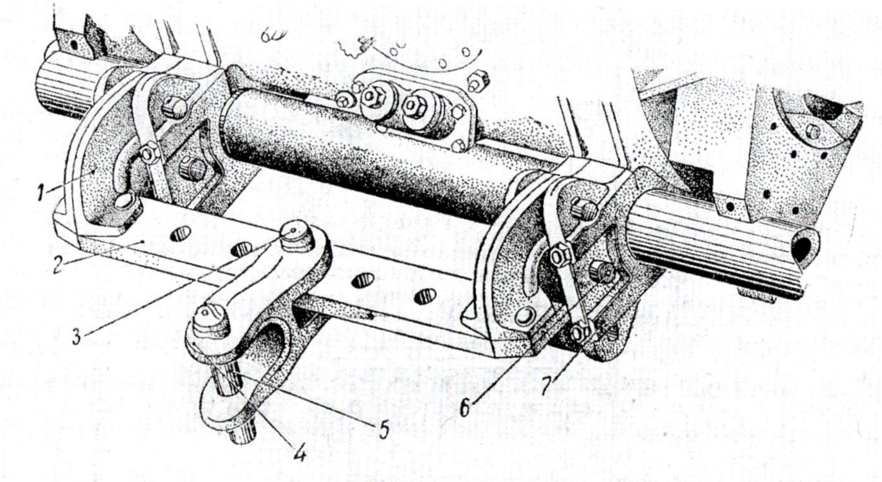

BOTTOM RIGHT The KhTZ-3 tow hook. The tow hooks on tractors originally built for the Red Army were provided with spring amortization.

from 1937 until 1942. Machine tooling was evacuated from STZ to Rubtsovsk in the autumn of 1941, with further machine tooling evacuated from STZ the following year. After the start of series production, the STZ-NATI

(STZ-NATI 1TA) (СТЗ-НАТИ 1TA) was known at STZ as the STZ-3 (СТЗ-3) and as produced at KhTZ in Kharkov designated SKhTZ-3 (СХТЗ-3), sometimes abbreviated to KhTZ-3 (ХТЗ-3). The Kharkov-produced tractor was also variously known as the SKhTZ-NATI, KhTZ-3 SKhTZ and KhSTZ. In Red Army service both tractors were often designated simply as 1TA taking the name from the original STZ-NATI 1TA design, which was also how it was referred to in the official operator manuals.

The STZ-NATI 1TA was assembled at STZ in Stalingrad from 1937–42 as the STZ-3, at KhTZ Kharkov from 1937–41 as the KhTZ-3 and later at the Altai Tractor Plant (ATZ) from August 1942 until 1952 as the ATZ-3.

Total SKhTZ-3 (KhTZ-3/ STZ-3) production from 1937–38 to the outbreak of war in 1941 was approximately 16,000 '1TA' tractors, of which approximately 4,000 or 25 per cent of production was delivered for service with the Red Army, with STZ being the primary producer of STZ-3 tractors intended for service in the Red Army.

Production ceased at KhTZ in the autumn of 1941 with the evacuation of the plant and its subsequent capture, with production continuing sporadically for another year at STZ where T-34 tank assembly was henceforth the primary production focus. The tractor was used in the Red Army to tow divisional and often heavier artillery. Operational service with the Red Army included combat deployment during the Soviet–Finnish Winter War of 1939–40, with both the STZ-3 and KhTZ-3 versions deployed, before the onslaught of Operation *Barbarossa* in 1941. Being used in front line operations, initial losses were considerable, but the huge losses of 1941 were as with other tractor types largely replaced by civil tractors pressed into Red Army service as artillery and general transport tractors. The STZ-NATI (STZ-3/KhTZ-3) tractor was not ideal for the purpose, not being a dedicated tyagach with a load area for ammunition, but it was reliable, easy to maintain and served a useful role in filling in for a deficit of artillery towing vehicles. In addition to use by the Red Army, STZ-3/KhTZ-3 tractors captured intact were used by Finnish, German, Hungarian and Romanian forces for artillery movement and general transport.

Production of the SKhTZ-NATI (STZ-3/KhTZ) was according to official records restarted, and massively increased, in August 1942 at the Altai Tractor Plant in the Altai region (primarily for civil use, with full production from 1944) as the ATZ-NATI (AShKhTZ-NATI) or ATZ-3. Production of the modified design began on 24 August 1942 and continued until 1952, with post-war production on a massive scale as the post-war Soviet Union ramped up assembly for agricultural production recovery. Production was restarted at KhTZ in Kharkov and at STZ in Stalingrad at the end of 1944, continuing until 1949 at both original plants and until 1952 at ATZ. The STZ-NATI 1TA design under its various production plant designations was the most widely employed tracked tractor of its time, with a total of 210,744 having been built when production finally ceased in 1952.*

Both STZ-3 and KhTZ-3 variants of the STZ-NATI were used during the 1939–40 Soviet–Finnish Winter War, with 1,733 artillery tractors deployed during the Soviet operation against Finland, of which 48 per cent were the STZ-3, with fewer than 20 STZ-5 tractors deployed. The majority of STZ-NATI tractors used against Finland were returned to the Soviet Union in 1945.

As of 1 January 1941, there were 3,658 SKhTZ-NATI tractors serving in Red Army artillery units, with a recorded 9,073 of both '1TA' types in service overall, at a time when there were approximately 32,000 such tractors in agricultural service. Operational feedback from the Winter War resulted in the standard provision of a fabric thermal jacket for the engine compartment. After the fall of Kharkov, the STZ-3 continued to be produced at Stalingrad alongside T-34 medium tank production. The machine tooling for the STZ-3 was however evacuated from Stalingrad to the new ATZ plant in Rubtsovsk before that plant and city also came under threat of capture, with the tractor being re-established in production in August 1942 based on tooling evacuated from Kharkov and Stalingrad. Wartime production at STZ from 22 June 1941 until evacuation was an additional 1,851 STZ-3 tractors. On 1 September 1942 the Red Army had in service 9,704 SKhTZ-NATI tractors on all Fronts, more than in June 1941 due to mobilization. As examples of distribution, 431 remained on the Karelian Front, 745 on the Western Front and 289 on the Stalingrad Front.

According to prevailing Statutes at the time when the AShKTZ-NATI entered production at ATZ in August 1942, the tractor was intended for towing the 37mm M-1939 anti-aircraft gun, 76.2mm M-1902/30 divisional gun, 107mm M-1910/30 corps gun, and 122mm M-1938 (M-30) and 152mm M-1938 (M-10) howitzers, with a travel order weight of up to 4,500kg. In the reality of war, the tractors were used as available for any task required.

STALINETS-60 (S-60)

The Soviet Zernovoi Trest (Zernotrest – Grain Trust) in the 1920s purchased 20 'Caterpillar Sixty' (Caterpillar-60) tractors for evaluation in Soviet conditions, resulting in the Soviet Union contracting for the purchase of another 1,929 tractors from Caterpillar in 1929. As production of the Caterpillar-60 was in

* Sources on total STZ/KhTZ/ATZ production are inconsistent, with stated total production varying from 191,000 to 210,744 tractors. The fact that 19,744 tractors can be 'lost in statistics' is however indicative as to the sheer scale of production.

(A) An S-60 plinth mounted outside the ChTZ plant offices in 1983 on the 50th anniversary of the start of production at the plant.
(B) (C) S-60 tractors on parade in Stavropol on 7 November 1935.
(D) S-60 tractors at the same parade. The distinctive horizontal fuel tank distinguishes the S-60.

D

TOP RGHT An S-60 captured during the 1939–40 Winter War in service with the Finnish Army. (SA-Kuva)

BELOW RIGHT The fate of many Red Army vehicles, entrapped on narrow forest roads by Finnish forces with local knowledge of the terrain, and with no ability to disperse. (SA-Kuva)

OPPOSITE The Finnish Army captured a significant number of S-60 and S-65 tractors and used them during the Winter and Continuation Wars. (SA-Kuva)

1931 coming to an end in the United States, successful negotiations were concluded to establish production of a Soviet version of the tractor at a new-build green field site plant in the Soviet Union. As described earlier, the plant was established in Chelyabinsk with American production tooling and technical assistance as the Chelyabinsk Tractor Plant (ChTZ). The S-60 was used as both an agricultural/civil engineering and a military tractor. It was powerful, reliable, simple to maintain, but slow, which was not relevant in civil use but limited its military application, hence the immediate development of an 'S' (skorostnoi) fast-tractor version, which would ultimately enter production as the S-2 artillery transport tractor.

(A) An abandoned S-60, most likely abandoned due to lack of fuel.
(B) An S-60 being used for tank recovery.
(C) An S-60 in Red Army service in 1942, towing a 152mm M-1937 (ML-20) corps howitzer.
(D) An S-60 tractor towing a captured Pz.Kpfw.III in Stalingrad, 1942.

A

B

C

D

TOP LEFT This captured S-60 in Axis forces service has a significantly modified ZiS-5 cab.

LEFT S-60 tractors in Finnish Army service towing a BT-5 fast tank.

Construction of the ChTZ Prototype Plant began south of the main rail tracks in Chelyabinsk in February 1930, with the first pre-series S-60 completed on 15 February 1931.* On 27 April 1931 Prototype No. 1 was sent to Moscow for demonstration to the Soviet leadership, with Prototype No. 2 sent the same summer. Prototype No. 3 became the 'Stalinets-3', fitted with a four-speed gearbox, while Prototype No. 4 reverted to what would become the standard three-speed gearbox. In the summer of 1931 and the winter of 1931–32 the S-60 prototype was tested at the NATI polygon near Moscow together with the US original. Prototype No. 3 with the four-speed gearbox was dropped, as was, for the meantime, the 'S' fast tractor variant. Prototype No. 4, with a ligroin engine developing 60hp at a low 650rpm, was accepted as the basis for the series production Stalinets-60 (S-60).

* The official designation 'Stalinets-60' was often subsequently shortened to S-60, with the designation ChTZ-60 also being used, but official manuals and documents retained the full designation. The same prefixes were used on the future S-65 and S-2.

ABOVE AND RIGHT An S-60 undergoing restoration in Rostov, May 2009. The layout of the ligroin fuelled engine and the driver's controls are in significant contrast to the later diesel engine S-65.

Over the next two years, while the main plant (completed in 1933) was being built north of the rail tracks, ChTZ delivered 525 tractors. The first S-60 series production tractor completed by the main plant was delivered by ChTZ on 15 May 1933, with a further 12 tractors delivered by 1 July 1933. The S-60 production start date is however recorded as 1 June 1933, when the first series production S-60 officially left the production line. Production ramped up dramatically thereafter, with 1,650 S-60 tractors delivered in 1933 (against a target of 2,000 for the year). By the end of 1934, ChTZ had delivered nearly 10,000 S-60 tractors, with full scale production continuing until 20 June 1937 when the first series production S-65 left the production line at ChTZ, with 68,997 S-60 tractors built in only five years before the S-60 was replaced in production by the S-65 in 1937.*

* Original Soviet document sources are slightly contradictory, ranging from 68,997 to 69,261.

LEFT An S-60 located at the Urals Military Glory Museum, Verkhnyaya Pyshma, Ekaterinburg. (John Ham)

BELOW LEFT A Red Army S-60 towing a Lend-Lease M5 Stuart light tank.

BELOW An S-60 towing a 152mm M-1937 (ML-20) gun-howitzer across the River Narev, 1st Belorussian Front, 1944.

The S-60 was powered by a four-cylinder carburettor engine which used ligroin (heavy gasoline, gas-oil) or kerosene as fuel; the S-60 being described in service as a 'ligroinovy traktor' (i.e. running on ligroin fuel). The engine developed 60hp at a moderate 650rpm, the S-60 being designed to deliver high output torque rather than speed. The tractor had a nominal 10,000kg towing capacity and a towing speed of 3–8.4km/h according to differing original sources, but despite a 390-litre fuel tank had a limited 75km range as the fuel consumption was 3–5 litres/km. The 500mm wide tracks provided excellent mobility in soft ground, resulting in a tractor that despite its multi-purpose use origins was also a powerful artillery tractor. Some tractors were by special order fitted with a front towing hook, for linking tractors for tank recovery and towing road trains.

TOP RIGHT S-60 artillery tractors towing 280mm M-1939 (Br-5) heavy mortars during the Victory Parade in Kiev, 1945.

BELOW RIGHT This S-60 artillery tractor is plinth mounted outside the ChTZ administration building. (Alexander Morzhitsky)

The S-60 was primarily developed as a powerful tractor for use in agriculture and civil engineering rather than for military use. The Red Army employed the S-60 for towing heavy artillery such as the 152mm ML-20 and the tracked 203mm B-4 broken into carriage and barrel loads. The combat debut of the S-60 was, together with the Komintern tractor, against Japanese forces at Lake Khasan in 1938, where both tractors were used to tow heavy artillery pieces. The S-60 was operationally deployed in Finland during the short Soviet–Finnish Winter War of 1939–40, with there being 5,559 S-60 tractors in Red Army service on 1 January 1941. Due to the huge losses of material as a result of Operation *Barbarossa* in the summer of 1941, large numbers of ostensibly civil

S-60 tractors were requisitioned into service with the Red Army where they continued to be used for towing heavy artillery and trailers. There were differences between the agricultural S-60 tractors drafted into military service and those built for military use, not least there being no compensation mechanism on the tow mechanism on the civil version. The S-60 as developed and tested had an open driver's position with a canvas roof for sun and rain protection, which was not ideal for a tractor towing artillery in frontal areas, especially as the canvas roof was in practice rarely fitted. Wooden construction cabs were fabricated for some of these tractors when drafted into wartime Red Army service, and captured foreign truck cabs, most notably of Opel-Blitz origin, were also retrofitted to many S-60 tractors.

The S-60 was generally used to tow at moderate speed artillery up to 14,000kg in transport order. In Red Army service it was used to tow the 107mm M-1910/30 and M-1940 guns, the 122mm M-1910/30 howitzer, the 122mm M-1931/37 (A-19) gun, the 152mm M-1909/30, 152mm M-1938 and 152mm M-1937 (ML-20) howitzers, as well as anti-aircraft artillery pieces. The tractor was also used on airfields to tow TB-3 and other heavy aircraft.

Feedback on the S-60 from Red Army artillery units was not always complimentary; for example, the commander of the 68th Army Artillery Brigade noted the slow and noisy process of towing 152mm gun-howitzers. But the tractor was what was available, it was reliable, and would continue to serve to the final days of the war. Captured S-60 tractors were used by Wehrmacht forces for towing artillery and trailers, but were not formalized as standard service vehicles and hence did not receive a foreign vehicle identification designation.

Though initial losses in 1941 of Red Army S-60 tractors were huge, many survived the war, with S-60 tractors participating in the Victory Parade on Kreshchatik in Kiev in 1945.

STALINETS-65 (S-65)

The S-65 was developed as a collaborative effort between NATI and ChTZ via a series of prototypes, with the diesel/kerosene powered S-65 replacing the ligroin/kerosene powered S-60 in series production at ChTZ in 1937. The main improvement over the earlier S-60 was the use of a four-cylinder M-17 (DM-17) diesel (multi-fuel) engine which had also been collaboratively developed by NATI and ChTZ from February 1935 under the design leadership of A. Lebedev and V. Lomonosov respectively, with work on the later prototype engine, now known as M-17, directed at ChTZ by Eh. Gurevich. The M-17 engine had a slightly increased power output of 65–75hp at 850rpm (depending on fuel) and increased torque, but with a 25 per cent reduction in fuel consumption for the

(A) An S-65 at the All-Union Agricultural Exhibition (VSKhV) which was completed in October 1939. Post-war VSKhV was renamed VDNKh. **(B)** An S-65 with standard factory cab abandoned in a Finnish forest. Finnish photographic records of Red Army vehicles used in the Winter and Continuation Wars are more comprehensive than those of the Red Army. (SA-Kuva) **(C)** An S-65 apparently being used as a shelter by Finnish troops, with Soviet Moisin-Nagant M-1891/30 rifles propped against the tracks. (SA-Kuva) **(D)** S-65 tractors with open cabs abandoned in a Finnish forest. Although the S-65 in the foreground is in ostensibly 'civil' configuration, it is fitted with a military tow hook with amortization. (SA-Kuva) **(E)** The Finns captured a significant number of S-60 and S-65 tractors during the 1939–40 Winter War, which were pressed into service under new ownership. (SA-Kuva)

(F) Another abandoned S-65 on a forest road. This S-65 has the standard enclosed cab as fitted at ChTZ to tractors intended for delivery to the Red Army. (SA-Kuva)
(G) The engine covers for the M-17 diesel engine were often removed in service to provide additional cooling. This particular S-65 is shown in Hungarian service after capture. (Sergei Popsuevich)
(H) A Finnish officer poses by an abandoned S-65. The hinged front and rear windows all opened for cooling and ventilation purposes. (SA-Kuva)

same outputs. The first factory trials of the new engine, mounted in an S-60, were conducted on 14 August 1935. The main diesel engine was started by a V-20 petrol engine developing 20hp, in turn started by a front mounted hand crank mechanism. The S-65 during state trials had a stately 6.95km/h maximum towing speed, which remained the main Red Army complaint in an otherwise powerful, reliable and simple to maintain artillery tractor. The M-17 diesel engine was accepted for production at ChTZ in accordance with SNK Resolution No. 866 dated 23 May 1936, as the engine for the forthcoming S-65, coupled to a three-speed gearbox.

(A) An S-65 with enclosed factory cab abandoned on the Omelia–Rukajärvi road, 24 July 1941. (SA Kuva)
(B) Captured S-65 tractors and early production 152mm M-1937 (ML-20) gun-howitzers in a Finnish storage yard. (SA-Kuva)
(C) This rear view of captured S-65 tractors in Finland shows the difference between the ostensibly 'civil' and 'military' versions of the S-65 tractor as they left the ChTZ plant. (SA-Kuva)
(D) An S-65 abandoned in a forest on the Omelia–Rukajärvi road, 24 July 1941. (SA-Kuva)
(E) Finnish forces salvaging Red Army equipment, Somee, 2 September 1941. (SA-Kuva)

(F) Red Army S-65 tractors on parade during the Soviet occupation of Bessarabia and Northern Bukovina in 1940.
(G) An S-65 tractor on the streets of Odessa, autumn 1941.
(H) An S-65 recovering a T-34-76 M-1942 from marshland near Sukhinichi, Belorussia, summer 1943. Photographer: G. Khomzor.
(I) A Red Army S-65 emplacing a 203mm B-4 tracked howitzer.
(J) A column of S-65 tractors with the standard factory fitted cab and engine covers in place.

(A) This photograph of an S-65 tractor column crossing a damaged bridge shows the mix of S-65 types used by the Red Army. **(B)** S-65 tractors of the 3rd Belorussian Front, 27 January 1945. The 203mm B-4 tracked howitzers are in camouflage paint, but not the S-65 tractors. **(C)** An S-65 without cab operating in the Stalingrad region, winter 1943. **(D)** A rare photograph of an S-65 tractor with a substantial designer wooden cab in use for ground compaction on a Soviet airstrip in the DDR (East Germany) in 1954. The aircraft is an Ilyushin Il-4. **(E)** An S-65 crossing a makeshift wooden bridge, Western Front, 1942. The 152mm M-1937 (ML-20) gun-howitzer, with early spoked wheels from the earlier M-1910/34, is painted in winter camouflage but not the tractor. **(F) (G) (H)** An S-65 tractor with an Opel Maultier cab and 122mm M-1938 (M-30) 1st Ukrainian Front. Photographer: Arkady Shaikhet.

Reflecting its agricultural and civil engineering origins, the S-65 entered service with a maximum towing speed of only 7.5km/h (albeit at the time the horse remained the transport for light and medium artillery in the Red Army and the Wehrmacht), but, as noted, the tractor was powerful and reliable, albeit with a limited range of 60–75km. The horizontal cylindrical fuel tank that was a distinguishing feature of the S-60 was replaced by a large 300-litre fuel tank mounted ahead of the cab. The running gear consisted of five road wheels and two return rollers, with rear drive sprocket and front idler and with 34 links per track.

(A) An S-65 tractor with coupled 76mm M-1939 USV guns, Western Front, May 1942. **(B)** This S-65 without cab and as usual in summer months missing its engine covers is towing trailers with N2P pontoon sections; these were usually transported singly on modified ZiS-5 trucks. **(C)** An S-65 tractor and 152mm M-1937 (ML-20) gun-howitzer on a rail flat car, August 1941. **(D)** Another Red Army S-65 with Opel-Blitz cab, towing a 152mm M-1937 (ML-20) gun-howitzer. **(E)** An S-65 with field cab conversion, towing a 152mm ML-20 gun-howitzer in terrain that necessitated tractors such as the S-65 for operational movement. **(F)** An S-65 with Opel-Blitz cab conversion and acquired Axis origin fuel can.

An S-65 with original factory cab restored by the Shamansky Workshops and located at the Motors of War Museum, Moscow.

An S-65 engine compartment. The engine block has the surface corrosion resulting from several decades sunk in a marsh.

(A) S-65 tractors at the Victory Parade in Kiev, 1945. **(B)** S-65 tractors towing 122mm M-1931/37 (A-19) corps guns, Victory Parade, Harbin, 1945. **(C)** The front tow hook on the S-65 was used for gun positioning or for linking two tractors in tandem. **(D)** A rear view of S-65 tractors towing 122m M-1931/37 Corps guns, Victory Parade, Harbin, 1945. **(E)** The S-65 rear drive sprocket and track arrangement. **(F)** The tow hook on S-65 tractors originally built for Red Army service was provided with a shock absorber/compensator.

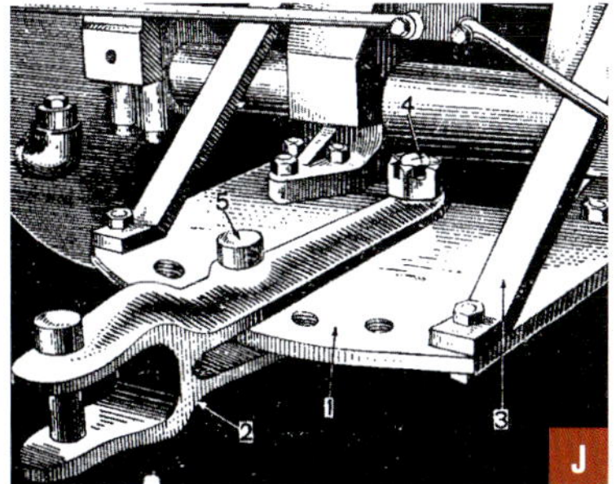

(G) A restored S-65 tractor on display in Red Square, Moscow, November 2023.

(H) The Shamansky Workshops military specification S-65 at an open day at the Motors of War Museum, Moscow.

(I) Wooden cab detail on the S-65 displayed in Red Square, Moscow, November 2023.

(J) (K) The S-65 'civil' version tow hook without shock absorber/compensator. From S-65 ChTZ manuals.

In contrast with the open driver's position on the S-60, with at best a canvas roof, the S-65 was latterly provided with a substantial factory-built wood and metal cab. Early production S-65 tractors were built without a cab, but cab options had been considered from the outset. In 1938, an enlarged ZiS-5 type cab was built and tested but rejected, with the large and distinctive wood and metal box construction factory fitted cab with sliding doors being standardized the following year on S-65 tractors built for Red Army service. Although ersatz cabs sourced from captured (again primarily Opel-Blitz) trucks were sometimes fitted to S-65s built without cabs, these modifications were less common than on the S-60. The distinctive radiator with 'X' struts across the front used on the S-60 was replaced on the S-65 by a more conventional radiator grille with five vertical columns.

The first pre-production S-65 tractor left the production line at ChTZ in March 1937, with full series production starting four months later on 20 July 1937; a total of 37,626 S-65 tractors were produced from 1937 to 1941.* In February a batch of 60 S-65 tractors were exported.

* Production numbers vary slightly depending on source.

As of 1 January 1941, 10,603 of the 37,626 tractors produced were in service with the Red Army, such that the S-65 was the most numerous artillery tractor in Red Army service at the time despite not being a specialized tractor. After 22 June 1941 S-65 tractors built specifically for the Red Army were complemented by large numbers of civil tractors drafted into military service. The S-65 thereby remained one of the most common tractors in service with the Red Army throughout 1941 and for the duration of the war. Drafted civil tractors had minor differences from those tractors originally built for military service with the tow hook fitted on military S-65s being provided with shock absorption by means of an enclosed spring mechanism.

As of 1 May 1945, according to official records, there were 9,631 S-65 tractors still in service with the Red Army, of which 8,220 were in working order. This was almost the same number (10,603) of tractors that were in service with the Red Army on 1 January 1941, the huge losses encountered in 1941–42 having been made up by the large quantity of civil tractors drafted into military service. At the end of 1941, there were 4,795 S-65 tractors in service with the Red Army, which may reflect a backlog on repair work or the return of many tractors to civil duties. Like the S-60, the S-65 transported tracked artillery over long distances broken down into two loads towed by separate tractors – namely tracked carriage and barrel, the latter transported on a tracked B-29 or wheeled Br-10 povozka carriage. There were two variants of the B-4 tracked howitzer as towed by the S-65, with barrel lengths of 4.29m and 4.91m and respective travel order weights of 15,796kg and 17,700kg.

A typical Soviet military summary defined S-65 and SG-65 gas generator variant distribution in the immediate pre-war era by ministry (with additional SG-65 tractors in brackets where applicable):

Ministry	Purpose	No. of tractors
NKO (Ministry of Defence)	Red Army	324
NKVMF (Ministry of Military Naval Forces)	Naval forces	25
NKVD (Ministry of Internal Affairs)	Military units	8 (5)
NKVD (Ministry of Internal Affairs)	GULAG, remote construction	8 (9)
NKAP (Ministry of Aviation Production)	Aviation construction	8
NKSP (Ministry of Ship Building)	Shipping vessel construction	(1)
NKB (Ministry of Ammunition Production)	Ammunition production	2 (1)
NKV (Ministry of Armaments)	Armaments	3 (2)
GVS (Main Military Council of the Red Army)	Military construction	1

ABOVE AND NEXT PAGE The S-10 during military trials, 13 July 1942. The intent was to increase the road speed of the S-65 by incorporating the running gear from the purpose designed S-2 'tyagach' artillery tractor.

S-10 AND S-11

In the spring of 1942, ChTZ (now renamed ChKZ reflecting its amalgamation with the LKZ (Kirov) plant in Leningrad) terminated the production of S-65 and S-2 artillery tractors, initially to retool for KV-1 heavy tank assembly. The KB at ChKZ nevertheless continued in collaboration with NATI to design potential new artillery fast tractors intended for towing corps artillery at a road speed of at least 30km/h. One such design developed to prototype stage based on new Tactical Technical Requirements (TTTs) was the S-10, a modification of the S-65, with the cab and engine compartment mounted on the Stalinets-2 (S-2) 'fast' transport tractor chassis recently removed from production. The S-10 was powered by an MT-17 diesel engine uprated to 125hp from the 65hp of the M-17 engine used on the S-65 and the 115hp of the later MT-17 engine used on the S-2.

СТАЛИН
СТАЛИНЕЦ
НИЗАЛ

Three prototype S-10 tractors were built, and evaluated from 6 to 14 June 1942, with prototypes No. 2 and No. 3 travelling over 400km on various surfaces. During trials, the S-10 tractors towed the (wheeled) prototype 203mm BL-39 corps howitzer at a steady 16km/h, with a maximum towing speed achieved during trials of 23.7km/h and an average fuel consumption of 190 litres/100km. The test protocol was signed on 19 June 1942 by V.Ya. Slonimsky as chief designer on behalf of NATI, General-Major Kholkov, Deputy Chief of GAU KA, and Colonel Vasiliev, Military Commissar Artkom GAU KA (Artillery Committee GAU KA). The S-10 tractor was recommended for production and adoption by the Red Army albeit with a clause requiring a cab capable of accommodating an eight-man gun crew. GKO Resolution No. 1923/s *About Production of the Tractor-Tyagach S-10 at the Kirov Plant NKTP* dated 22 June 1942 and addressed to ChKZ in Chelyabinsk required delivery of 150 S-10 tractors in July, 200 in August and 300 in September 1942 respectively. The new S-10 never entered production, however, due to other priorities at ChKZ rather than anything related to the S-10 design. In July 1942 ChKZ also began assembly of the T-34 medium tank in addition to the KV-1 heavy tank, and for the second time in a year tank production was prioritized over tractor production at ChKZ with no spare capacity for other assembly work. Hence the slow but dependable S-65 tractor would remain the primary Red Army heavy artillery tractor to the end of the war.

A further variant of the S-10, the S-11, powered by a D-11 diesel engine developing 160hp and with a higher drawbar capacity and 26km/h projected road speed, was also evaluated by the KB at ChKZ, but did not progress beyond the paper design stage.

CHAPTER 4
TRACKED TRANSPORTER-TRACTORS

The name 'Komsomolets' as applied to the armoured artillery tractor used for moving anti-tank guns appears more than once in the history of Red Army artillery tractors. The original tractor to bear the Komsomolets name was designed under the direction of N.G. Popov at NATI as a light artillery and general purpose military transport tractor, with the prototype being completed at STZ in Stalingrad in 1932. The Komsomolets Type A, which featured a forward cab and rear load area arrangement that would later be adopted on the series production STZ-5, was heavily based on British Carden-Loyd designs purchased and imported for evaluation purposes. The unarmoured Komsomolets Type A prototype was primarily used to test the new M-7 diesel engine developing 50hp; the testing of prototype diesel engines on tracked tractors being a recurring theme in the early to mid-1930s as the Soviet Union worked to perfect diesel engine technology with its power, fuel economy and safety advantages in military applications. However, the power output relative to tractor weight and the overall reliability of the M-7 diesel engine were not considered adequate for series production. NATI continued work on the 'universal' tractor theme, but the potential M-7 diesel engine was shelved as being insufficiently fettled for series production.

A pre-series prototype STZ-5 2TV (later known in production and service as the STZ-5).

STZ-5 artillery tractors towing 76.2mm M-1927 regimental guns through Kiev, 1938. The tractor accommodated the driver and gun commander, with 12 gun crew located in the rear load area and a further three seated on the gun limber.

(A) STZ-5 artillery tractors towing 152mm M-1938 (M-10) howitzers at the same parade, Kiev, 1938.

(B) STZ-5 tractors towing 76.2mm M-1939 USV divisional guns through Red Square, Moscow, 1 May 1940. Photographer: Sergei Korshunov.

(C) STZ-5 tractors towing 152mm M-1938 (M-10) howitzers through Red Square, 1 May 1940.

(D) STZ-5 tractors towing 122mm M-1938 (M-30) howitzers through Red Square, 7 November 1940.

(E) STZ-5 tractors towing 76.2mm M-1939 USV divisional guns through Red Square, 1 May 1940.

Note the rubber road wheel rims, fabricated cab roof and red star on the door of this STZ-5 on parade in Red Square, Moscow, 1 May 1940.

In mid-1933, development work continued at NATI and STZ on the Komsomolets Type A and Type B prototypes, under the overall direction of V.G. Stankevich. The prototypes were competitively tested, with the name changing during development to STZ-NATI, reflecting the two design teams involved. The Komsomolets prototypes were used to test the engines, transmissions, running gear and layout of what might be described as a universal tractor design; this led to the later series production STZ-NATI 1TA, produced as the Stalingrad STZ-3 and Kharkov KhTZ-3 tractors with a rear cab and a forward control, rear cargo area variant, the STZ-NATI 2TV transport tractor that more closely resembled the early Komsomolets prototypes and would ultimately enter series production as the STZ-5. The tractor types were developed with maximum parts interchangeability between the 'agricultural' and 'military' designs, with the design work concentrated in the experimental KB at STZ. The engine chosen for both tractor types was the four-cylinder 1MA engine, which was started with petrol and ran on a combination of kerosene or ligroin, essentially a multi-fuel engine.

As the two related designs matured, a NATI team of 30 engineers under the direction of V.Ya. Slominsky was sent to STZ in Stalingrad to assist in preparing the plant for series production of what would become the STZ-3 'agricultural' tractor and the STZ-5 military transport tractor variant. NATI engineers involved on production preparation included A.V. Vasiliev and I.I. Trepenenkov sent from NATI and I.I. Drong, V.A. Kargopolov, G.F. Matyukov and G.V. Sokolov located at STZ, with other designers including V.Ye Malakhovsky, D.A. Chudakov and V.N. Tulaev, with overall design work overseen by V.G. Stankevich. The result of this work would be the previously related series production versions of the

STZ-NATI 1TA (the KhTZ-3 and STZ-3) and the forward control cab STZ-5. The Komsomolets name would meanwhile re-appear in later years as an armoured tractor design.

STZ-5

A new medium general purpose transport tractor, based on Soviet evaluation of Vickers Carden-Loyd prototypes purchased from Great Britain and evaluated for service with the Red Army the previous year, was developed at STZ in Stalingrad from June 1932 in collaboration with engineers from NATI in Moscow. The new tracked transport tractor was to be used for towing medium artillery together with the gun crew and ammunition, or to operate as a tracked transporter. The first prototype was completed in May 1933, and subjected to plant trials fitted with a diesel engine, but overall reliability was deemed unacceptable and the project terminated in favour of a design developed at NATI in Moscow, which would ultimately be developed via the STZ-NATI 2TV prototype into the series production STZ-5.

In the summer of 1933, engineers at NATI had, as related, previously begun work on two tracked tractors, the NATI-1TA with a rear cab, ostensibly for agricultural but also for artillery tractor use, and NATI-2TV,* a transport tractor variant with forward control cab and rear cargo area, more specifically aligned with a Red Army requirement for a general purpose artillery and transport tractor with better road speed than the 1TA 'agricultural' variant. The two tractor types, which incorporated the best components of the earlier Komsomolets 'Type-A' and 'Type-B' prototypes, maximized the use of standard components, for assembly on a single assembly line.

Developing the designs for series production was undertaken at STZ in Stalingrad, with the NATI-1TA developed via the STZ-NATI 1TA into the SKhTZ-3, assembled at STZ and KhTZ as the STZ-3 and KhTZ-3 respectively, while the NATI-2TV was developed via the STZ-NATI 2TV into the STZ-5 (the STZ factory designation) built only at STZ in Stalingrad.

The STZ-NATI 2TV (STZ-5) 'transportny-traktor' (TT) variant was developed as a collaborative effort between NATI and the aforementioned special design group (SKB) established at STZ in Stalingrad with 30 NATI and STZ engineers working on the STZ-NATI 1TA and STZ-NATI 1TA designs, their distinct roles falling under the ultimate direction of the NATI engineer V.Ya. Slominsky.

* In Russian the НАТИ-2ТВ (NATI-2TV) which later became the production СТЗ-5 2ТВ (STZ-5 2TV), is often mis-translated as TB in English.

(A) An STZ-5 towing a 122mm M-1938 (M-30) howitzer and limber, Western Front, December 1941. Note the radiator thermal jacket.
(B) A winter camouflaged STZ-5 with 122mm M-1938 (M-30), abandoned during the 1939–40 Soviet–Finnish Winter War. (SA-Kuva)
(C) (D) A column of STZ-5 tractors in the Moscow Oblast in the early winter of 1941.
(E) A captured STZ-5 in Finnish army service. The original STZ radiator has been exchanged for a KhTZ-3 radiator with the cast XT3 radiator symbol. (SA-Kuva)

Two prototype STZ-NATI 2TV (later STZ-5) tractors underwent plant trials at the beginning of 1935, followed by an endurance trial with two prototypes being driven to Moscow from Stalingrad, which was successfully completed with a typical list of technical issues (findings) to be resolved before series manufacture. An improved third prototype was developed based on the findings from testing the earlier prototypes. On 16 June 1935 the STZ-NATI 2TV (the forthcoming production STZ-5) was demonstrated together with the STZ-NATI 1TA (STZ-3) at the NATI polygon near Moscow to the senior Soviet hierarchy including Stalin, with all members of the Politburo taking turns to ride around the polygon on the tractors. The 1TA (STZ-3) and 2TV (STZ-5) prototypes were both approved for series production by the leadership present, subject to elimination of faults and defects identified during the final trials. The first pre-series batch of 135 STZ-5 tractors was built at Stalingrad in late 1935, ahead of final approval, as was not unusual in the Soviet Union.

The STZ-5 was built at STZ in Stalingrad alongside the T-34 medium tank until the plant was overrun in October 1942. These photographs of STZ-5 tractors awaiting delivery show detail such as the cargo area sides without gaps and the fuel tanks behind the cab. The T-34 tanks have a mix of cast and welded turrets and steel and rubber rimmed wheels, reflecting the assembly of components as delivered to the plant.

On 10 December 1935 two NATI-2TV (STZ-5) transport tractors which had travelled from Stalingrad to Moscow without breakdown were again

(A) A captured STZ-5 with remnants of winter camouflage in Finnish Army service as vehicle SA-16363 in a panssaripataljoona (armour battalion or tank battalion) located at Äänislinna (Petrozavodsk), summer 1942. (Esa Muikku)
(B) An STZ-5 with high cargo area sides and camouflaged with bushes, towing a 122mm M-1938 (M-30) howitzer, Western Front, summer 1942. This STZ-5 is fitted with steel road wheels and a 'solid' rear cargo area without a gap in the planking. Note also the (not uncommon) guitarist seated on the limber.
(C) The STZ-5 was often used to tow heavier than design 122mm A-19 and 152mm ML-20 'corps duplex' artillery pieces. The Axis signpost indicates the location with the front line as it existed in the summer of 1943. Note this STZ-5 also has steel STZ-3 road wheels rather than the rubber rimmed STZ-5 type.
(D) This STZ-5, also with steel road wheels, towing a 122mm M-1938 (M-30) howitzer, cited in differing sources as Kursk Oblast in the summer of 1943 and Minsk Oblast in 1944.

demonstrated to the Soviet leadership, with final service approval received subject to elimination of defects found during testing. As these issues were resolved, series production gradually increased, with STZ delivering 173 STZ-5 tractors in 1936, with full series production starting in late 1937. In 1938, production continued to be slow as modifications were undertaken as a result of ongoing defect resolution, with full series production starting at the beginning of 1939 (at which point only 309 STZ-5 tractors had been built in total) with 1,256 STZ-5 tractors built that year.

(A) An STZ-5 with rubber rimmed road wheels and a thermal radiator jacket destroyed while towing an 85mm M-1939 (52-K) anti-aircraft gun in the region of Kharkov.

(B) An STZ-5 towing an 85mm M-1939 (52-K) anti-aircraft gun through Vitebsk, 1944.

(C) A well-loaded STZ-5 with 'complete' cargo body sides towing a 122mm M-1938 (M-30) howitzer across a log bridge over a stream. This STZ-5 also has all-steel rather than rubber rimmed road wheels.

(D) STZ-5 general schematic, as shown in the Operator's Manual.

(E) STZ-5s towing 76.2mm M-1939 USV divisional guns, Western Front, July–August 1944. Photographer: Aleksandr Ustinov.

Testing of new designs tended to be an ongoing matter rather than a single event. In the summer of 1939, long after the STZ had entered full series production, the STZ-5 underwent Red Army proving trials at Medved in the Novgorod region, with satisfactory performance, no breakdowns during testing and achieving a steady 14km/h road speed in battery column towing order, reducing to 10km/h on dirt roads. The STZ-5 successfully completed Red Army acceptance trials, and with the STZ-5 formally if belatedly accepted for service, tractor assembly continued apace, with peak production being achieved only in 1940. As development continued and the design accepted for Red Army service, the designation was shortened from STZ-NATI 2TV to the plant designation STZ-5 2TV, or STZ-2TV, and latterly to STZ-5.

The STZ-5 was a cab over engine full track militarized version of the essentially agricultural STZ-3, specifically developed as an artillery tractor and ammunition transporter. It featured a forward control wood framed metal two seat cab for the driver and tractor/gun crew commander, with the engine mounted centrally between them. Behind the cab was a load area with drop sides and tailgate and a canvas tilt. The configuration would set the standard for all future transport tractors. The STZ-5 had a 4,500kg towing capacity and 1,500kg load capacity. The tractor was however often used with heavier loads driven at slower speeds.

The running gear of the STZ-5 as with the STZ-3 consisted of oscillating bogies with horizontally mounted coil springs. There were however significant changes to the running gear compared with the STZ-3, including the use of rubber tyred road wheels and return rollers, and new smoother profile 'road tracks'. These changes resulted in a higher road speed and smoother road travel with less vibration than the STZ-3, but with less off-road traction, in line with a vehicle intended primarily for long-distance road transport. Some late production STZ-5 tractors were however in the summer 1942 fitted with the all-steel STZ-3 type road wheels, reflecting the shortage of rubber at STZ, which also resulted in T-34 tanks being assembled with steel wheels without rubber tyres at the same plant.

The original plan to mount a diesel engine in the STZ-5 having been abandoned, the tractor was instead powered by a standard 1MA four-cylinder carburettor and nominally petrol engine,* as used in the SKhTZ-3 (STZ-3/KhTZ-3), but with a higher 9.8 compression ratio (as against 2.1 on the STZ-3) coupled to a five-speed gearbox with two-speed transfer box more suited to higher speed road travel. The engine provided maximum torque at low revolutions, with much work undertaken on eliminating prior detonation of low grade fuel ('pinking') under load in summer temperatures, and was built for reliability and longevity. The STZ-5 had a 14-litre petrol fuel tank for starting purposes, and a 148-litre main fuel tank. In contrast with the STZ-3, the STZ-5 used an electric start with a hand crank as a back-up. The drawbar capacity was in practice restricted to 4,000kg, sufficient for 'high speed' (road) towing of wheeled artillery in the calibre-range 76–152mm. The engine and gearbox ratios allowed the tractor to tow heavy overloads at speeds as low as 1.9km/h, with track traction being a limiting factor rather than available torque.

* The 1MA engine carburettor was started with petrol, then once at 90°C operating temperature would run on kerosene or ligroin fuel, and was thereby in modern parlance a 'multi-fuel' engine – an important consideration in military operation. The highly reliable engine remained in production until 1953.

TOP RIGHT By 1944, the STZ-5 was rarely destroyed in significant numbers, as had been the case in the summer 1941 when this burned out STZ-5 and 122mm M-1938 (M-30) were destroyed.

BELOW This STZ-5, restored to running condition by the Shamansky Workshops in Mytischi, is located at the Motors of War Museum in Moscow, which is open to the public and often has mobile displays of recent restorations.

An operational nuance of the STZ-5 was that the cylinder block and upper engine components of the 1MA petrol engine were located between the cab seats. Summer temperatures in the cab could reach 50°C, hence the STZ-5 cab was provided with opening windscreen and cab rear windows. The upper engine compartment within the cab also had steel sandwich plates filled with sand to minimize heat transfer from the engine into the cab. A vertical capstan winch was located under the load platform for positioning, loading or self-recovery. Although the STZ-5 was produced only at STZ in Stalingrad, there were variations in many components such as the driver-mechanic's instrumentation panel and the location of fuel filler caps, indicating the different sub-component suppliers that fed into the production line at STZ.

This side view of the STZ-5 at the Motors of War Museum clearly shows how remarkably compact the versatile STZ-5 artillery tractor was as a 'tyagach' artillery tractor design.

A lengthened and modified version of the STZ-5, with five road wheel pairs rather than four per side, a front mounted engine and central cab arrangement, designated STZ-2TD, was developed to prototype stage but did not enter series production. The STZ-6 was a lengthened STZ-5 with four bogie sets and eight wheel pairs on each side and a greatly lengthened load area. The STZ-8 was a 'bolotny' (marshland/swamp) tractor with wider tracks developed and tested for service in 1936–37.

The ambitious STZ production plan for 1937 originally included 9,300 STZ-3 general service tractors, 4,775 STZ-5 transport tractors and 600 STZ-8 bolotny tractors, plus 225 STZ-5 chassis and 12 STZ-6 lengthened chassis.

In 1938, STZ delivered 309 series production STZ-5 tractors (technically all the combined 'pre-series' production to that date) to artillery units attached to tank and motorized rifle divisions. A further 1,256 STZ-5 tractors were delivered in 1939, and 1,274 in 1940. As of 1 January 1941, 2,839 STZ-5 tractors were serving with Red Army artillery units, well short of the paper Statute requirement of 5,478 at that time. That number in service was however 13.2 per cent of all specialist artillery tractors in service at that date. Production was ramped up exponentially after the outbreak of war. Plant records show that STZ in 1941 delivered STZ-5 tractors to three ministries – NKO (4,540), NKVMF (180) and NKVD (10), albeit this number is conflated with production in other years and total production, so may include a significant number of tractors built in 1940. From 22 June 1941 until the end of the year, the same plant records show

(A) (B) A fuel tanker version of the STZ-5 was also developed for refuelling tanks in front line locations. **(C)** The BI-9 was a mobile drilling rig used by the Red Army for bridge piling and other engineering roles. **(D)** A Soviet drawing of the BI-9 mobile drilling rig from the Operator's Manual.

that 3,100 STZ-5 tractors were built at STZ, and 3,359 in 1942. Production continued at STZ as the Battle of Stalingrad edged closer to the plant. Even as fighting raged close to the production facilities with the enemy literally 'at the gates', 30 STZ-5 tractors were delivered in the period 28 August to 13 September 1942, the date on which the last STZ-5 was delivered before the plant was destroyed in fighting. As of 1 September 1942, there remained 4,678 STZ-5 tractors in service with the Red Army.

The STZ-5 was generally used to tow 76mm regimental and divisional artillery pieces, 122mm M-1938 (M-30) and 152mm M-1938 (M-10) howitzers and 76mm (and later 85mm) anti-aircraft guns. Being one of the most common Red Army artillery tractors, it was used to tow most artillery pieces as dictated by operational needs, particularly in late 1941. The STZ-5 was generally underpowered for the roles it performed in wartime conditions, with its relatively narrow tracks providing less all-terrain traction than the heavy grouser tracks of the STZ-3. The STZ-5, being based on proven standard components, proved to

TOP LEFT A TRM (PM-3) field repair workshop with jib crane, mounted on the STZ-5 chassis.

ABOVE Another specialized PM-3 workshop developed at NATI on the STZ-5 chassis.

be very reliable in service despite being frequently overloaded. There were some design limitations, including the vulnerable position of the oil sump which was frequently damaged during cross-country travel. There were minor upgrades in some components over the short production period, but in general the STZ-5 remained in production as originally designed. In 1939, KhTZ in Kharkov worked on the modified D-8T diesel engine for installation in the Stalingrad-built STZ-5, but although further developed at a later date, the engine was not installed in the wartime STZ-5.

On 1 January 1941, the Red Army had, as noted, 2,839 STZ-5 tractors in service. In the autumn of 1941, with the production of artillery tractors stopped at all other plants due to evacuation and relocation or to concentrate on tank production, the STZ-5 remained the only artillery tractor still in series production, assembled at STZ in Stalingrad alongside the T-34 medium tank. From 22 June 1941, the absolute priority at STZ was also tank production, but from that date to the end of 1941 STZ nevertheless delivered 3,146 STZ-5 tractors, and in 1942 it delivered 23–35 tractors daily. Production was terminated at Stalingrad on 13 August 1942 when Axis forces overwhelmed the plant, at which time a total of 9,944 tractors had been assembled at the plant, of which 6,506 were delivered after the outbreak of war on 22 June 1941. As of 1 September 1942, just over two weeks after production ceased at STZ, only 4,678 remained in service, a significant loss in the overall STZ tractor park in 15 months of operational deployment. Losses declined proportionally thereafter due to the changing war situation, with a significant number of STZ-5 tractors surviving the war and being used in military and civil roles in the Soviet Union into the early 1950s.

Several specialized versions of the STZ-5 were produced, including PM-3 and other TRM workshop vehicles, a command/communications vehicle and a BI-9 mobile drilling (piling) rig, of which 50 were mobilized in 1941 and 15 used in Red Army service. The KI-3 was an STZ-5 with an A-frame crane mounted on the front of the chassis. In the late autumn of 1941, the STZ-5 chassis was used to mount the BM-13 MRS, as detailed separately. The chassis and/or STZ-5 components were also used for the KhT-16, NI-1 and IZ armoured tractors produced in Kharkov, Odessa and Leningrad respectively.

SKhTZ-NATI ARTILLERY TRACTOR PROTOTYPE

In late June 1941, a team at NATI in Moscow under the direction of D.A. Chudakov developed to prototype stage a tracked artillery tractor based on the agricultural tracked SKhTZ-NATI, intended for potential mass conversion of agricultural tracked tractors (or use of their components) to more specialized artillery tractor application. This was based on earlier pre-war developments related to problems with the STZ-5 modernization programme in Stalingrad and as a means of adding additional production capacity in the event of war. The prototype featured a modified drivetrain with STZ-5 type 'road' tracks and a modified and enlarged open cab which could accommodate the driver and gun crew. The prototype was not developed further, with drafted standard STZ-NATI 1TA (STZ-3/KhTZ-3) tractors used in the role without modification. In the autumn of 1941, as KhTZ prepared for evacuation, there were also as many as 1,500 KhT-16 'bronetraktor' (armoured tractor) chassis – using elements of and related to this SKhTZ-NATI conversion prototype – at different stages of assembly at KhTZ, with 55–70 KhTZ-16s having been completed as armoured tractors before the plant in Kharkov was evacuated. The SKhTZ-NATI derived series of tractors, including the STZ-5 and the armoured KhTZ-16 (KhT-16), were all based on a common design with maximum parts interchangeability, such that but for the evacuation of KhTZ, the prototype developed in June 1941 would likely have been series assembled as an unarmoured artillery tractor.

ATZ-3T

The wartime KhTZ-16 bronetraktor chassis built in Kharkov in late 1941 using SKhTZ-NATI components almost had a second lease of life in Red Army service later in the war. Part of the machine tooling evacuated from KhTZ in the autumn of 1941 was sent by train to the city of Rubtsovsk in the mountainous Altai region where tracked tractor manufacture was re-established within the newly formed Altai Tractor Plant (ATZ). The chief design engineer at the plant was M.S. Sidelnikov, who had worked on SKhTZ-NATI (KhTZ-3) production at KhTZ and had managed development of the KhTZ-16 bronetraktor at the Kharkov plant prior to its partial evacuation. In August 1942, the ATZ plant began series production of the ATZ-NATI (SKhTZ-NATI) tracked tractor,

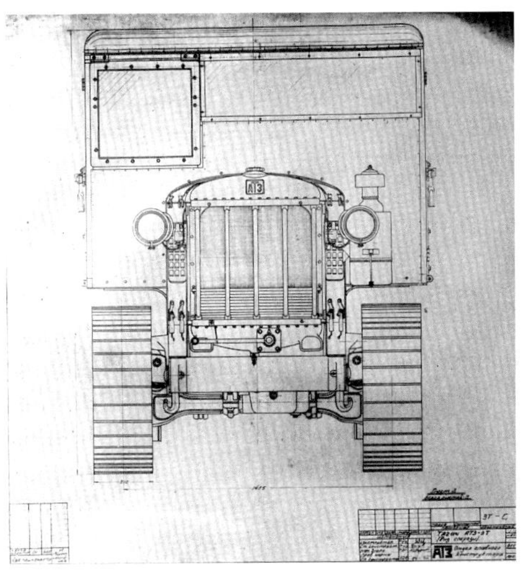

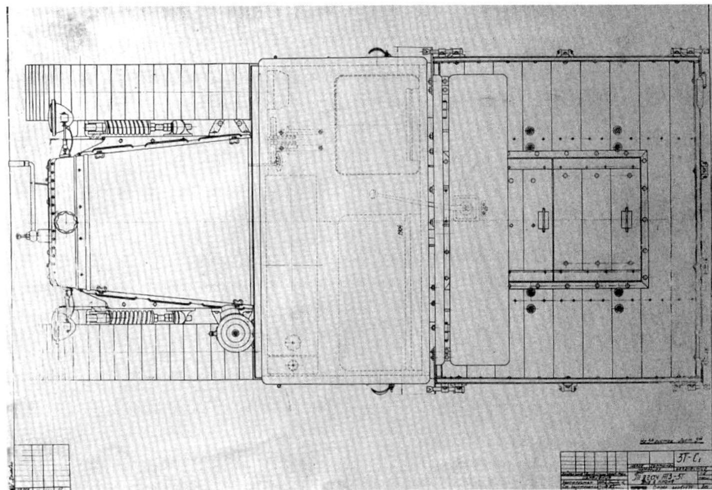

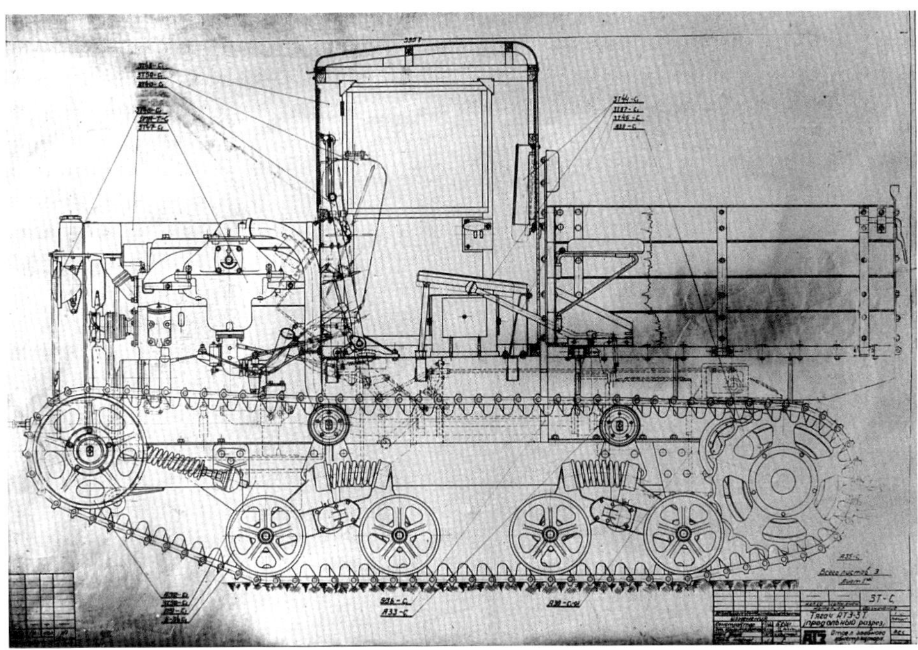

ATZ factory drawings of the proposed ATZ-3T artillery tractor, based on the ATZ-3 tractor that had started life as the pre-war agrarian SKhTZ-NATI 1TA, built at KhTZ and STZ as the KhTZ-3 and STZ-3 respectively. It did not enter production.

a derivative of the Stalingrad-built STZ-3 and Kharkov-built KhTZ-3, being closer to the latter design, with a fully enclosed cab.

At the time, the need for dedicated artillery tractors (tyagachi) remained a priority and so, having established series production of the ATZ-NATI, the KB at ATZ under the direction of Sidelnikov in 1943 developed a new unarmoured tracked transport tractor, the ATZ-3T. The new tracked artillery tractor was similar to the Stalingrad-built STZ-5 but incorporated changes made in the KhTZ-16 chassis when modifiying it from the KhTZ-NATI agricultural base chassis, including the uprated engine developing 58hp. The cab was located centrally behind the engine compartment, with the fuel tank moved to the left and the driver located on the right, with a load area behind the cab for a gun crew and a limited amount of ammunition.

Surviving plant documents show that a single prototype ATZ-3T was built in the early summer of 1943. On 1 July 1943, the head of GAU, General-Colonel Yakovlev, approved the production of a pre-series batch of ATZ-3T tracked artillery tractors for military evaluation purposes. The ATZ-3T was not however accepted for series production, as by 1943 a new generation of dedicated artillery tractors, specifically the Ya-11 (and its series production Ya-12 modification introduced after the Luftwaffe destruction of the GAZ engine plant) was now entering series production. The Yaroslavl-built tractors had a road speed able to maintain pace with Red Army tanks, now an important consideration as the Soviet Union moved over to offensive operations. The ATZ-3T design was thereby shelved, ending the history of a vehicle chassis which had started life as the agricultural SKhTZ-NATI tracked tractor, had been developed into the wartime KhTZ-16 armoured tractor with its 45mm tank gun armament, and later in the war had almost had a third incarnation as a specialized tracked artillery transport tractor.

KOMINTERN

Work on the first designs of 'transport tractors' specifically designed as artillery tractors began in 1930, when the General Technical Bureau of the GUVP (the Main Directorate of Military Industry) together with engineers from the then under construction Kharkov Tractor Plant (KhTZ) undertook several artillery tractor design projects in accordance with Red Army requirements, namely: 'small tractor for RKKA', 'medium tractor for RKKA' and 'large tractor for RKKA'. The tractor types, designed to tow artillery while also transporting crews and ammunition – tyagachi or transport tractors – were all to be based on tank chassis proven in Red Army service. The development of artillery tractors was however actually undertaken at the Kharkov Steam Locomotive Plant (KhPZ) rather than KhTZ, as KhPZ had experience in heavy machine building and had recently also begun tank production at a time when the new KhTZ tractor plant was still under construction. The GAU order to design a medium artillery tractor to replace the Kommunar was accordingly given to the KB at KhPZ under the direction of Boris N. Voronkov, with work commencing in October 1930.

The Kommunar, though an efficient design, was more 'tractor' than 'tractor-transporter'. In January 1930, KhPZ had tested the T-12 tank prototype developed in Kharkov, and was working on potential series production of the modified T-24,

A restored to running condition Komintern artillery tractor at the Motors of War Museum, Moscow.

B.N. Voronkov in the cab of the original BNV (Komintern Obrazets No. 1) prototype, 1931.

hence the running gear, components and expertise related to these tanks became integral to tracked tractor developments at the same plant. The initial prototype, designated BNV at the time, remained of classic 'tractor' rather than 'tyagach' design, having an open driver's seating arrangement and no gun crew or load area, the prototypes resembling the earlier Kommunar tractor rather than the later series production Komintern. The first prototype was later renamed as the Komintern No. 1 medium tractor.

Three prototypes of the first BNV design with its open cab arrangement were completed in November 1931 and tested through the winter to the spring of 1932. The trials indicated that the Komintern was underpowered, with limited tractive effort and the maximum road speed of 18km/h being considered still slow for its intended role. The first prototypes did not have a cab, load area or winch, and were thereby not considered a significant improvement on the Kommunar. A redesign was initiated, incorporating the Mechanization and Motorization Command of the Red Army (UMM RKKA) requirement for 'development of a heavy tracked transport tractor' for which the TTTs were for all-terrain tractors capable of towing an 11,000kg load at 15km/h or a road train of up to 30,000kg at slow speed, with a load area with 3,500kg

ABOVE The T-24 manoeuvre tank was the mechanical basis for the Komintern artillery tractor.

RIGHT Komintern artillery tractors towing 152mm M-1910/34 corps guns through Red Square, Moscow, 7 November 1938.

capacity and a 100hp engine (medium tractor) and 150hp (heavy tractor), along with maximum parts interchangeability between tractors. The tractors were to be capable of operating across a temperature range of -30˚C to +40˚C, reflecting the geography and climate of the Soviet Union. The original prototype was redesigned, resulting in a new, enlarged tractor with what would become the classic 'transport tractor' or 'tyagach' configuration, with a fully enclosed central cab and rear load area, with modified suspension and running gear components now taken from the T-24 M-1929 manoeuvre (medium) tank recently manufactured at the plant. The second prototype was powered by a front-mounted

ABOVE LEFT A Komintern illustration, from the Operator's Manual.

ABOVE The Komintern during evaluation trials.

LEFT A Komintern and an S-65 during tank recovery rials with a T-28 medium tank.

four-cylinder nominally petrol KIN engine developing 131hp,* providing a nominal tow capacity of 14,000kg (and greater at reduced speeds), a load platform capacity of 2,000kg, a maximum road speed of 31km/h and a range of 170km.

Voronkov was reassigned to another plant in 1931 and his name removed from further developments, with the second prototype, developed under the direction of chief designer N.G. Zubarev, being designated Komintern No. 2 (the BNV prototype having been Komintern No. 1). The modified transport tractor prototype designated was tested at the newly established Scientific Experimental Auto-Armoured-Tank (NIABP) polygon at Kubinka over the period 4–12 June 1934, separately towing a 203mm B-4 carriage for 50km at a constant 14.5km/h, and the 203mm B-4 barrel on its Br-10 povozka carriage for 69km at a constant 12.4km/h.

* The Komintern KIN engine was able to run on any grade of petrol or with a mix of ligroin and kerosene – effectively a 'multi-fuel' engine. The engine for the Komintern was developed in parallel with early work on the BD-2 (the future V-2) and BD-14 diesel engines. The electric magneto type starting system operated effectively even in cold weather.

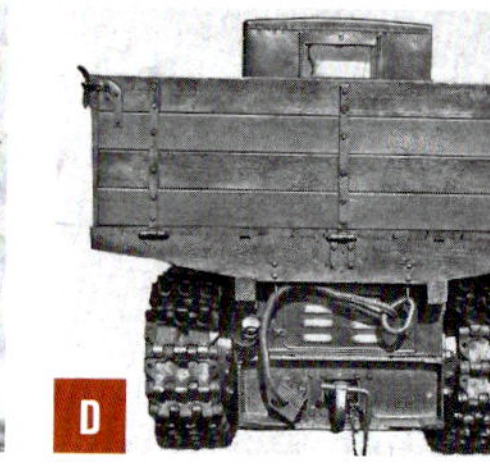

(A)–(D) The Komintern artillery tractor was the first purpose designed 'tyagach' artillery tractor, with crew cab and a rear cargo area with benches, drop sides and tailgate to accommodate the gun crew and a quantity of ammunition. **(E)** Komintern artillery tractors traverse Red Square during the 7 November 1937 military parade. In parade configuration the Komintern transported 12 seated gun crew/infantry. **(F)** Komintern artillery tractors on Red Square during the same 7 November 1937 military parade. **(G)** Komintern artillery tractors towing 203mm B-4 tracked howitzers through Red Square, 7 November 1938. **(H)** A Komintern tractor and captured Japanese 150mm M96 howitzer during the battles of the Khalkin Gol, 1939. **(I)** Komintern tractors exit Red Square during the 7 November 1938 military parade. **(J) (K)** Komintern tractors traverse Red Square, 7 November 1940.

A meeting of the 3rd Department UMM RKKA on the result of testing two Komintern prototypes at the NIABP (tank) and NIAP (artillery) polygons noted that the Komintern could tow the 203mm B-4 tracked carriage (16,500kg) at a steady 12.4km/h on roads over a tested road range of 50km and the associated Br-10 loaded barrel carriage at a higher recorded speed of 19.1km/h. The wheeled 152mm M-1910/30 howitzer could be towed at a steady 20.3km/h and a 5,000kg trailer at 25.4km/h. Maximum unladen speed was 29km/h, and 34km/h over short distances. The Komintern met all the original TTT requirements during the trials, with the tractor capable of towing all wheeled 122mm and 152mm calibre artillery types. Negative commentary included a notable gap in ratios between the third and fourth gears, but the proving trials were considered successful and the prototype was accepted for Red Army service as the 'Komintern' (Communist International) artillery tractor.

The Komintern 'fast' transport tractor, based on the chassis of the abandoned T-24 'manoeuvre tank' (according to the old Soviet classification), was the first Soviet series production specialist tyagach (artillery tractor). The tractor was capable of towing all calibres of wheeled and tracked artillery. The significantly heavier tracked 152mm M-1935 (Br-2), 203mm M-1931 (B-4) and 280mm M-1939 (Br-5) weapons with travel order weights of up to 19,000kg were in Red Army service split into barrel and carriage loads for towing by two separate Komintern tractors. At low speed the tractor could also tow the tracked 203mm B-4 howitzer while mounted on its tracked gun carriage.

As was typical per Soviet norms, the Komintern was accepted into production in accordance with NKTP Order No. 146 dated 31 March 1933 and into service with the Red Army in accordance with Revolutionary Military Council of the USSR (RVS SSSR) Order No. 5249ss dated 10 June 1933, before the final proving trials were undertaken. A single prototype Komintern tractor (No. 617) was thereafter subjected to a 2,000km endurance trial to ascertain any potential further remedial work required before establishing full series production.

ABOVE A Komintern tractor towing a 76.2mm M-1931 (3K) anti-aircraft gun at the 7 November 1941 military parade in Kuibyshev, which was at the time the destined second capital in the event that Moscow fell to Axis forces.

ABOVE RIGHT A winter-camouflaged Komintern tractor and captured 105mm WZ29 Schneider howitzer on the Troitsky bridge in Leningrad during the siege.

RIGHT An abandoned Komintern artillery tractor.

A Komintern tractor towing a 122mm M-1910/34 corps gun during military evaluation trials.

According to plant and Red Army records the first pre-series batch of five tractors built for operational trials was delivered in the final quarter of 1934, with a further batch of 50 produced in the second half of 1935 and full series production starting only in 1936.

The Komintern was of conventional layout, with a long engine compartment and a central two-door fully enclosed wood framed metal cab taken from the ZiS-5, but with the driver seated on the right, and with all windows opening. The rear cargo area accommodated the gun crew and ammunition. The suspension, inherited from the T-24 tank, consisted of four vertical spring mounts with eight small rubber rimmed road wheel pairs each side, with rear drive sprocket, front idler and four return rollers.

The Komintern heavy artillery tractor was widely used for transporting all types of field artillery and howitzers, primarily heavy wheeled artillery. The tractor was also employed as a tank recovery vehicle, and was provided with a winch, which for the first time had a pulling capacity equal to a typical trailer weight, with forward and rear winching capability.

The combat debut of the Komintern tractor was with the Far Eastern Military District against the Japanese at Lake Khasan in 1938, where together with the S-60 the tractor was used in small numbers. The following year the Komintern saw service in the same region during the battles of the Khalkin Gol. The Komintern was used in very small numbers during the Soviet–Finnish Winter War of 1939–40, where it operated as both artillery tractor and tank recovery vehicle.

A total of 1,798 Komintern artillery tractors were built between 1934 and 1940, of which 1,712 entered operational service with the Red Army, others being allocated to NKVD, GULAG, Forest and other organizations. The 'Komintern' was replaced in production by the larger and far more powerful

ABOVE A Komintern tractor restored by the Shamansky Workshops at the Motors of War Museum, Moscow.

ABOVE RIGHT The same tractor at the Motors of War Museum, Moscow, May 2025.

RIGHT The distinctive Komintern radiator with 'Komintern' and Plant No. 183 SSSR cast into the radiator housing.

'Voroshilovets' in 1940. A total of 1,581 Komintern tractors were listed as in service with the Red Army on 1 January 1941; the largest number of Komintern tractors (153) were deployed in the Zabaikalsky Military District in the far east of the Soviet Union, with 147, 139 and 109 located in the Moscow, Western and Kiev Military Districts respectively, and smaller numbers in other districts. In service the Komintern was reliable, relatively fast on made roads and easy to repair in field conditions with a typical 2,000km endurance between capital rebuilds. The Komintern was however relatively long and narrow with a high centre of gravity such that stability was sometimes an issue on rough ground, while being based on T-24 tank suspension and components fuel consumption was high. A total of 568 Komintern tractors remained in service in 1945. Captured Komintern tractors were used by the Wehrmacht under the designation Artillerieschlepper Kom-604(r).

VOROSHILOVETS

With the introduction of significantly heavier tracked heavy artillery pieces into Red Army service in the mid-1930s,* their transport and positioning also required a new technical solution. The tracked S-60 and later S-65 were adequate towing tractors, but particularly slow, and with no ability to transport gun crews and ammunition, while the new Komintern still required tracked artillery pieces to be broken down into two loads for adequate speed road transport. There was thereby an urgent requirement to develop a transport tractor similar to the Komintern, powered by a tank engine, and capable of towing heavy artillery of up to 22,000kg in travel order at up to 30km/h. The increased combat weight of medium and heavy tanks also required a powerful new tracked recovery tractor capable of recovering medium tanks with a combat weight of up to 28,000kg.

These considerations formed the basis for the development of a new heavy transport tractor (tyagach, developed under the combined auspices of two Soviet military command structures – GAU (artillery) and ABTU (armoured vehicles).† The new tractor, originally designated simply as TT – 'tyazhely traktor' (heavy tractor) was developed from the summer of 1935 at the tractor KB (Department 200) of KhPZ (from 1936 re-designated Plant No. 183) in Kharkov in response to the combined ABTU and GAU requirements as a replacement for the Komintern, which had at the time only just entered series production at the plant, with responsibility for production also to be at the same plant. The name 'Voroshilovets' was given slightly later, following the Soviet tradition of naming military vehicles after Soviet leadership figures.

Development was under the supervision of chief designer N.G. Zubarev, his deputies D.F. Bobrov and D.M. Ivanov, and a large team of designers led by P.E. Libenko and I.Z. Stavtsev (engine design), V.M. Krichevsky assisted by S.Z. Sidelnikov and V.P. Kaplin (transmission), P.G. Efremenko and A.I. Avtomonov (chassis and running gear) and I.V. Dudko and Yu.S. Mironov (auxiliary equipment), with overall design layout under the direction of D.M. Ivanov.

* Namely the 152mm M-1935 (Br-2), 203mm M-1931 (B-4), 210mm M-1939 (Br-17) and 280mm M-1939 (Br-5).

† UMM RKKA became ABTU from 22 November 1934 and was reorganized as GABTU from 26 June 1940.

(A) The Voroshilovets was the most powerful Red Army artillery tractor used during the 1941–45 'Great Patriotic War', powered by a de-rated version of the V-2 diesel engine used in the T-34 medium tank. **(B)** The Voroshilovets could tow any Soviet artillery piece, but the complex running gear required constant lubrication and field maintenance to maintain operational capability, with lack of spares being a constant problem. **(C) (D) (E)** The Voroshilovets replaced the Komintern in production at Plant No. 183 in Kharkov, but was an altogether larger and more powerful artillery tractor than its predecessor. **(F)** A pre-series production Voroshilovets tractor during trials in the Leningrad Military District. During development the Voroshilovets was known as the 'TT' (heavy tractor). **(G)** A Soviet drawing of the Voroshilovets from the Operator's Manual. **(H)** A Soviet side drawing of the Voroshilovets.

(I)–(L) A Voroshilovets towing what appears to be a 280mm Br-5 tracked heavy artillery piece without disassembly into separate carriage and barrel loads. Differing original captions indicate Central Front, winter 1943 and (more likely) winter trials.

The Voroshilovets was of the now standard tyagach or transport tractor layout, similar in layout to the earlier Komintern, but larger in scale; it had a significantly shorter engine compartment with the engine mounted near the front of the vehicle under the cab floor, as with later tractors, and a larger central cab, also from the ZiS-5 but widened, accommodating the driver and two passengers. For ventilation and communication with the gun crew, there were two hatches in the cab rear. The two fuel tanks were mounted behind the cab at the front of the load area. The engine was mounted below the cab, with maintenance via side panels and access panels within the cab. The load area was used for ammunition and accommodating the gun crew, with three benches that could accommodate 13–16 personnel or 3,000kg of ammunition. The tow hook was specifically designed for towing artillery on roads, with spring amortization.

The Voroshilovets was designed from the outset to be powered by a prototype V-12 aluminium block four-stroke direct injection 12-cylinder BD-2 diesel engine (the future V-2 tank engine) developing 400hp. The new tank diesel engine had been completed at Department 400 at Plant No. 183 under the direction of chief designer K.F. Chelpan in the summer of 1938 for use in the

(A) Voroshilovets tractors towing 152mm Br-2 tracked artillery pieces through Red Square, Moscow in 1939 or 1940. Photographer: Vladislav Mikosha.
(B) Voroshilovets tractors towing 203mm B-4 tracked artillery pieces through Red Square, Moscow in 1939 or 1940. Note the difference in gun carriage auxiliary wheel types.
(C) A captured Voroshilovets tractor in Wehrmacht service.
(D) A rare colour photograph of a Hungarian soldier posing with a captured Voroshilovets tractor with German markings in the summer of 1942.
(E) An Axis forces soldier, likely Hungarian, poses with a captured Voroshilovets tractor.
(Sergei Popsuevich)

E

T-34 medium tank then nearing series production, and the first prototypes were fitted with this engine, subsequently replaced by the later V-2V development. The tractor incorporated many features taken from tank assembly experience, including the provision of four separate engine air/oil filters (two of them in the cab). Engine starting was by means of two 6hp electric motors, with compressed air accumulators providing for cold and emergency starting. An engine pre-heater was also provided for very low temperatures.The BD-2 engine was linked to a four-speed automobile type transmission with two-speed transfer case according to Plant No. 183 tradition. The main clutch was a multi-disc dry, steel-on-steel clutch tank type. The side clutches, brake bands and final drives were taken from the BT fast tank then in production at Plant No. 183. The engine and drivetrain provided a maximum unladen road speed of 42km/h, a drawbar capacity of 22,000kg and a load capacity of 3,000kg. As such the tractor could tow any Soviet heavy artillery piece, including the 152mm M-1935 (Br-2), 203mm B-4 and 280mm M-1939 (Br-5) tracked artillery systems, albeit with significantly reduced speed off-road. The towing mechanism was as with all military designs fitted with spring amortization. The electrical system had both 12v and 24v circuits, with 12v for the lights and other systems.

The chassis was constructed of two main beams with numerous cross-pieces for rigidity, with sheet steel panels for impact damage shielding on the lower sections. The rear tow hook was of the 'military' type with amortization intended for shock reduction and increased traction. The tractor had a reversible 12,000kg capacity horizontal capstan winch mounted under the cargo platform, with 30m of 23mm steel cable, used for attaching gun carriages and trailers, and for self-extraction from mud if necessary.

A Voroshilovets tractor towing a 15cm sIG 33 Sfl. auf Pz.Kpfw.I Ausf B captured by the 16th Army during the Battle of Skirmonovo Heights in October–November 1941.

ABOVE LEFT A Voroshilovets tractor towing a 203mm B-4 tracked howitzer as a single piece, as the Red Army moves through Axis territory in early 1945.

ABOVE This detail view of the same tractor shows that the original upper cargo area with tarpaulin cover has been replaced by a wooden structure with windows and a curved sheet metal roof, providing better living arrangements for the crew.

The running gear consisted of two pairs of balancer bogie assemblies with lever spring scissors type coil suspension with four small road wheels per unit, for a total of eight road wheel pairs per side, providing good ground floatation and acceptable road performance with minimal vibration, along with rear 14-tooth drive sprocket, front idler and five return rollers. The running gear, though somewhat anachronistic, provided even load distribution and smooth operation on and off-road, with the rubber tyres fitted on the roadwheels and return rollers reflecting the 'high speed' orientation of the tractor chassis.

The tank type track, with 71 links when new, had limited traction on dirt roads due to its small grouser profile, and particularly on icy and snow-covered roads, a problem that afflicted all pre-war transport tractors. The Voroshilovets could not fully utilize its high power in operation as the engine power output was not matched by ground traction. Track grousers were developed for the Voroshilovets, but were rarely used as they typically had a service life of less than 50km.

The technical documentation was released at the end of the year, with a small number of pre-series vehicles subsequently built for evaluation and testing purposes. Two prototype Voroshilovets tractors fitted with BD-2 engines were completed at Plant No. 183 in 1936 which subsequently underwent two years of plant and polygon trials confirming compliance with the original TTTs, including successfully towing a T-35 heavy tank, confirming capability in the tractor's secondary role. In March 1937, one of the prototypes was driven from Kharkov to Moscow where it was demonstrated in the Kremlin to the People's Commissar of Defence, Marshal K.E. Voroshilov, and approved for service with the Red Army. The prototype completed the round trip back to Kharkov without breakdown, confirming the reliability shown during the extensive earlier trials. Testing, as expected, revealed some defects requiring remedy, such as the rubber on the road wheel rims quickly disintegrating at speeds of 30–35km/h. After rework, one of the Voroshilovets tractors was handed over to ABTU by the plant for conducting a further 2,500km of endurance runs to determine chronic weak points.

Meantime, in the summer of 1938, the new V-2V version of the V-2 engine being prepared for the forthcoming T-34 medium tank under development at KhPZ was officially tested in the Voroshilovets at the NIABP tank proving grounds at Kubinka. The V-2V was a de-rated version of the V-2 developing 375hp and designed specifically for artillery tractor use and, with two 6hp electric motors providing engine starting. Trials with the Voroshilovets tractor now fitted with the V-2V engine proved the tractor to be both powerful and particularly reliable for its intended role, economical, easy to start and not capricious under various test conditions. The trial report noted an average road speed of 29km/h, a maximum unladen road speed of 42km/h and the required ability to tow a 20,000kg load at a consistent 30km/h on roads, in line with the earlier trials with the BD-2 powered prototypes. The tractor employed a dry sump lubrication system which provided certain advantages in extreme operating conditions, together with four oil-air filters, two of which were in the cab, and a six-bladed cooling fan. Considerable design effort was undertaken to increase transmission reliability and minimize mechanical stresses resulting from the use of the new V-2V diesel engine with its unprecedented torque output for tractor application.

From 17 April to 8 July 1938 the V-2V diesel engine powered prototype covered 1,425km, revealing further defects requiring rectification. The engine trials were deemed highly successful, and on 16 August 1938 the chief of ABTU, Dmitry G. Pavlov, wrote to the Ministry of Armaments (NKV) with an update on progress with the Voroshilovets. The tractor was approved for production fitted with its new V-2V diesel engine, with a pre-production batch of 50 tractors to be completed by December 1938. The tractor did not however enter service with the Red Army until 1939, due to ongoing design changes as new components became available. The new V-2 engine would meanwhile become the basis for Soviet tank engines for many years ahead, with the V-2V modification being used to power medium and heavy tractors for the next four decades.

The Voroshilovets was, as noted, accepted for production in August 1938 but still, as was typical, required Red Army service acceptance, with the Voroshilovets finally being ready for Red Army evaluation trials in the summer of 1939. These trials were again undertaken at the NIABP Kubinka tank proving ground near Moscow, where it was tested towing the 152mm M-1935 and 203mm M-1931 howitzers, the 210mm M-1939 (Br-17), the 280mm M-1939 (Br-5) mortar and also the 305mm M-1939 (Br-18) howitzer, all as

LEFT A rear view of the same Voroshilovets tractor.

INSET ABOVE This detail rear view of the same tractor shows the elaborate nature of the cargo area conversion.

separate carriage and barrel loads. The tractor was also tested towing the T-28 medium and T-35 heavy tanks, the latter at the time the heaviest Soviet tank in service, to evaluate tank recovery capability. The tractor could provide a nominal 17,000kg towing capacity, making the Voroshilovets the most powerful tractor ever developed for the Red Army. One of the prototypes was also operationally tested in Leningrad Military District.

During the trials at the Kubinka tank polygon the Voroshilovets achieved a 42km/h maximum road speed, an average fully loaded road speed of 20km/h, and 16km/h across open ground, the highest speeds achieved among all tractors tested. The average battery column road speed was 18km/h, and 13km/h as part of a 'regiment column'. The relatively economical diesel engine allowed the Voroshilovets to undertake a full day of road travel without refuelling. The nominally diesel engine could run on diesel, gas oil or in extremis a mixture of engine oil and kerosene/ligroin. The achieved road range with cargo load only was 390km, reducing to 240km with load and trailer, and to 125–200km on dirt roads with load and a trailer. Red Army artillery troops finally had a powerful tractor which could adequately tow any Soviet artillery type.

The Voroshilovets heavy artillery tractor was eventually accepted for service with the Red Army on 19 December 1939, entering series production at Plant No. 183 in the last days of the year, but with slower than planned initial output of one tractor per day. The Voroshilovets was at the time of its introduction the largest, heaviest and most powerful artillery tractor in service with the Red Army, a status it would maintain throughout the war. The tractor was used primarily to tow heavy tracked 152–305mm calibre heavy artillery pieces with a travel order weight of up to 22,000kg, particularly the tracked 203mm B-4 and 280mm Br-5. It was also used for recovering medium and heavy tanks, being able to recover and tow the T-28 and T-34 medium tank, and at slower speed also the T-35 and KV heavy tanks. The tractor could also transport ammunition loads of up to 3,000kg and was provided with a 12,000kg winch for positioning.

As of 1 January 1941, there were 470 Voroshilovets tractors in service with the Red Army, with 228 serving in artillery units, against planned Statute expectations for 733 such tractors to be in service by April 1941. This number was achieved only as war broke out on 22 June 1941; by 1 July it had increased to 975. Production output continued apace after the outbreak of war, with three to four tractors completed daily as the plant attempted to make up for the desperate overall shortage of artillery tractors. In total, from 22 June 1941 until the end of production with evacuation of the plant to Nizhny Tagil at the end of August 1941, Plant No. 183 delivered an additional 170 Voroshilovets tractors to the Red Army, with 706 delivered to the army by the end of 1941.

Pre-war production Voroshilovets tractors were fitted with the V-2V diesel engine, but with the outbreak of war production at Plant No. 75 in Kharkov was prioritized on V-2 engine assembly for the T-34 medium tank rather than the V-2V engine for the Voroshilovets tractor. V-2V engine production ceased altogether on 1 August as the engine plant prepared for evacuation from Kharkov to Nizhny Tagil. As an interim measure, Plant No. 183 thereafter installed other engines in the Voroshilovets, namely the six-cylinder V-4 engine developing 300hp, as originally developed for the T-50 light tank, and in August 1941 installed the M-17T petrol engine from the BT-7 fast tank, developing 400hp, as also installed in some T-34 and KV tanks. As KhPZ prepared for evacuation from Kharkov to Nizhny Tagil, Voroshilovets production dropped off dramatically and then ceased altogether due to a lack of components, not least engines.

During the Siege of Leningrad, an unknown number of Voroshilovets tractors were retrofitted with an armoured cab and engine compartment, as seen on the tractor behind the standard Voroshilovets.

During the war, the Voroshilovets was used on all Fronts, primarily for towing RVGK heavy artillery, the tractor being the largest and most powerful of all Red Army artillery tractors in service with artillery and tank units during World War II. A small number of Voroshilovets tractors captured in 1941–42 were used by German, Hungarian and Romanian forces, with the Wehrmacht employing captured Voroshilovets under the designation Stalin-607(r).

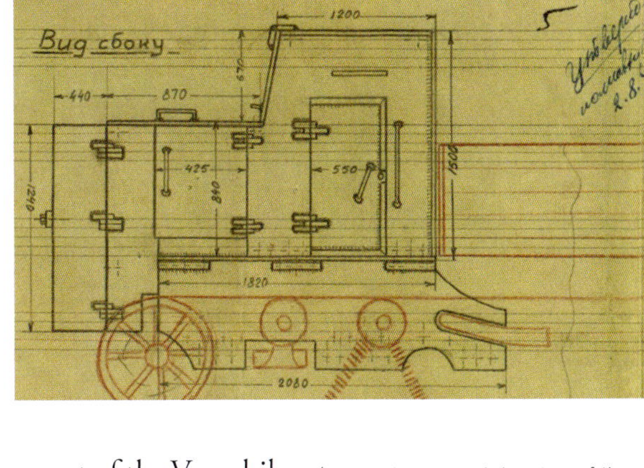

An original drawing of the Voroshilovets conversion.

Some of the shortcomings noted during state trials were confirmed in subsequent operational deployment of the Voroshilovets. The engine power output and available torque was outstanding, but the waffle design track plates did not provide optimum traction on soft ground and gravel roads. Mud and wet snow build-up around the drive sprocket also led to the track often disengaging from the drive teeth, with the build-up of mud and snow in the running gear causing frequent track-shedding in service. Main clutch failures could occur after only 200–300 hours of operation. Drive shaft and transfer-box gear failures were not uncommon, especially on early production tractors. After 300–400 hours of operation, bearing wear on the main drive gears was noted. Oil seals leaked (a Plant No. 183 manufacturing tradition), as did fuel and coolant line couplings due to vibration from the powerful diesel engine, requiring frequent retightening. When driving over rough ground, the lower strike plates were often damaged, while driver-mechanics noted the winch was difficult to use.

The Voroshilovets suffered from rapid wear of the running gear, particularly the suspension axle bushings, due to the design of the labyrinth seals of the road wheel bearings, return rollers and idlers, exacerbated by irregular lubrication under wartime operational conditions. To reduce abrasive wear to the road wheels after moving through deep mud, the road wheels had to be frequently disassembled, washed and lubricated with grease, an inordinate task undesirable in field conditions. Inefficient bearing sealing was a known problem at Plant No. 183 that remained unresolved with early T-34 medium tank production at the same plant. There were also problems with the compressed air back-up system used to start the tractor at temperatures below -20°C, as the cold air supplied to the cylinders super-cooled the engine when released, such that the 550–600°C temperature required for fuel self-ignition could not be attained. The cold start pre-heating procedure for the V-2V engine with its repeated heating and draining of water and oil often delayed the movement of artillery columns by three to four hours. Red Army operational feedback indicated the

ABOVE This captured Voroshilovets tractor in a Wehrmacht field workshop has a more substantial armour layout.

ABOVE RIGHT The BYe (БЭ) high speed rotary trenching machine was built and tested for Red Army service in 1937. It could cut trenches up to 1.5m deep at a rate of 800m/h.

primary drawbacks of the Voroshilovets to be insufficient range and the fact that the tractor was high maintenance; the tractor required a complete engine and mechanical overhaul – 'capremont' – after 1,200 running hours, with a general lack of spare parts due to the aforementioned early production termination at Kharkov and assembly not being re-established elsewhere, resulting in the need to cannibalize damaged tractors to maintain other vehicles in service. This was common wartime practice, but for most other artillery tractors the available park to draw spares from was exponentially larger.

Despite combat losses, wear and attrition, 528 tractors remained in Red Army service on 1 September 1942. The Red Army would henceforth move from defensive to offensive operations, with some 336 of the 528 tractors in service in September 1942 remaining in service at the end of the war in Europe. Voroshilovets tractors that survived the war were used in the post-war Soviet Army for towing heavy artillery until replaced by the AT-T tractor in the early 1950s.

The Voroshilovets was powerful, capable of towing up to 22,000kg and with a cargo load of 3,000kg, with good mobility, being able to tow the 203mm B-4 tracked howitzers at 18km/h on made roads. Operational feedback indicated that the Voroshilovets was generally reliable, but the long and relatively narrow track and track shoe profile was problematic in self-recovery in mud and snow, with brake failure after 200–300km and transmission failure after 300–400km common. The Voroshilovets was in its time a well-designed, powerful and well-accepted machine in service, and much in demand, as there were also few modern Komintern transport-tractors in service. Though classified as an artillery tractor, the Voroshilovets was also used as a tank recovery vehicle. Many Voroshilovets tractors were lost in combat during tank recovery operations, hence projects developed later in the war, as tank production allowed, that considered a semi-armoured heavy recovery tractor on the T-34 (and later T-44) medium tank chassis.

A total of 1,123 (1,128 per some sources) Voroshilovets tractors were built from late 1939 to August 1941 when production was terminated (170 being built after the outbreak of war). At the beginning of 1941, Red Army records show that there were 470 Voroshilovets tractors in service, with 706 tractors delivered in 1941 before Plant No. 183 and the nearby KhTZ plant were evacuated by rail to Nizhny Tagil in the autumn of 1941, where production was not re-established. There had been consideration of restarting Voroshilovets production at STZ, with the tractor reconfigured on the T-34 chassis as assembled at STZ (essentially the AT-45 design principle as developed in Nizhny Tagil in 1944), but this did not materialize due to other priorities at STZ, which already produced the smaller STZ-5 alongside the T-34 medium tank.

As of 1 January 1941, 85 Voroshilovets tractors were located in the Moscow Military District, with 75, 59 and eight Voroshilovets tractors located in the Kiev, Western and Leningrad Military Districts respectively. Red Army records also show that as of 1 September 1942, 528 Voroshilovets remained in Red Army service, with artillery tractor losses being minimal compared to 1941–42. As at the end of the war in Europe in May 1945, 336 (some sources state 306) Voroshilovets tractors were recorded as remaining in inventory, of which 251 were in running order.

In the autumn of 1941, a small batch of self-propelled guns were produced by Artillery Factory No. 8 by mating Voroshilovets tractors with the 85mm M-1939 anti-aircraft gun. A variant of the Voroshilovets developed in accordance with instruction from the Engineering Command (IU) of the Red Army in 1937 was the BYe (БЭ) high speed rotary trenching machine built and tested for service the same year.

STALINETS-2 (S-2)

In the mid-1930s the first purpose designed 'transport tractors' or 'fast tractors', with a rear cargo area for transporting gun crews and ammunition and with greatly improved road speed, had been designed by NATI in collaboration with STZ and KhPZ (Plant No. 183) resulting in the STZ-5, Komintern and later Voroshilovets. The powerful but slow Stalinets-60 and later Stalinets-65 agricultural/industrial tractors produced at ChTZ in Chelyabinsk were not so well suited to such developments, but early design work on a heavy 'fast tractor' at ChTZ actually pre-dated the work undertaken by the other tractor plants. Development of such a specialized artillery tractor using parts from the imported 'Caterpillar' tractor had actually been reviewed before work on building the ChTZ plant had even commenced, with RVS Resolution No. 29 dated 17–18 June 1929 approving the project, later reviewed by UMM RKKA in January 1931, for a tractor design that would ultimately become the S-2 at the end of the decade.

(A) The S-2 artillery tractor with a typical 'tyagach' artillery tractor layout.
(B) A destroyed S-2 and 85mm M-1939 anti-aircraft gun combination.
(C) A Soviet drawing showing the S-2 (but with the S-2 Obrazets No. 1 cab and engine compartment arrangement).
(D) A T-26 M-1933 being towed by two S-2 artillery tractors, winter 1941–42.

In accordance with the above noted RVS resolution, designers at NATI in Moscow in collaboration with the KB at ChTZ in Chelyabinsk developed a 'fast' transportny-traktor-tyagach, or specialized military artillery tractor, based originally on the Caterpillar-60 and then the Soviet domestic S-60 variant. Work proceeded sporadically as ChTZ concentrated on mass production of the S-60 tractor. But in 1935, as early work on the S-65 production replacement for the S-60 was underway in Chelyabinsk, the NATI design bureau in collaboration with designers at ChTZ began work on a new heavy artillery tractor with a forward control cab and rear cargo area, specifically designed as a 'gruzovoi' or military transport (load) tractor. The project was led by V.Ya. Slominsky.

The S-60 was a rugged and powerful tractor, but with a 7km/h maximum road speed it was particularly slow. Although the chassis could be reconfigured with a forward control cab and rear cargo area for more useful application as an artillery tractor, it was optimistic to expect that a higher towing speed of up to 20km/h could be achieved using the existing chassis. The decision was therefore taken to modify the running gear taking into consideration technology used on other tractors such as the contemporary Komintern and STZ-5. The standard S-60 suspension was changed out for T-26 balancer-type assemblies with rubber rimmed road wheels and lighter tracks, providing increased road speed and better ground floatation on varied surfaces. A four-speed gearbox replaced the standard three-speed gearbox of the S-60 for better road performance. The resulting prototype, based on the S-60 but with modified running gear, and designated the NATI S-1 (S-1) with the S at the time standing for 'skorostny' (fast) rather than 'Stalinets', was completed and tested in the spring of 1935 as the first ChTZ development of a heavy 'transportny-traktor-tyagach' for the Red Army. During trials the ligroin powered S-1 achieved a maximum speed of 21km/h, reducing to 11km/h with a towed load of 12,000kg, an improvement on the S-60; but the ligroin fuel engine was deemed underpowered and the suspension required strengthening. The S-1 was apparently demonstrated to the Soviet leadership in Moscow on 10 December 1935 together with other tractor designs, but without any immediate result. In early 1936, the S-1 was again modified, with an engine uprated to 120hp and other changes made; it was resubmitted for polygon trials in the winter of 1936–37. Performance was much improved, with an unladen road speed of 22km/h achieved, reducing to 17km/h with a 7,200kg artillery piece in tow, and to 11km/h with a 12,000kg towed load. The S-1 had however reached the end of its development potential as the S-60 on which it was based had been replaced in mass production by the diesel S-65.

While the S-1 had continued to be refined and tested, the inevitable decision had in 1935 already been taken as the diesel powered S-65 was close to entering series production to develop the S-1 design further on the new S-65 chassis.

A new prototype, designated NATI S-2 (S-2), was developed to prototype stage in 1936 in collaboration between NATI and the Prototype plant at ChTZ as a transport tractor (tyagach) version of the Stalinets S-65, configured with a forward control cab allowing for a load platform at the rear for the gun crew and ammunition. The S-2 prototype was powered by an M-17 (MT-17) diesel engine developing 115hp at 1,350rpm, with a redesigned 'high speed' chassis, suspension and running gear developed under the direction of A.A. Kreisler. The tractor now had three fuel tanks, for a total of 222 litres. The engine was coupled with a four-speed gearbox for better road performance. The rear cargo platform had a load area of 5.09m^2 and a load capacity of up to 1,500kg. The S-2 was fitted with a rear mounted amortized tow hook and a front mounted fixed hook for tandem tractor towing. The S-2 was designed to tow loads of up to 12,000kg at a maximum road speed of 25km/h and up to 19,000kg at lower speeds, with a 25 per cent fuel consumption saving relative to the ligroin powered S-60.

Trials began in early 1938, showing improvements and a moderate increase in maximum speed of 22.5km/h. At some point during the later transition to S-2 series production, the designation S for 'skorostny' morphed into S for 'Stalinets' as per the S-60 and S-65 from which the design was derived. The final configuration of the S-2 was again mounted on two T-26 type balancer trolleys, the front one with four rubber rimmed road wheel pairs, the rear with two, with the band braking system also inherited from the T-26 tank. The track type was as used on the KhPZ developed tractors.

A destroyed S-2 at the roadside, a typical scene in the summer and autumn of 1941. (Sergei Popsuevich)

Factory trials of the S-2 were completed in August 1938, followed by a return proving run from Chelyabinsk to Moscow where it was demonstrated to a commission including the heads of ABTU, GAU and NKSM. The 12-day endurance trial, covering 2,000km of road and all-terrain travel, showed up further defects that required redesign. A small number of S-2 artillery tractors was built at ChTZ in the autumn of 1938, with a small pre-series batch of 12 S-2 tractors built at ChTZ in the autumn and early winter of 1939.

In August 1939 a NATI S-2 prototype had meantime been subjected to field trials including a second extended road march from Chelyabinsk to Moscow, the trials again conducted over 2,000km of varying ground conditions in 12 days, during which the tractors proved reliable, if slightly slower than intended. Further tests were conducted with two NATI S-2 tractors at the NIABP proving grounds at Kubinka near Moscow from September to December 1939, with the S-2 being able to capably tow the 203mm B-4 tracked howitzer as a single unit (i.e. without disassembly into barrel and carriage loads) at 15km on made roads and 10km/h on dirt roads. The Red Army demanded some further changes, not least moving the driver and his tiller controls to the left side of the cab, with other improvements required to the braking system and winch construction. A 10,000kg/f winch was mounted between the engine and gearbox, with a 30m cable.

The S-2 was accepted for service with the Red Army on 19 December 1939, with some final approvals belatedly received in the spring of 1940. Series production began only in September 1940, remaining relatively slow; 23 were built to the beginning of 1941, with the tractors delivered to training establishments for familiarization. The original factory production plan to the end of December 1940 envisaged 535 tractors to be delivered to NKO, 100 to NKVMF, 45 to NKVD and five to NKV. The official NATI history notes that 23 S-2 tractors were actually delivered to the Red Army by the end of 1940.

S-2 assembly was leisurely pre-war in part due to the designers working to increase the reliability of the running gear which in a 'fast' tractor endured rapid wear. Despite the complexities of establishing S-2 series production, modernization of the design was already underway as war broke out. Two prototypes with new running gear developed at NATI were tested at the Kubinka polygon in August 1941, but due to the need to maintain existing S-2 production output, these developments were shelved.

According to recent research in original archives it would appear that on 1 January 1941 only four S-2 tractors had actually been delivered to the Red Army, with shipments well behind schedule when war engulfed the country in June 1941; by this time ChTZ was producing six to nine S-2 tractors per day, with full series production achieved from August 1941. The production increase at ChTZ was such that as of 1 September 1941 there were 892 S-2 tractors

TOP An S-2 artillery tractor in Red Army service, towing a well camouflaged 122mm M-1931 (A-19) gun.

BOTTOM An S-2 tractor with armour shielding during trials of the Mugalev PT-2 mine trawl, 1–3 July 1941. The system is seen being tested operating at 2–3km/h against TM-35 anti-tank mines.

recorded in Red Army service, with 383 recorded as lost in combat since 22 June 1941. A total of 1,179 S-2 tractors were delivered by November 1941 when S-2 production was terminated at ChTZ as the plant retooled for increased tank production.* Red Army sources indicate that 1,161 tractors remained in service at the end of 1941, which in part reflects the small number that were in operational service in June–July 1941, hence smaller losses, with the majority of production and delivery to front line units being after the outbreak of war.

GKO Resolution No. 1693 *About Production of the ChTZ S-65 and S-2 Artillery Tractor at the Kirov Plant NKPT* dated 20 May 1942 instructed the plant to continue S-2 and S-65 production alongside the production of 15 tanks per day, but tank production took precedence in the critical war situation that existed in 1942, with all tractor production at ChTZ terminated in lieu of tank

* S-2 production numbers are conflated in original sources, showing an overall 1,179–1,275 built.

assembly. A final batch of five S-2 tractors was completed at ChKZ in early 1942 from available parts, by which time the plant had entirely moved over to KV-1 heavy and also T-34 medium tank production. The plant continued to produce spares for the S-2, which gave the tractor certain advantages over the Plant No. 183 produced Komintern and Voroshilovets in service.

The Stalinets-2 (S-2) was a huge and heavy tractor, with the engine alone weighing 2,200kg, but it could tow any Soviet heavy artillery piece including tracked types. The S-2 was in service used for towing medium and heavy artillery, the latter including the tracked 152mm Br-2 gun-howitzer, 203mm M-1931 (B-4) howitzer and 280mm M-1939 (Br-5) mortar, and the wheeled 122mm A-19 and 152mm ML-20 corps artillery pieces at typical road convoy speeds of 15km/h, so proved eminently fit for purpose. The majority of S-2 tractors were deployed on the South West Front.

The S-2 is often maligned due to the number pictured by Wehrmacht forces having been destroyed in combat in the early months of the war, but Red Army records show that in May 1945 there remained 81 S-2 tractors in service, of which 43 were in running order with the other tractors awaiting repair. Due to the short engine compartment and engine location, the S-2 was more difficult to maintain than other artillery tractors. A small number of S-2 tractors, also referred to as ST-2 in some sources, remained in service with the post-war Soviet Army until the beginning of the 1950s.

LT-1 AND LT-2

With the Komsomolets in series production, in 1939 a group of designers at Plant No. 37 under the direction of G.S. Surenyan in collaboration with a design team at NATI developed an unarmoured tractor variant for towing light artillery in non-forward positions and on long road marches, using the automotive components and running gear of the T-20 Komsomolets tractor. The philosophy behind the unarmoured design was that the armoured Komsomolets, powered by a GAZ-M engine from the GAZ-MM 4x2 truck, was slightly underpowered for its role, but for an artillery transport tractor without armour, operating mainly on roads in rear areas, the same engine would provide better drawbar capacity and speed. Armour plate was in great demand for tank and SAU production, hence an unarmoured tractor provided artillery transport for rear area operations without drawing on scarce armour plate resources. Moreover, and critically, the new design could be assembled in large numbers at automobile plants, hence overall artillery tractor production capacity could be greatly increased in line with Red Army needs – bearing in mind the shortage of such specialized tractors even in pre-war years. The philosophy of assembling at lighter

production plants without in-house foundry and plate-rolling capability would in the years ahead be exactly as applied to production of the T-60 small tank at assembly plants not previously specializing in armoured vehicle production.

Design work resulted in the development of two prototypes, the LT-1 and LT-2, both fitted with a conventional GAZ-AA/MM type cab and a rear cargo area for transporting ammunition. The LT-1 (Light Tractor-1) was powered by the same GAZ-M, four-cylinder petrol engine as the Komsomolets, developing 50hp, while the LT-2 was powered by a six-cylinder GAZ-11 petrol engine developing 76hp. Prototypes of both models were built and tested, but by the time of its development the use of a GAZ-M engine developing 50hp was considered inadequate for any tracked vehicle, restricting the role of the LT-1 to towing anti-tank guns and light artillery. The LT-2 with its more powerful engine could also be used for towing heavier divisional artillery. The LT-2 was almost identical in appearance to the LT-1 but had a larger engine compartment with a ZiS radiator badge, and small detail differences such as the return roller spacing. The LT-2 was also evaluated but not accepted for production.

The LT-1 was built by Plant No. 37 in 1939 based on the running gear of the T-20 Komsomolets as an alternative to the armoured T-20 Komsomolets for operation in rear areas, with improved towing capacity.

The LT-1 and LT-2 closely resembled the later GAZ developed GAZ-20 (Komsomolets-2) which also used T-20 Komsomolets suspension, running gear and tracks, and the later GAZ-22 (T-22) which used a GAZ-11 engine and running gear components from the T-40 amphibious reconnaissance tank.

GAZ-20 AND GAZ-22

Design engineers at GAZ under the direction of N.I. Dyachkov and S.B. Mikhailov with engineers including S.A. Solovyev and I.G. Storozhko in 1940 developed a similar unarmoured tractor prototype to the earlier Plant No. 37 / NATI developed LT-1 and LT-2. The GAZ-20 (Komsomolets-2) light tractor, powered by a GAZ-M engine uprated to 60hp and using T-20 Komsomolets suspension and running gear, was fitted with the cab and cargo body of the GAZ MM 4x2 truck. It was designed, as with the Plant No. 37 developed LT-1, to tow anti-tank guns, divisional artillery and anti-aircraft guns together with crew and ammunition in rear areas and on long road marches. The GAZ-20 prototype was tested under the direction of A.F. Khmelevsky but ultimately was not accepted for production.

(A) (B) The GAZ-20 and later GAZ-22 were developed to prototype stage at GAZ in 1940 and 1941 respectively as non-armoured tractors utilizing standard automotive components. The later GAZ-22 (T-22) pictured here used running gear and torsion bar suspension components taken from the T-40 amphibious light tank.
(C) The GAZ-22 (T-22) during winter trials at GAZ in Gorky in the winter of 1940–41.

A further tracked light tractor developed by the same design team at GAZ was the GAZ-22 (T-22) developed to prototype stage in the autumn of 1941 under the direction of S.B. Mikhailov (with the chief designer being M.I. Kazakov – who had also been associated with the earlier and almost identical Plant No. 37/NATI designs – per the GAZ official history). This was powered by a GAZ-11 (GAZ-202) petrol engine developing 76hp. Like the LT-1 and LT-2, the GAZ-22 was intended to tow 76.2mm divisional artillery and anti-aircraft pieces together with crew and ammunition. Trials for service with the Red Army were conducted in January–March 1941, with two prototypes towing the 122mm M-1938 (M-30) howitzer and limber. The trials showed that the GAZ-22 with a weight of 3,300kg was adequate for towing loads of up to 1,500kg on roads at up to 36km/h and could attain a speed of 45km/h unladen, but the prototype proved inadequate at towing artillery cross-country. As with the GAZ-20, the GAZ-22 maintained the conventional GAZ-MM truck cab and rear cargo body layout, but used the running gear and torsion bar suspension components of the T-40 amphibious light tank. An armoured cab with 16mm armour plate was also considered for the design. Subject to resolving some minor technical issues revealed during testing, the GAZ-22 was accepted for production. This did not however materialize, because the outbreak of war resulted in more immediate production priorities at GAZ and a defecit of tank running gear components for secondary roles.

AT-45

A significant number of Voroshilovets tractors that survived the fighting of 1941–42 continued in service where parts and maintenance allowed until the end of the war, with attrition losses declining as the war continued. The tractor did however suffer significant losses when operating in its secondary role as a tank recovery vehicle, often under fire, such that the TTTs for a new tracked artillery tractor based on the T-34 tank chassis were drawn up as early as 1942. With medium tank production at the relocated Plant No. 183 in Nizhny Tagil at maximum output and the Red Army on the offensive, in early 1944 a design team at the KB of the Kolomensk Machine Building Plant (KMZ) in the name of V.V. Kuibyshev in Nizhny Tagil (the relocated Plant No. 183), headed by N.G. Zubarev, began work on such a new tractor, which would later become known as the AT-45, and also as the 'New Voroshilovets'. The tractor was intended as a replacement for the pre-war Voroshilovets, designed by Zubarev's KB when earlier based in Kharkov.

An AT-45 prototype leaving the assembly workshops. Only a small pre-series batch of AT-45 tractors was built, but the design was ultimately the basis for the later AT-T heavy artillery tractor.

An AT-45 during operational trials towing a 203mm B-4 tracked howitzer in a single piece load.

The AT-45 incorporated elements of the armoured AT-42 design developed from 1940 on the T-34 chassis at Kharkov before its wartime relocation to Nizhny Tagil. The AT-45 was based on T-34 tank chassis components, and powered by a V-2V diesel engine developing 375hp, with a towing capacity of 22,000kg, a load capacity of 6,000kg and a maximum road speed of 42km/h. The all-steel cab and engine compartment of the Voroshilovets was utilized, but with a new load area constructed of sheet steel. As the KB at Plant No. 183 developed the AT-45 design to prototype stage, the plant location for series production remained outstanding. Tank production would clearly remain the priority at Plant No. 183 in Nizhny Tagil but Kharkov had been retaken by the Red Army on 23 August 1943, and by 16 October Order No. 616/s was issued regarding the rebuilding of the original Plant No. 75 in Kharkov in three stages. The first stage included the instruction to assemble a pre-series batch of AT-45 tractors by March 1944, with ten tractors to be completed by the end of the year.

On recapture, the site of Plant No. 75 had initially undertaken tank and armoured vehicle repairs, with the subject of artillery tractors continuing to have secondary importance. However, the plant began to be re-established as an assembly facility, with existing and additional replacement machine tooling being in place by June 1944. In the spring of 1944 the plant had already begun assembling the first six AT-45 prototypes, which were completed by the end of June as preparation continued for series production. After plant trials, two AT-45 tractors were sent for Front operational testing with the Red Army, with the other tractors sent to the Kuban region of the northern Caucasus for long term evaluation.

Plans for AT-45 production were however disrupted by GKO Resolution No. 6209/ss issued on 18 July 1944 *About Organizing Production of the T-44 Medium Tank at Plant No. 75 and Plant No. 264 NKTP*, which established that Plant No. 75 should immediately prepare for series production of the T-44 medium tank then in development as the Obiekt-136 prototype. In June 1944

An AT-45 towing a T-34T ARV during trials.

machine tooling was relocated from Plant No. 38 (Kirov) to Plant No. 75, but the primary aim of this relocation was to establish T-44 medium tank production, the NKTP resolution as per Soviet norms following the de facto preparations on the ground. Tank production at the time remained the outright priority, and development of the T-44 proved more complex than originally envisaged, hence there was no available capacity at Plant No. 75 for AT-45 series assembly. Plant No. 40 in Mytischi was being prepared to take over production of the Ya-12 and Ya-13 series of medium artillery tractors from Yaroslavl (with the later tractor designations M-12, M-12A and later M-2) so it could not also entertain AT-45 production. In September 1944, two or more AT-45 tractors were meanwhile sent to the Front for service evaluation with the Red Army, with another sent to the NIBT* test polygon at Kubinka for trials purposes. At the end of the year NKTP determined that AT-45 series production could be started at the evacuated site of Plant No. 174 in Leningrad, but the design did not make the transition from Kharkov to Leningrad during the war years. In the immediate post-war era, the AT-45 theme continued to be developed via a series of prototypes into the post-war series production AT-T heavy artillery tractor.

AT-K

In April 1944, with Kharkov recaptured and the industrial capacity of the city rebuilt, GKO Resolution No. 5773 dated 30 April 1944 and NKTP Order No. 289 dated 4 May 1944 issued a requirement for the development of a new fast medium tracked tractor. The KB at the re-established Plant No. 75 in Kharkov was tasked with development of the new tractor as a potential successor to the pre-war Komintern and Voroshilovets. The GAU provided TTTs specified a 4,000kg tow load, an optimistic 55km/h maximum road speed and an 18hp/tonne power to weight ratio. The project was designated AT-K (Artilleriisky

* The NIABP test polygon term was also referred to as the NIBT (auto-armoured-tank) polygon, with the latter name becoming standardized in later years.

Tyagach Korpusnoi), i.e. a forward control cab monocoque type design. The tractor featured a cab-over engine layout similar to the STZ-5, but with a 5,000kg capacity load platform. The AT-K was to be powered by a T-200 diesel engine (a downrated variant of the V-2 tank engine designed at Plant No. 37 in Moscow developing 200hp at 1,500rpm) providing the envisaged 15,000kg tractor with a maximum convoy towing speed of 21km/h. The design was reviewed by both the Technical Committee of NKTP and GAU in October 1944, with the decision to build a pre-series batch for military trials. The project was however terminated due to lack of engine availability and other more critical workloads being allocated to the plant, not least development of the T-44 medium tank.

HEAVY ARTILLERY TRACKED TRACTOR-TRANSPORTER – PLANT No. 183 (NIZHNY TAGIL)

Plant No. 183 in Nizhny Tagil had in late 1944 declined being the base for series production of the AT-45 artillery tractor due to T-34-85 medium tank production remaining the overwhelming priority at the plant. The plant management was nevertheless already considering what to do with excess production capacity in the post-war era. As the end of the war approached, much thought was given as to how the workforce skills could be maintained in situ when the demand for military production inevitably reduced. This dilemma faced all military production facilities, which is why, for example, SU-100 production was transferred from Sverdlovsk to Omsk immediately post-war, in order to maintain skillsets in place pending new design developments maturing to series production. The majority of the workforce at Plant No. 183 in Nizhny Tagil had been evacuated from Kharkov in 1941, but after recapture and re-establishment of the production plants in Kharkov, the evacuated workers' places there had been taken by a new workforce.

At the beginning of 1945, a plant initiative was developed at Plant No. 183 in Nizhny Tagil under the direction of plant director Yu.E. Maksarev for a heavy artillery transport tractor based on the T-44 medium tank then slated for series production at Plant No. 75 (Kharkov) and Plant No. 264 (near Stalingrad). The design drawings were for a large tractor with a front mounted cab and a particularly long (5.6m) load platform, mounted on an extended T-44 chassis with six road wheels per side; they were entitled *Tractor-Transporter for 122/152mm Artillery and 500 Rounds of Ammunition.* The 6,000kg load area capacity of the AT-45 was increased to 20,000kg for the planned new tractor. The design was intended as a multi-purpose chassis, with several variants considered, including with a fully enclosed cargo area. A full scale working model was completed in the spring of 1945, based on a T-34 chassis but with T-44 running gear. Trials were successful, with significantly improved characteristics compared to the AT-45, and with a projected engine life of 20,000km between capital rebuilds. The working model was reviewed by GAU and NKTP on behalf of the artillery and armoured forces respectively, and the design tacitly approved. However, Commissar V.A. Malyshev at NKTP apparently did not sign off on further development, and the project was abandoned. Nevertheless, in December 1945, Malyshev did approve the production of a new artillery tractor as a continuation of the wartime AT-45 theme, to be produced at the re-established (former engine) Plant No. 75 in Kharkov based on the planned T-54 tank chassis. This tractor, developed as the ObiekT-401, would become the post-war AT-T.

Ya-11

The pre-war shortage of specialized military artillery transport tractors in the Red Army was sharply exacerbated in the months after the outbreak of war in 1941. With S-65 and S-60 production terminated at ChTZ in Chelyabinsk in lieu of tank production, and with Kharkov captured, by the end of 1941 only STZ in Stalingrad continued to produce artillery tractors, with that being secondary to T-34 tank production at the same plant. As much of Soviet tank production had been evacuated to new locations, Soviet industry was mobilized nationally, with armoured vehicles such as the T-60 small tank and the SU-12 (SU-76) SAU being developed specifically due to their utilization of standard truck engines, gearboxes and components. This allowed vehicle manufacturers without armour plate production capability or heavy machine tooling to assemble armoured vehicles with steel plate supplied from other plants, increasing the number of plants capable of light armoured vehicle assembly.

Artillery tractors were also urgently required in quantity, and the same thinking was applied to a new artillery tractor design. Accordingly, a TsK level decision required the development of a new tracked artillery tractor type which could if necessary be assembled at any Soviet automotive plant.

The task of developing the new artillery tractor intended to tow artillery pieces of up to 8,000kg transport order weight, together with gun crew and 1,500–2,000kg of ammunition, was undertaken by NATI in Moscow, with its significant experience in developing military tractors, from the short-lived pre-war Pioner to the STZ-5 and S-2 developed in cooperation with the STZ and ChTZ plants respectively. The new tractor was developed to replace the pre-war Komintern and Voroshilovets tractors, being of similar layout, with automotive cab and rear load area, but lighter in construction and also in towing capacity. The working drawings of what would later become known as the Ya-11 were developed at NATI from February 1942, under the direction of E.G. Popov, as the 'Tyagach D' (Transport Tractor Type D) (D – dvukh motorny – twin engine). The design was based on work conducted by the same team at NATI in 1939–40 (namely the LT-1/LT-2 and more specifically the GAZ-20 and later GAZ-22). These earlier prototypes had considered the development of an artillery tractor latterly (in the case of the GAZ-22) based on the running gear of the T-40 amphibious light tank. Several engine options were considered for the prototype, including the GAZ-202 developing 85hp and its automobile variant, the GAZ-11 developing 72hp, and the ZiS-5 and ZiS-16 engines developing 73hp and 85hp respectively, with a road speed of 35km/h being the principal design requirement.

The Tyagach D prototype was ultimately powered by two standard engines from the GAZ-MM 4x2 truck, mounted in parallel (an engine configuration also used on the SU-12 (the early SU-76) SAU, developing a total of 86hp at 2,800rpm, which provided the designated towing capacity of 8,000kg. The tractor also used a twin GAZ-MM truck gearbox and the torsion bar suspension and tracks from the T-60 small tank. The twin engine arrangement in practice produced a combined output of 72–75hp, not significantly better than a single ZiS-5 engine, with a more complex drive arrangement that suffered the same synchronization problems as the early SU-12 SAU. The parallel engines also made a front mounted STZ-5 style driver's cab impractical, with the engines offset 159mm to the right of the centre-line to allow the driver a modicum of working room. Due to engine and gearbox synchronization issues, the practical towing capability was reduced to 5,000kg; this was still adequate for the 122mm M-1938 (M-30) howitzer and 85mm M-1939 anti-aircraft gun, divisional artillery and heavy mortars, with a maximum road speed of 26.7km/h achieved during trials.

The single 'Type-D' prototype, developed by NATI designers including I.F. Verzhbinsky, I.I. Drong (who latterly took over as chief designer from E.G. Popov), A.A. Dushkevich, N.I. Korotonoshko, V.P. Petrov, V.G. Rozanov and A.A. Seslavin, was completed at NATI in August 1942. It was subjected to trials in Yaroslavl the following month overseen by NKSM, with the trials concluding on 9 November 1942. During subsequent trials at the NATI polygon the 'Type-D' showed good overall mobility, towing characteristics and reliability, achieving a road speed in fourth gear of 26.4km/h, significantly better than most other artillery tractors then in service. The working drawings together with the single prototype were duly transferred to the Yaroslavl Avtomobilny Plant (YaGAZ, renamed YaAZ from mid-1943) at Yaroslavl which had been producing small numbers of Ya-6A trucks, with the plant ordered by Chief of Artillery of the Red Army, N.N. Voronov, to have the new tractor design ready for series production within three months. The original prototype was modified for production at YaAZ under the direction of chief engineer V.V. Osepchugov and chief designer G.M. Kokin, in collaboration with Drong and Slominsky under the ultimate supervision of E.G. Popov, with the plant preparing for series production of the tractor as the Ya-11 under NKSM direction.

The Ya-11 was primarily intended to tow artillery up to 8,000kg in travel order, namely the 122mm M-1931/37 (A-19) and 152mm M-1937 (ML-20) 'Corps Duplex' artillery pieces. Changes made in preparing the Ya-11 for series production included increasing the chassis steel thickness from 8mm to 11mm and using the running gear and tracks from the T-70M rather than the now obsolescent T-60. Development of the Ya-11 was particularly protracted due to other wartime priorities. In March 1943 five prototypes now officially designated Ya-11 and fitted with twin six-cylinder GAZ engines developing 70hp were subjected to further testing, with three of the prototypes undertaking a proving run from Yaroslavl to Moscow in April under the supervision of plant director A.A. Nikanorov. This run was undertaken as the state trial of the new tractor, which was accepted for service with the Red Army. Long term tests of the Ya-11 were meanwhile undertaken at the NIABP tank polygon at Kubinka from May to June 1943 with the Ya-11 approved for production by GABTU and GAU. Assembly of a pre-series batch of 50 Ya-11 tractors was undertaken between April and June 1943, at which point production ceased due to a lack of engine inventory from GAZ, as the engine assembly plant at GAZ (Engine Workshop No. 1) was damaged in Luftwaffe air raids just as the Ya-11 was entering series production. Further production of the Ya-11 was not undertaken, but a solution for the lack of GAZ engines was found in the availability of Lend-Lease four-cylinder GMC-4-71 diesel engines and associated Spicer gearboxes, the combination having been ordered from the United States in 1941 and subsequently warehoused in Soviet inventory. Production of the modified design, designated Ya-12, began in August 1943.

The Ya-11 was almost identical in external appearance to the later series production Ya-12. The Ya-11 had solid disc wheels from the T-60 small tank (as did the early production Ya-12) whereas the later Ya-12 had spoked roadwheels. Other minor detail changes included simplified track guards without rounded leading edges on the production Ya-12.

Ya-12 illustration from the Operator's Manual.

Ya-12

The Ya-11 had proven a rugged and effective design, but, as noted, production was terminated and the design modified because of the lack of engine supply from GAZ due to Luftwaffe bombing. The Ya-11 was thereby redesigned to use another engine. NATI had

LEFT The Ya-12 during evaluation trials.

BELOW LEFT The Ya-12 could tow the 122mm M-1931/37 (A-19) and 152mm M-1937 (ML-20) 'corps duplex' heavy artillery pieces.

BELOW A Ya-12 towing a 122mm or 152mm corps artillery piece crossing a log bridge in 1944.

significant experience in diesel engine development, having designed the M-6, MD-23 and MD-25 engines in addition to the engines used in several Soviet artillery tractors, but in 1943 the question was one of immediate availability, and crated imported GMC-4-71 engines were available stored in warehouses. These engines had been delivered to the Soviet Union as a result of an order for 1,500 GMC-4-71 engines requested by YaAZ plant director A.A. Nikanorov in December 1941 and approved by Stalin, ostensibly for use in the YaG-6 truck which had earlier been powered by imported Hercules engines, with a view to increasing truck output at the plant. For reasons that remain obscure, these engines were never used for their intended purpose and were thereby available for installation in mid-1943. The Ya-11 was accordingly redesigned to be powered by the imported Lend-Lease GMC-4-71 diesel engine developing 110hp,

A

B

C

D

E

F

(A) A Ya-12 (or Ya-13) in the Latvian SSR, 1944. The radiator grille differs from the standard Ya-12 type. **(B)** This Ya-12 (or Ya-13) in the Latvian SSR in 1944 also has a different radiator from the standard Ya-12 type. **(C)** A column of Ya-12 tractors towing 122mm M-1910/34 corps guns. **(D)** Ya-12 artillery tractors towing 122mm M-1910/34 (A-19) corps guns through Red Square, 1 May 1945. Photographer: Shipokov. **(E)** Ya-12 tractors towing 122mm M-1931/37 (A-19) corps guns through Red Square. Photographer: Kiselovsky. **(F)** Ya-12 tractors and 122mm M-1931/37 (A-19) corps guns in Red Square during the Victory Parade in Moscow, 26 June 1945.

coupled to a Long-32 clutch and Spicer-5533 gearbox, with some components such as the band brakes now being taken from the contemporary production T-70M and SU-76M rather than the earlier T-60, and other detail changes.

Prototype development was rapid considering that the Ya-12, designated as a tractor-transporter (tyagach) artillery tractor, was a re-engined modification of the existing Ya-12 design, retaining the front mounted engine, central two door fully enclosed cab and rear stake type cargo body and running gear arrangement of the Ya-11. The Ya-12 had a towing capacity of 8,000kg and a useful 3.37m^2 load platform with wooden stowage panniers and an ammunition load capacity of 2,000kg.

Trials confirmed that the tractor remained capable of towing up to 8,000kg at acceptable road speeds, with a maximum road speed of 38km/h, reducing to 16km/h on dirt roads and further reducing to only 4.7km/h towing heavier artillery across terrain. The Ya-12 had two fuel tanks, a 124-litre main tank and a 176-litre reserve with dual filter systems, providing a road range of 290km. The Ya-12 was considered suitable for towing the 122mm M-1931/37 (A-19) and 152mm M-1937 (ML-20) corps artillery pieces, and could tow the 152mm, 203mm and 280mm tracked artillery pieces broken down into two loads over short distances under duress if required. In June 1943, the plant accordingly prepared the Ya-12 for series production, which began in August 1943, with 285 Ya-12 tractors built to the end of 1943 and 1,666 built to the end of the war.

Operational feedback noted that the Ya-12 was both capable and reliable. The engine had a plant guarantee of 700 working hours and the transmission and running gear a plant guarantee of 3,000km; these were met in service,

Ya-12 tractors being greeted by sportswomen pass the Central Telegraph office on Gorky Street (today Tverskaya), Moscow, 7 November 1947.

ABOVE LEFT AND RIGHT A Ya-12 towing a 152mm M-1943 (D-1) howitzer in the Belorussian SSR, 1954. Note that all but one of the original road wheels have been replaced with earlier T-70/SU-76 solid disc wheels.

BELOW This rear view of the same Ya-12 in Belorussia in 1954 clearly shows the wooden rear cargo area with double-gate type rear door and bench seating for the gun crew.

making the Ya-12 particularly durable. Its relatively narrow T-70/SU-76 derived tracks had poor traction on icy roads (grousers were available but rarely fitted), with the small ground clearance and lack of winch also noted as not ideal. Engine starting in very cold conditions was not always straightforward, and the running gear wore out quickly if overloaded.

The Ya-12 was in series production at Yaroslavl from 1943 to 1945. Early production Ya-12 tractors were 5.03m in length and had solid disc road wheels, like the Ya-11; late series Ya-12 tractors were slightly shorter at 4.89m in length, with the majority of tractors having spoked road wheels. Series production was initially at a pace of two to three tractors a day. By August 1943, 218 had been completed (including prototypes), with 965 built in 1944 and 1,046 built to the end of war in Europe on 9 May 1945, at which point there were 1,270 'Ya' series tractors (including the Ya-11, Ya-12 and later Ya-13) serving in the Red Army.

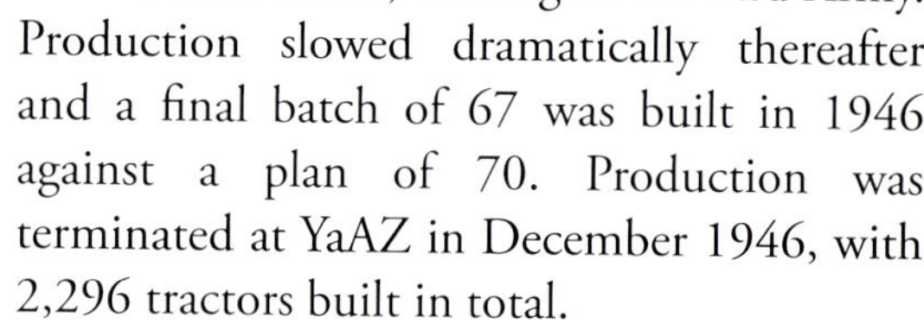

Production slowed dramatically thereafter and a final batch of 67 was built in 1946 against a plan of 70. Production was terminated at YaAZ in December 1946, with 2,296 tractors built in total.

The Ya-12 served on all operational Fronts, partook in the Soviet Victory Parade held on 24 June 1945 and subsequent military parades on Red Square, and served with the post-war Soviet Army into the early 1950s alongside small numbers of M-12A and M-13A tractors before being gradually replaced by the series production M-2. The Ya-12 also served post-war with the armies of Poland and Czechoslovakia.

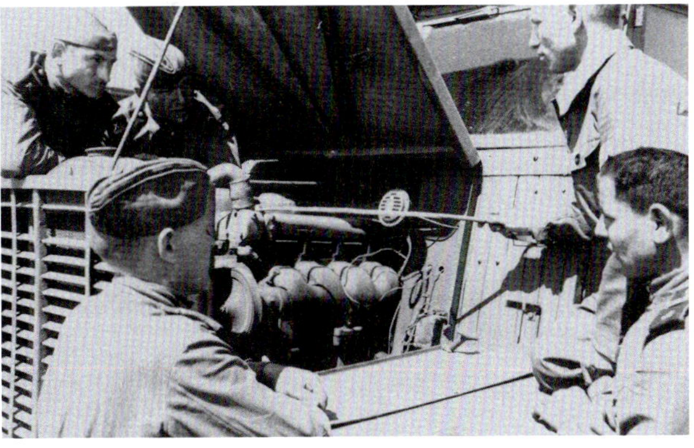

ABOVE LEFT The same Ya-12 artillery tractor in the Belorussian SSR in 1954 with a mix of spoked and solid road wheels on the other side of the tractor also. The cab door is painted with crossed barrels, unit number 2-74-00 and 'ТЯГАЧ' (tractor).

ABOVE Driver-mechanics receiving engine maintenance instruction on a Ya-12, Belorussian SSR, 1954. Post-war, some Ya-12 tractors had their original GMC-4-71 engine replaced by the analogous Soviet domestic YaAZ-204 type.

LEFT At the end of the war, Ya-12 production was moved from Yaroslavl to Mytischi near Moscow where the modified M-12A, M-13A and later the M-2 were built, in order that YaAZ could concentrate on heavy truck production. The YaAZ-200 (pictured) was originally produced at YaAZ, with production later moved to MAZ (Minsky Avtomobilny Zavod – Minsk Automobile (truck) Plant) in Minsk.

In the immediate post-war months, production of the Ya-12 was transferred to Plant No. 40 at its original location at Mytischi in the northern suburbs of Moscow, which had extensive experience of light tank and armoured vehicle production. The transfer of series production to Plant No. 40 was in order to enable YaAZ to return to mass truck production with the YaAZ-200 4x2 truck, with series production of the YaAZ-200 in due course transferred to Minsk as the MAZ-200. YaAZ, which pre-war had been a specialized truck manufacturer, made good use of the expertise gained in assembling the Ya-12 powered by an imported diesel engine. Designers at YaAZ modified the engine, which entered production at the engine workshops of the YaAZ plant in 1947 as the YaAZ-204 engine, also assembled from the following year at Minsk as the MAZ-204 engine. In 1958, YaAZ was renamed YaMZ (Yaroslavlsky Motorny Zavod – Yaroslavl Motor Plant), henceforth specializing in a variety of engines used in a wide range of Soviet wheeled and tracked military vehicles.

In October 1945, a single Ya-12 was sent into storage for the future NIII-21 Museum at Bronnitsy, where it remained until cut up for scrap in 1967 when the museum was closed. A single Ya-12 powered by a YaAZ-204 engine continued to work within the YaMZ plant in Yaroslavl, before being plinth mounted in front of the factory administration buildings, where it remains to the present day.

Ya-13 & Ya-13F

The Ya-12 had terminated production of the limited production Ya-11 due to a lack of engines from GAZ, with, as noted, the Lend-Lease GMC-4-71 diesel engine being installed as standard in the Ya-12. Due to GMC engines also becoming limited in supply by the end of 1943, coupled with the increasing availability of indigenous petrol engines, a modification of the Ya-12 was developed at YaAZ: the Ya-13, powered by a ZiS-5M petrol engine developing 77hp. The slightly lighter (8,000kg) Ya-13 fitted with a lower horsepower and less economical but available ZiS-5M petrol engine resulted in a tractor with a lower drawbar capacity of 5,000kg, a retained load capacity of 2,000kg and a design maximum road speed of 20km/h reducing to 3.2km/h crossing terrain. This was achieved with a higher fuel consumption of 115 litres/100km due to the less powerful engine, and a reduced road range of 180km. The Ya-13 as tested at Kubinka at the end of July 1943 and accepted for service as the Ya-13 could still capably tow most wheeled artillery, including the ubiquitous 152mm M-1937 (ML-20) corps howitzer, and could be used in the same roles as the more powerful Ya-12. A total of 71 (some earlier sources state 95) Ya-13 tractors were produced, the operational numbers of which were counted within Red Army statistics for the Ya-12.

The Ya-13 was followed at the end of the year by the Ya-13F, the prototype of which was completed in November 1943. The Ya-13F was powered by the Miass developed ZiS-5MF (MF-Miassky Forsirovanny – Miass plant Forced – i.e. uprated) petrol engine. This was developed under the direction of chief designer A.A. Aizenberg at the Miass plant where the wartime UralZiS-5V was produced, with the modified engine developing 95–99hp at 2,800rpm. The ZiS-5MF engine was sometimes simply designated ZiS-MF. The tilt over the cargo compartment on the Ya-13F was raised to a height of 2.3m. During trials the Ya-13F maintained the towing and load capacities of the Ya-13, with a slightly higher 23km/h maximum towing speed but a reduced terrain towing speed of 2km/h. The Ya-13F was subjected to GBTU (Main Armoured Directorate of the Red Army) trials at the Kubinka polygon in 1944, but with no conclusive outcome due to other priorities.

In accordance with the original GKO Resolution No. 5304 dated 5 March 1944 and GAU KA and NKSM Order No. 0147/3205 belatedly dated 10 August 1945, testing of two Ya-13F prototypes fitted with the ZiS-MF engine was finally undertaken at the GBTU polygon at Kubinka only post-war, between 5 August and 1 October 1945, by which time responsibility for the production of artillery tractors had been passed to Plant No. 40 at Mytischi, with YaAZ returning post-war to heavy truck production. A total of three Ya-13F tractors were built in 1944, and a further two in early 1945, for a total of five produced in total; series production was not undertaken, due to the aforementioned transfer of production from YaAZ to Plant No. 40. A total of 1,666 of all 'Ya' series tractors were produced from 1943 until 9 May 1945, of which 1,270 remained in service with the Red Army at the end of the war in Europe.

M-12A & M-13A

At the very end of the war, responsibility for production of medium artillery tractors (i.e. the Ya-12) was passed from YaAZ in Yaroslavl to Plant No. 40 in Mytischi in the Moscow suburbs, in order that YaAZ could concentrate on truck and engine production. N.A. Astrov and his design team at Plant No. 40 led by chief designer N.A. Popov (chief designer at Plant No. 40 from 1943 to 1946) modified the Ya-12 as the M-12 (Mytischi-12), powered by a ZiS-5M petrol engine. The M-12 was subsequently in August 1945 fitted with a diesel engine, and re-designated M-12A. As much of the design team had worked on the T-60, T-70 and T-80 and on the SU-76 SAU they were well versed in the

A rare photograph of a Plant No. 40 (Mytischi)-built M-12A. The limited production M-12A and M-13A are the least documented of all artillery tractors as the YaAZ built Ya-12 morphed into the later M-2 via the M-12A and M-13A. Note the front bumper, track guards, modified headlight mounting locations and larger cargo area.

The M-12A and M-13A would appear to have been built in small batches with ongoing changes before the M-2 entered series production. Note the headlight locations on this tractor compared to the standard series production M-2.

specifics of the components involved, and development was rapid. The M-12A (Mytischi-12A) was either powered by a YaAZ-204V engine or (according to some Russian sources) was again powered by a GMC-4-71 diesel engine developing 112hp. Development was rapid due to the aforementioned existing expertise in tracked vehicle development, with 15 pre-series production M-12A artillery tractors being completed in September 1945 (according to some sources these were M-12s, with the M-12A being built in early 1946). In the Red Army and post-war Soviet Army the tractor nevertheless retained the habitual Ya-12 designation. Like the previous Ya-12, the M-12A could tow an artillery piece of up to 6,000kg (some original sources state 8,000kg) in travel order. The M-12A was very similar to the Ya-12 but most had a cab sheathed in sheet steel and all had a modified load platform which was 305mm wider and with higher sides. The tractor also featured a new front bumper and had higher ground clearance than the Ya-12. The M-12A was additionally provided with a new, enlarged radiator and being 200kg heavier than the Ya-12 was provided with an additional 50 litres fuel capacity.

The M-12A was produced in small batches at Plant No. 40 from early 1946 (or perhaps slightly earlier as noted above) until 1948, with the plant being renamed MMZ the same year. In Soviet Army service the M-12A towed the 152mm D-1, 152mm D-20 and 122mm D-74 in addition to wartime artillery pieces. An M-12A was delivered to the NIII-21 Museum at Bronnitsy where it remained until it was scrapped in 1967.

Following on from the M-12A development of the Ya-12, the Mytischi plant a few months later also developed the M-13A variant, powered by a six-cylinder ZiS-MF engine developing 95hp, which underwent trials in February–March 1946. The M-13A, which had a slightly lower towing capacity of 6,000kg, was produced from 1946 until 1948, concurrently with the M-12A. Externally the M-12A and M-13A were indistinguishable and it would appear that the M-12A and M-13A were built in small batches, gradually acquiring the characteristics of the later series production M-2.

The M-12A and M-13A were both replaced in production by the Plant No. 40 designed M-2, which entered series production at Mytischi in 1948, powered by a MAZ-204V engine.

	M-12A	**M-13**	**M-13A**
Weight (kg):	6,740	5,710	5,905
Towing capacity (kg):	6,000–8,000	5,000–6,000	6,000
Load (kg):	2,000	2,000	2,000
Dimensions (L/W/H) (m):	4.87x2.45x2.29	4.89x2.44x2.29	4.88x2.45x2.30
Ground clearance (m):	0.35	0.48	0.49
Engine (hp/rpm):	95/2,800	99/2,800	95/2,800
Road speed (km/h):	35	24.5	28.2
Dirt road speed (km/h):	34	24	28
Range road (km):	415	250	295
Dirt road range (km):	295	200	240

CHAPTER 5
ARMOURED ARTILLERY TRACTORS

The armoured 'small tractor' prototype was based on the T-16 tank chassis.

The appearance of the tank on the battlefield in the second decade of the 20th century was followed by the inevitable development of the anti-tank gun, which in turn led to the conundrum as to how to manoeuvre these new weapons that were required to operate within a few hundred metres of their target. Across the world, the horse had been the staple means of moving artillery since its invention, but the increasing calibre and travel order weight of 20th century artillery had already begun to reduce the role of these animals in war. The situation was particularly acute as regards positioning and moving newly developed anti-tank guns in forward areas where the horse was particularly vulnerable, as the gruesome photographic records of the 1939–40 Soviet–Finnish Winter War demonstrate. What was needed was a mechanized means of moving such weapons across terrain within the range of enemy positions, which required the development of a small, tracked, manouvrable and preferably armoured transport tractor. The history of specialized armoured artillery tractors stemmed from the early development and use of tracked tractors in the Red Army both as tractors and as armoured fighting vehicles.

The Gulkevich bronetraktor or armoured tractor was developed to prototype stage in 1915 based on an Allis-Chalmers half-track chassis. The machine was however built as a combat vehicle – a tank – rather than an artillery tractor. In 1922 the Soviet engineer F.L. Khyslov designed a tracked tractor specifically intended for towing a new generation of 37mm and 45mm anti-tank guns,

A historically important albeit grainy photograph showing the T-16 based 'small tractor' (light tractor) during trials in 1931, with a Dyrenkov armoured tractor in the background.

but the project did not progress beyond concept stage. By the late 1920s it was clear that mechanization of the Red Army would require the series production of tracked tractors on a number of chassis, including armoured tank chassis, while there was a more general urgent requirement to increase the mechanization of artillery and thereby the number of artillery tractors in service, especially for the deployment and repositioning of towed anti-tank guns then in development. The Kommunar and the Bolshevik were the only indigenous Soviet tracked tractors in series production during the 1920s but neither was ideal for conversion to an armoured tractor role. One consideration made at the time, which would repeat in the years ahead, was to utilize new or mechanically worn light tank and tankette chassis for such purposes, with the development in the following decade of the T-20 Komsomolets armoured artillery tractor being preceded by a series of developments based on tank chassis.

In 1929, the Soviet State issued a resolution regarding the development of a series of specialized artillery tractors for service with the Red Army. The project was initiated by the GUVP and VSNKh in collaboration with OAT* and individual design bureaus as a national design effort driven as an essential matter for state and military development.

Work formally began in 1930 on a project entitled *Tracked Tractors for the Red Army* which required light (designated 'small'), medium, and heavy (designated 'large') tractors for the Red Army, based respectively on the chassis of light tanks or tankettes, medium and 'manoeuvre' tanks.

LIGHT ARMOURED TRACTOR (T-16 CHASSIS)

The first specialized armoured artillery tractor prototype resulting from the 1929 state resolution on tractor development was developed in 1930 at the Artillery Directorate Main Design Bureau (GKB GAU). The prototype 'Maly Bronirovanny Traktor' (small armoured tractor) was developed on the T-16 tank chassis as the 'gun crew (small) tractor of the Red Army', and built at the 2nd Automobile Plant (Plant No. 2). The prototype was completed in April 1931 and tested from 12 May 1931 and into early June at the RKKA Scientific Engineering Technology Polygon (NITP). The armoured tractor, retaining the 6–12mm armour basis of the T-16, had a combat weight of 3,930kg which was beyond its design parameters, and the 35hp engine proved underpowered to provide the specified 3,000kg towing capability requirement. Only four gun crew could be accommodated versus a requirement for six, and the fuel capacity,

* GUVP – Main Directorate of War Industry (to 1932). VSNKh – Supreme Council of the National Economy. OAT (Ordnance Arsenal Trust) – the central directorate for weapons development.

hence range, was determined as inadequate. The tractor was also difficult to operate. The prototype was not accepted for series production, but work immediately began on a tractor based on the T-23 chassis, with an engine developing 60hp from the T-20 variant of the T-18 tank. This project was also terminated in the autumn of 1931.

MEDIUM ARMOURED TRACTOR (T-19 CHASSIS)

An RVS resolution dated 18 July 1929 had required the urgent development of a new 'support' tank, the T-19, as a potential replacement for the T-18 (MS-1) tank. A prototype was completed in June 1931, but trials showed the construction to be over-complex, particularly the running gear, and expensive for a mass production tank, not least due to the vast cost of imported bearing assemblies. The T-19 tank project was thereby dropped, but the T-19 chassis was used as the basis for the medium tractor specified in the 1929 GUVP and VSNKh resolution, developed with the project name 'Borets' (fighter).

The Borets project, accepted for development in 1930, envisaged an armoured tractor on the basis of the T-19 light tank, powered by a T-19 or imported 'Hercules' engine, capable of towing up to 7,500kg with a maximum road speed of 20km/h, and accommodating an eight-man gun crew in addition to the driver. The armoured tractor was also intended as a potential armoured replacement for the Bolshevik and Kommunar tractors in specific roles within the Red Army. The Borets was developed to the stage of working drawings, but was ultimately cancelled as the T-19 chassis on which it was based was not approved for series production.

Further to the abandonment of the Borets tracked tractor, the decision was taken to develop future 'medium' armoured tractors on the basis of the next generation of Soviet light tanks then in the early stages of development. The new fully armoured design was intended to tow artillery of up to 4,500kg in travel order at road speeds of up to 20–25km/h. In February 1932 the Artillery KB within the Bolshevik plant in Leningrad developed two versions of such an artillery tractor, based on the new T-26 light tank chassis being produced at the same plant, one with a fully armoured casemate superstructure, the other with a canvas upper superstructure. Both versions (the T-26T and T-26T2) were accepted for production on 1 January 1933 with an original plan to produce 150 fully armoured and 200 semi-armoured artillery tractors, both based on the T-26 M-1931 chassis.

The heavy armoured tractor developed on the basis of the 1929 GUVP and VSNKh decision in collaboration with OAT was an unarmoured transport tractor intended to tow artillery of up to 11,000kg weight in travel order at up to 15km/h on roads. In 1933, this tractor received the name 'Komintern' and would be produced at KhPZ in Kharkov as the first Soviet series production transport tractor developed specifically for Red Army artillery units.

T-27 TANKETTE

After a hiatus in the 1920s, the subject of mechanizing artillery was returned to in the early 1930s as Red Army artillery grew in calibre and accordingly in travel order weight. The development of dedicated anti-tank guns also necessitated the requirement for a fast moving, and preferably armoured, light artillery tractor for moving such weapons between fire positions within 500–1,000m of enemy positions. Work thereby began at the turn of the decade on developing a light tracked tractor for towing 37mm M-1930 and 45mm M-1932 anti-tank guns and the 76.2mm M-1927 regimental gun. This would result in the unarmoured Pioner and the later armoured T-20 Komsomolets tractors. As an interim measure while specialized armoured artillery tractors were in their infancy, worn-out T-27 tankettes were in the early 1930s used as tracked anti-tank gun tractors. The T-27 had been introduced into service in 1931 and had been produced for only two years, but with a production run of 3,342 machines there was no shortage of mechanically worn-out and largely redundant tankettes which were removed from operational units and subsequently used by the Red Army as artillery tractors. The use of T-27 tankettes as artillery tractors is documented in Moscow Military District where a small number of machines served in such a tractor role during the

A T-27 tankette towing a 45mm M-1932 (19-K) anti-tank gun, 1st Proletariatskaya Division, Moscow Military District, autumn 1936.

A T-37A amphibious light tank and 45mm M-1932 (19-K) anti-tank gun abandoned during the 1939–40 Soviet–Finnish Winter War. (SA-Kuva)

winter of 1941–42. A surprising number of T-27s survived the war in such a role. Fifty-two T-27 tankettes were within the statutes of the 1st Far Eastern Front when it was formed on 8 August 1945, albeit with 46 of them in storage in various states of repair. The purpose designed Komsomolets artillery tractor was by contrast later deployed on occasion in the role of tankette, the role for which the T-27 had been designed. The use of tankettes and light tanks as ad hoc artillery tractors was a recurring theme in the years leading up to the outbreak of war with Germany in 1941. The T-37A amphibious light tank was also used as an artillery tractor during the 1939–40 Soviet–Finnish Winter War.

KOMSOMOLETS 'TYPE-A'

In 1932, the NATI tractor institute under the direction of N.G. Popov developed the unarmoured, forward-control cab Komsomolets 'Type-A', long before the better known armoured light fast artillery tractor of the same name. The vehicle was based on British Carden-Loyd designs which were well received and respected in the Soviet Union. The prototype 'Type-A' was built at STZ and was used as a testbed vehicle to trial the M-7 four-cylinder diesel engine, as also developed by NATI, which was ultimately not put into series production. Though unarmoured, the Komsomolets 'Type-A' set the stage for later amoured tractor developments.

An early T-20 Komsomolets artillery tractor during development. The running gear originally envisaged using the rear suspension unit road wheel as the idler wheel, but frequent track shedding led to the later incorporation of a dedicated idler wheel. The layout is otherwise close to the series production Komsomolets.

KOMSOMOLETS 'TYPE-B'

In 1933, NATI developed a further transport tractor, the Komsomolets 'Type-B'; as with the 'Type-A', the prototype was built at STZ in Stalingrad. The 'Type-A' and 'Type-B' prototypes were evaluated concurrently, resulting in a third prototype developed by a team of engineers at NATI in collaboration with design engineers at STZ incorporating the best elements of both designs and resolving defects uncovered during trials. This final transport tractor prototype, initially known as the STZ-NATI, was built at STZ based on mechanical components shared with the STZ-NATI 1TA (the later series production STZ-3/KhTZ-3) agricultural tractor. It would however be later developed specifically as a transport tractor for the Red Army under the designation STZ-5 2TV and would ultimately enter Red Army service under its better-known shortened factory designation: STZ-5.

ABOVE LEFT A later Komsomolets prototype, now with the box-shaped DT machine gun sponson used on the first production (M-1937) series Komsomolets, but with the rear bogie pair still acting as the track idler.

ABOVE AND LEFT The same Komsomolets prototype with the seats folded down to form a cargo area with a 500kg load capacity.

While NATI worked with STZ in Stalingrad on the Komsomolets prototypes, Plant No. 37 in Moscow had meanwhile received orders to develop an artillery tractor designed primarily to tow anti-tank and regimental artillery, which was developed under the direction of N.A. Astrov at the Plant No. 37 tank design department (later Department 22) as the 'Pioner' (Pioneer) which had a short production and service history as the unarmoured predecessor to the later armoured T-20 Komsomolets developed at the same plant.

PIONER

The first Soviet attempt to develop a small, highly manoeuvrable light artillery tractor primarily tasked with towing anti-tank guns to reach the stage of 'series' production was aptly named 'Pioner' (Pioneer). Although unarmoured, the Pioner was the starting point for the concept that resulted in the armoured T-20 'Komsomolets' artillery tractor. The Soviet requisitioning of foreign designs and

A

B

C

D

(A) The diminutive Pioner artillery tractor at the NATI design bureau. **(B) (C)** The driver sat centrally in the Pioner tractor, with only the engine compartment cover for protection; six gun crew were seated back to back behind him.

(D) Pioner artillery tractors of the Moskovskoi Proletarskoi Division parade through Red Square, 7 November 1936. Photographer: M. Kalashnikov. **(E)** Pioner artillery tractors during the same 1936 parade.

technology as deemed appropriate in the development of indigenous tank and tractor designs had included the procurement and testing of the British Vickers Carden-Loyd 'small tractor' and also the designs of the US company Marmon-Herrington. The designs were instrumental in the Soviet developmentin 1934–35 of the similar Pioner light fast tractor specifically designed for the towing anti-tank and infantry guns.

At the beginning of the 1930s the Red Army had begun to receive large numbers of 37mm M-1930 and 45mm M-1932 anti-tank guns, for which an all-terrain fast tractor was required to move the guns between fire positions within close range of enemy forces, with the tractor under fire from small arms and other weapons. The horse, the main transport means at the time and for centuries before, was highly vulnerable in such a situation. The tractor was also required to be of a design whereby it could be produced at an automotive plant in the event of wartime mobilization, with production output shared across several plants. The Pioner was accordingly developed to prototype stage in 1935 at the NATI design institute under the direction of A.S. Sheglov, based on evaluation of the American Marmon-Herrington fast tractor design (according to the NATI official history, based on the similar Vickers Carden-Loyd designs). The lead engineer on the project was E. Brusyantsev, with the design team including S.N. Osipov and N.I. Korotonoshko working on the general layout and towing arrangements.

The Pioner was powered by a front mounted GAZ-A engine from the GAZ-AA 4x2 truck, developing 40hp at the time of initial trials and later uprated

Pioner tractors with 76.2mm M-1927 regimental guns on parade in Moscow, 1 May 1937.

RIGHT The diminutive size of the Pioner artillery tractor is evident in this view. The engineering and operational concepts behind the development of the Pioner would carry over to the later armoured T-20 Komsomolets artillery tractor.

FAR RIGHT Pioner tractors in the Pervomaisky region of Moscow, September 1937. Photographer: Fishman.

to 50hp, coupled to a four-speed gearbox also taken from the GAZ-AA; this provided a remarkable (unladen) road speed of 50km/h. The Pioner weighed only 1,570kg (2,370kg in loaded combat configuration per polygon official test reports), with a towing capacity of up to 1,500kg under duress and a load (i.e. the gun crew) capacity of 500kg.

The engine, transmission and other components such as the differentials, bogie wheels, drive sprocket and tracks were taken from the T-37A amphibious tank. There was only one complete bogie set per side, with the rear road wheel also serving as an idler. The driver-mechanic sat centrally, directly above the gearbox, exposed to the elements and enemy fire protected only by the pressed steel engine compartment housing to his front. The gun crew sat behind the driver either side of the vehicle, in two rows of three seats mounted back to back, facing outward with their feet almost touching the ground, and with a canvas tilt providing basic protection from the elements. Additional gun crew could travel seated on the gun limber.

A single prototype was developed at NATI from 1935 and completed in early 1936, initially powered by a GAZ-A water cooled engine developing 40hp and designed to run on 2nd Sort low octane petrol. The Pioner was a short and narrow design, and noted during trials as unstable in rough ground, which would prove a liability during its limited operational service. The Pioner was not provided with defensive armament.

The Pioner was accepted for service with the Red Army, with the first pre-series production batch of 50 Pioner tractors assembled at Plant No. 37 (the Ordzhonikidze plant) in Moscow in 1936,* with the tractor participating in the 7th November military parade that year commemorating the 19th Anniversary of the October Revolution. Some sources state that the Pioner continued in production at a leisurely pace until 1937, which would indicate only 25 were built in 1936, but when production ceased nevertheless only 50 Pioner tractors had been built in total. The Pioner was again displayed at the 1 May 1937

* Some sources indicate the first batch was 25 tractors, but 50 was nevertheless the total number built.

The Pioner B1 and B2 were developed in collaboration between NATI and Plant No. 37, based on the unarmoured Pioner chassis. The main difference was that the gun crew faced outward on the Pioner B1 and inward on the Pioner B2.

military parade on Red Square before subsequently disappearing from public view. During these parades the Pioner was demonstrated towing the heavier 76.2mm M-1927 regimental gun rather than an anti-tank weapon.

Feedback from initial Red Army service was not entirely complimentary. With the tractor being intended for moving anti-tank guns in close proximity to enemy forces (typically as close as 500m from enemy lines) the vulnerable position of the driver-mechanic, and lack of armour protection for driver, crew, engine, radiator and fuel tank from small arms fire and shrapnel were considered unacceptable. The short and narrow tractor with a high centre of gravity was noted as less than stable when travelling cross-country, particularly when turning, in part due to limited track traction. The machine was described as very small and cramped, with limited towing capacity, and the lack of defensive armament was also noted. A test commission reviewed the issues raised in service, with the lack of armour being considered as the major concern for a tractor operating in forward combat areas. The Pioner served somewhat anonymously in the Red Army, apparently on an operational trials rather than a service acceptance basis. In the meantime, the Pioner was further developed at NATI addressing the issues raised during operational trials, with the design principles being the basis for the future Komsomolets armoured tractor.

PIONER-B1 AND PIONER-B2

The Pioner had in limited service adequately fulfilled its design role of anti-tank gun tractor, but the testing commission that reviewed its performance noted the lack of armour as being the most serious defect for a tractor intended to move anti-tank guns in forward areas. In 1936, as the unarmoured Pioner was being prepared for potential series production, two improved and now armoured

ABOVE The layout of the armoured tractor crew cab, seating and machine gun sponson on the Pioner B1 and B2 resemble the later series production T-20 Komsomolets tractor.

ABOVE RIGHT Rear view of the original Pioner.

variants of the Pioner, designated Pioner-B1 and Pioner-B2, were therefore developed at NATI under the direction of the design engineer Marinin in collaboration with Plant No. 37. The two lengthened prototypes were now provided with an armoured cab for the commander/gunner and driver-mechanic, with the only difference between the two prototypes being the crew seating arrangement. On the Pioner B1 the gun crew was seated back to back facing outward, as with the original Pioner, while on the Pioner B2 the gun crew was seated facing inward for better protection from small arms fire and shrapnel.

The prototypes were tested for Red Army service; however although they now provided armoured protection, the stability and towing capacity issues remained unresolved and the new tractor variants did not meet Red Army service requirements. Plant No. 37 had meanwhile begun assembly of the T-38 amphibious reconnaissance tank to replace the T-37A and work had already started on a new tractor utilizing modernized T-38 components. Although the original unarmoured Pioner and armoured B1 and B2 were not ultimately successful, the Pioner was further developed by NATI from the end of 1936, resulting in the series production T-20 Komsomolets armoured artillery tractor. Slightly later, a new torsion bar suspension developed by specialists from Leningrad Plant No. 185 in Leningrad was in 1938 tested on one of the later Pioner prototypes, but without further development.

T-20 KOMSOMOLETS

The Komsomolets was the first series production Soviet armoured artillery tractor. It was developed to prototype stage from late 1936, immediately after the earlier Pioner had entered limited production and received initial operational service feedback from the Red Army. Developed at the KB of Plant No. 37 in Moscow under the direction of chief designer N.A. Astrov, the prototype was quickly completed, in part because components and assemblies of the T-38

(A) 1st production series (M-1937) Komsomolets artillery tractors towing 76.2mm M-1927 regimental guns through Red Square. **(B)** This view of an early (M-1937) series Komsomolets, now with separate rear idler, clearly shows the tarpaulin which was the only protection from the elements for the gun crew. **(C)** 1st production series (M-1937) Komsomolets artillery tractors towing 45mm M-1932 anti-tank guns through Red Square, Moscow, 7 November 1940.

(D) The 1st production series Komsomolets featured a single radiator louvre, as shown on this tractor captured by Finland during the 1939–40 Winter War and pressed into service as vehicle Ps755.8. **(E)** A 1st production series (M-1937) model Komsomolets in Finnish service. Finland slightly modified the tractors, with the flame-cut clipped track guards being one of the first changes made on this particular tractor.

(A) Komsomolets 2nd production series artillery tractors towing 45mm M-1932 (19-K) anti-tank guns during a parade believed to be in Kishinyev. Note the small rounded machine gun mantlet without a pistol port. **(B)** Komsomolets 2nd production series artillery tractors with 45mm M-1932 (19-K) anti-tank guns on parade in Minsk, 1939. **(C)** Komsomolets 2nd production series artillery tractors on parade in Kuibyshev, 7 November 1941. Had Moscow fallen in 1941, Kuibyshev was the designated Soviet second city and military command centre. **(D)** A Komsomolets 2nd production series artillery tractor and multiple limber road train captured by Finnish forces during the early stages of the Continuation War. (SA-Kuva) **(E)** A 2nd production series Komsomolets artillery tractor destroyed in Finland. Note that the folding bench seats are fitted with seatbelts. (SA-Kuva) **(F)** Another 2nd production series Komsomolets tractor captured in Finland. The radiator cooling arrangements were modified on the 2nd production series Komsomolets, and were in later production series again slightly modified. **(G)** A 2nd production series Komsomolets, Kalinin Front, winter 1941–42. Photographer: A. Kapustyansky.

LEFT A 3rd production series Komsomolets artillery tractor with tilt erected. The additional pistol port on the DT gun sponson is just visible.

BELOW The modified DT gun sponson with pistol port most readily distinguished the 3rd production series Komsomolets.

amphibious reconnaissance tank which had just entered series production were widely incorporated into the design. The new semi-armoured tractor (the vehicle crew and engine compartment being armoured but the gun crew unprotected) used the mechanical components of the T-38 tank, including the running gear with its more compact suspension, transmission, final drives and brake bands, but with the engine and gearbox taken as before from the GAZ-AA (MM). The tractor was known during initial development by the plant index '020' and latterly as the T-20 (Tyagach-20) (Tractor-20) Komsomolets.

As with the earlier Pioner tractor, the Komsomolets was designed as a transport tractor for towing the 37mm M-1930 and 45mm M-1932 anti-tank guns and also regimental guns, with a nominal towing capacity of 1,500kg. The primary difference from the earlier Pioner was the provision of a riveted and welded armoured cab for the driver-mechanic and vehicle commander/machine gunner, each provided with a separate roof hatch. The lot of the gun crew

(A) This fully restored 3rd production series Komsomolets is at the Museum of Russian Military History, Padikovo, near Moscow. **(B)** A Komsomolets tractor with anti-tank gun and twin limbers in tow in late 1941. **(C)** A 3rd production series Komsomolets tractor restored by the Shamansky Workshops at the Motors of War Museum, Moscow. **(D)** A column of Komsomolets tractors including 1st and 3rd production series models destroyed on the Ratte Road, Suomussalmi, during the 1939–40 Soviet–Finnish Winter War. **(E)** A column of Komsomolets tractors destroyed at Rautalahti during the Continuation War against Finland, 21 August 1941. (SA-Kuva) **(F)** The first Komsomolets to be recovered and restored in the post-Soviet Russian Federation was a later 4th production series model, seen here displayed at Paklonnaya Gora in Moscow on 9 May 1993. The 4th production series was almost identical to the 3rd production series but with new stamped hatches and greater use of welding. **(G) (H)** A 3rd production series Komsomolets with seats folded into 'cargo' configuration abandoned in a Finnish forest. (SA-Kuva)

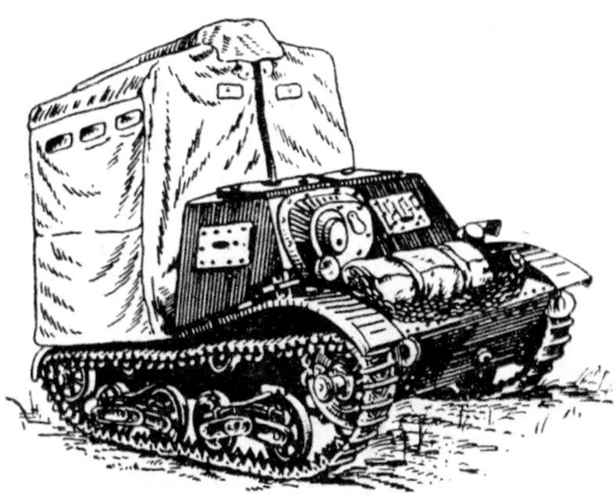

A Soviet technical manual drawing of the Komsomolets tractor.

remained unaltered, with two rows of back-to-back bench seats open to the elements, shrapnel and enemy fire. The rear seats could be inverted to form a load area, allowing the Komsomolets to transport 500kg of ammunition or cargo in forward areas.

The early prototype as evaluated for service was as with the Pioner fitted with a four-cylinder GAZ-AA engine developing 40hp which could run on 2nd Sort petrol, coupled to a four-speed gearbox taken from the GAZ-AA (MM). The testing commission noted that the Komsomolets could also be fitted with the GAZ-M engine developing 50hp at 2,800rpm, as would occur in series production. The early prototype and pre-production series Komsomolets featured running gear with the rear wheel of the second bogie wheel pair also acting as the return roller, but during prototype trials the suspension bogies would often 'flip' and shed the tracks. The problem was resolved by adding a conventional rear idler, which was mounted on series production models. During development, a 'silent' reinforced rubber track with metal shoes similar to that developed for Soviet half-tracks was also evaluated for use with the Komsomolets, but not accepted for production.

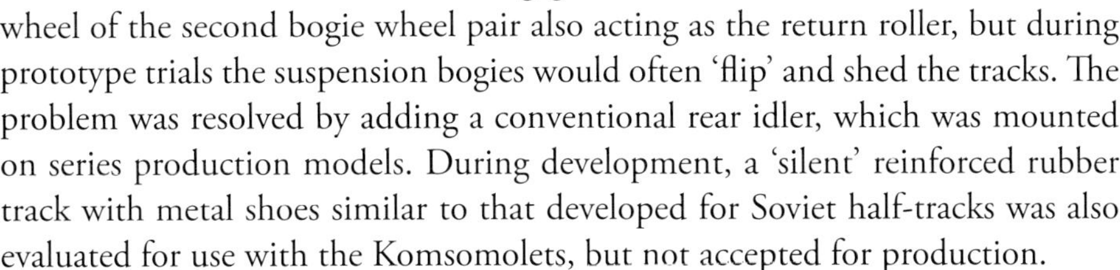

The Komsomolets was the first series production armoured vehicle to be produced in the Soviet Union and accepted for service with the Red Army for the movement of anti-tank guns between firing positions, replacing the gun crew and the horse in such a role. The tow hook on the Komsomolets was fitted with spring amortization and designed specifically for towing wheeled artillery. The four-cylinder GAZ-M engine, developing 50hp installed on series production Komsomolets tractors nevertheless proved underpowered for the vehicle weight and required towing capacity. The Komsomolets could travel at 40km/h towing 1,500kg on made roads, with a road range of 200km. The transfer box and gearing also allowed for towing loads of up to 3,000kg under duress to move at a minimum speed of 2–2.5km/h over short distances. The underpowered engine was a known design deficiency, and in service this, combined with the engine location and armoured housing, would lead to frequent overheating. The air intakes, originally on the vehicle sides near the track, provided insufficient airflow for cooling, hence the intake was moved to provide cleaner air and the exhaust grilles on the rear armoured plate redesigned more than once, leading to three (effectively four) distinctive production model recognition features.

The Komsomolets tractor had some remarkable design features. The tractor was fitted with partial dual controls, such that in the event that the driver-mechanic was incapacitated, the commander-gunner could operate the vehicle, though

ABOVE A 3rd production series Komsomolets tractor that with modifications served in the Finnish Army as Ps756-82, located at the Parola Armour Museum in 1985. (Esa Muikku)

RIGHT An overhead view of the driver-mechanic's compartment of a Komsomolets artillery tractor in Finnish service. (SA-Kuva)

not change gears, from his own position in order to escape immediate danger. The Komsomolets had an armour basis of 7–10mm. Armament consisted of a 7.62mm DT sponson mounted on the right side of the glacis, which was also modified several times during production.

The Komsomolets prototype was tested for Red Army service from August to November 1937, with the prototype meeting the specifications of the original design parameters (TTTs). The T-20 showed good overall performance, including an average tested road convoy speed of 15–20km/h with towed load, reducing to 8–11km/h cross-country; during trials it also knocked over small trees of up to 18cm in diameter. The turning radius was only 2.4m, as might be expected from a tracked vehicle with brake and skid turning. But the GAZ-M derived engine, the MM-6002, which was not designed for long term operation on a tracked tractor, was, as noted, overloaded. During the trials, the engine often overheated inside its centrally mounted armoured compartment, and was considered not ideal for a front line armoured vehicle; premature failure of connecting rod bearings, the head gasket and miscellaneous seal leaks was also noted. There was however no available alternative engine installation and the design compromise was accepted. Subject to the elimination of certain defects, the tractor was found suitable for towing the designated artillery systems and the Komsomolets was accepted for service with the Red Army. The viewing devices were taken from the BT-7, with most production models fitted with Triplex glass in the vision devices. Series production began in 1937 at Plant No. 37 in Moscow.

LEFT Finnish soldiers inspecting a destroyed 3rd production series Komsomolets, Kirjavalahti, 27 July 1941. (SA-Kuva)

BELOW Rear view of a 3rd production series Komsomolets, also lost in combat in Finland. Note the tow hook arrangement. (SA-Kuva)

(A) Recently captured and unmodified Komsomolets 3rd production series and T-37A amphibious light tanks in Finnish Army Service. (SA-Kuva) **(B)** A 3rd production series Komsomolets artillery tractor, Roavaniemi, Finland, 31 January 1940. (SA-Kuva) **(C)** A Red Army Komsomolets abandoned in a forest, Simpele, Finland, 3 August 1941. (SA-Kuva) **(D)** A Red Army 3rd production series Komsomolets artillery tractor with tilt in place, destroyed in fighting of 1941–42. **(E)** A Komsomolets tractor captured by Finland during the 1939–40 Winter War. **(F)** A 3rd production series Komsomolets tractor at a display of Soviet equipment in Budapest, Hungary, 1942. **(G)** A Komsomolets tractor, time and location unknown. **(H)** A Komsomolets Series 3 tractor restored by the Shamansky Workshops on display during an open day at the Motors of War Museum, Moscow.

The Komsomolets was series produced at Plant No. 37 from late 1937 until July 1941, with production being stopped after the outbreak of war in order for the plant to concentrate on light tank production. The Komsomolets was originally intended to be produced at STZ in Stalingrad, which did not materialize, and was also assembled at the special production (i.e. non-series production) workshop at GAZ, under the direction of M.I. Kazakov) from 1937 to 1938, albeit in very small numbers (only 40 were built), with some components provided by STZ.

The Komsomolets was produced in three (essentially four) production series, differing in the machine gun sponson mounting, load platform and folding seat arrangement, engine cooling system, suspension and running gear, vision devices, and many other details. A total of 7,780 Komsomolets tractors were built before production was terminated in 1941.

The first production variant, sometimes known as the Komsomolets M-1937, had riveted and welded armour, a box-shaped DT machine gun sponson mounting, almost rectangular hatches, bench seating for the gun crew and a large louvred air intake at the hull rear. The engine also had a hand crank mounted at the rear of the vehicle. The second production variant, sometimes known as the Komsomolets M-1938, also had riveted and welded armour, but with a round stamped sponson for the DT machine gun, without a pistol port; it had the same near rectangular hatches and bench gun crew seats as the earlier model, but a modified hull rear plate with several smaller engine air intakes rather than a single large intake. The third production variant had an oval-shaped sponson with pistol port to the left side of the DT machine gun, riveted and welded armour construction, and the previous rectangular stamped crew hatches, but 'sectioned' benches for the gun crew (i.e. with three separate seats on each side). The hull rear plate was again modified. The fourth and final production variant, sometimes known as the Komsomolets M-1940, had increased use of welding in its hull construction, a large oval DT machine gun sponson with pistol port as introduced on the third production variant, stamped crew hatches with distinctly rounded corners and individual seating for the gun crew, but with the same hull rear layout as the third variant. The engine hand crank was relocated to the front of the vehicle.

The driver-mechanic and commander/gun crew commander were located in the armoured front compartment together with the GAZ-AA/MM derived four-speed gearbox, supplemented with a transfer box from the 6x4 GAZ-AAA, providing traction and transport gear ranges, as well as a single-disc main dry friction clutch, two multi-disc dry friction clutches and two final drives and band brakes. The driver-mechanic was seated on the left and the commander on the right. The T-20 was armed with a 7.62mm M-1929 (DT) machine gun ball

ALL RIGHT This 4th Series production model Komsomolets, at Paklonnaya Gora in Moscow, was restored with a combination of available parts.

mounted in on the right in front of the commander, with 1,008 rounds of ammunition in 16 disc magazines placed in stowage racks.*

The riveted (and later increasingly welded) armoured body was assembled from rolled armour sheets with a thickness of 10mm (glacis) and 7mm (sides). Two hatches were located on the control/fighting compartment roof for the vehicle crew. For observation from the cab, three folding flaps with viewing devices were installed, one in front of the driver and two on the cab sides. Later machines were provided with Triplex glass devices in lieu of the earlier viewing slits.

The engine was mounted under armour centrally behind the armoured control compartment with the gun crew seated above in the open. The tractor was powered by a GAZ MM-6002 liquid cooled petrol engine (a modified GAZ-M engine as used in the GAZ M-1 light vehicle) with a Zenit carburetor and developing 50hp, with twin fuel tanks. The nominally petrol engine was able to run on low grade 2nd Sort petrol, or if required on a 50/50 mix of petrol and ligroin (tractor kerosene). The engine could be started from an electric starter or manually with a handle. The suspension and running gear consisted of four small (400mm diameter) spoked and rubber rimmed road wheels mounted

* Some sources state 12 drums and 756 rounds located on two racks, one with six discs behind the driver's seat, another with three discs to the right of the commander/gunner.

LEFT Komsomolets 1st and 4th Series production model artillery tractors towing 45mm M-1932 (19-K) anti-tank guns in the Soviet city of Kuibyshev (today Samara).

ABOVE Komsomolets 4th Series production model tractors abandoned in Finland. Note the rounded hatch edges and welded lower vehicle crew compartment sides.

on two leaf spring balancer assemblies, with front drive sprocket, rear idler and two rubber rimmed return rollers. The Komsomolets had a road range of 200km reducing to 150km on dirt roads – significant by tractor standards.

In total, according to different estimates, from 7,338 to 7,780 T-20 Komsomolets tractors were manufactured, with 7,780 produced to June 1941 being the generally accepted total. According to pre-war statutes, each infantry division should have had at least 60 T-20 Komsomolets tractors in service. This was never achieved in practice, and Komsomolets tractors were used primarily by motorized infantry units within rifle divisions, provided with (in theory) 21 Komsomolets tractors each.

The T-20 Komsomolets proved to be simple, reliable and versatile in Red Army service. The use of standard motor vehicle and T-38 tank components in the design had allowed for both rapid development and ease of repair and maintenance in service. The T-20 was particularly versatile, and could if required transport not only 45mm anti-tank and field guns, but also heavier divisional guns. The small dimensions, armour (for the vehicle crew) and mobility maximized battlefield survivability, while the machine gun armament provided limited defensive or infantry fire support. The Komsomolets also had a built-in

The first Komsomolets to be recovered and restored in the Russian Federation, later located at Paklonnaya Gora, Moscow.

engine compartment fire suppression system, and rear-view mirrors fitted within the side vision hatches. The tow hook with spring amortization was designed specifically for military use.

The combat debut of the Komsomolets tractor is sometimes noted as being in 1938 during the Soviet counter-offensive against the Japanese at Lake Khasan; however, the Komsomolets is not specifically listed as being in the inventory of the 39th Rifle Corps and the 2nd Mechanized Brigade of the Far Eastern Military District, which at the time was equipped with S-60 and Komintern tractors. The following year, the Komsomolets was however definitely used in combat against the Japanese at the battles of the Khalkhin Gol River fought from May to September

BELOW A typical scene on the Eastern Front in the years 1941–42, a destroyed Series 4 Komsomolets tractor at the roadside.

BELOW RIGHT This 4th series production model tractor destroyed in action in 1941 is readily identifiable by the turret hatches and the use of welded rather than riveted armour at the lower cab and track guard join.

A 4th Series production model Komsomolets tractor in what would appear to be Soviet partisan service.

1939, with eight or nine T-20s lost in combat. The Komsomolets did not participate in the invasion of Poland in September the same year, but was widely deployed during the short 1939–40 Soviet–Finnish Winter War. The Soviet 9th Army faced severe challenges in the vast region of light forest, lakes and marshland of Karelia and in the more concentrated Karelian Isthmus. The combination of cold, deep snow, light birch and pine forests and the need to navigate through otherwise impassable areas on narrow forest roads – with which the Finnish were intimately familiar – led to frequent ambushes where tracked and wheeled vehicles alike were trapped in pre-determined fire-pockets. In the first weeks of the war Red Army losses were particularly high. In Karelia the Red Army lost a large number of artillery tractors including 21 Komsomolets tractors damaged in combat, of which seven were abandoned on Finnish territory. In the Karelian Isthmus north of Leningrad losses were similar, with five of the 24 Komsomolets tractors in service with the 15th Rifle–Machine-Gun Brigade on 1 December 1939 being lost in combat during the later weeks of the short war. Losses in the 1st and 13th Tank Brigades were approximately 20 per cent of tractors deployed.

The primary role of the Komsomolets was as an anti-tank gun tractor for use in forward areas, but there were few Finnish tanks in service against which to deploy Soviet anti-tank guns. Instead, hardened concrete (DOT) and soil (DZOT) defence points were the main focus of Soviet artillery, which required the use of heavy calibre weapons firing high-explosive fragmentation or specialist ammunition. This led to a change in the operational deployment of Komsomolets

TOP A 4th Series production model Komsomolets tractor moving at speed, Kalinin Front, 1942.

ABOVE Two captured 4th Series production model Komsomolets tractors in service with their new Wehrmacht owners.

artillery tractors in Finland, with the tractors being allocated to towing 76.2mm M-1927 regimental guns, with 45mm anti-tank gun movements being reverted to the horse. In the far north on the Murmansk Front, the situation was more stable: three tank battalions employed a total of 35 T-20 Komsomolets tractors, with 19 T-27 tankettes also used as artillery tractors, and the Komsomolets occasionally deployed as a reconnaissance tankette, all with minimal losses. The Komsomolets was occasionally also used as a recovery vehicle, something it was never designed for, and in winter conditions its capabilities were limited even for recovering T-26 light tanks, a role for which the relatively rare Komintern tractor was better suited. Combat experience in Finland led however to development work at Plant No. 37 and GAZ on unarmoured transport tractors with a secondary recovery role. The T-37A amphibious reconnaissance tank and the T-27 tankette were both also used as artillery tractors during the Soviet–Finnish Winter War as they could not, as noted, be usefully employed where earth and log or concrete fixed defence structures were often the main targets to be overcome.

The Finnish army captured a total of 62 Komsomolets tractors during the 1939–40 Winter War and adopted them into service, of which six were recaptured by the Red Army during the same war. Between the Winter and Continuation wars Finland captured some 200 Komsomolets tractors that were adopted into Finnish service, the last batch of ten tractors leaving Finnish service as driver training vehicles as late as 1961.

Experience of the 1939–40 Winter War in Finland led to changes in divisional and corps level artillery park structures, with an urgent requirement issued for a further 7,000 artillery and transport tractors. Plant No. 37 did not have excess workshop and tooling capacity to rapidly ramp up production, but expected to reach full series production by 1 January 1943, which subsequent events would preclude. Per Soviet Statutes, 21 Komsomolets tractors were intended for each rifle division, which was only partly achieved despite production increases. The equipment fulfilment for new mechanized corps was however in 1940 well behind schedule for all artillery tractor types. The 1st Mechanized Corps should have had 41 T-20 Komsomolets in service by 15 April 1940, but in fact had none at all available. As war neared, there were in January 1941 some 4,401 Komsomolets tractors in service with the Red Army, with production rapidly increasing. By mid-June 1941, the Red Army had 6,672 Komsomolets tractors in its inventory, of which 6,668 were with operational units. A small number were in service with the NKVD and VMF (naval) forces. Official Red Army records show 1,770 such tractors still in service on 1 January 1942, a catastrophic loss of 4,920 tractors in six months.

In the first days of Operation *Barbarossa* against the Soviet Union, the 3rd, 6th, 8th, 13th, 14th and 17th Mechanized Corps, which took the brunt of the Axis onslaught, were destroyed with nearly all their equipment, with another ten corps suffering high losses. The 41st Mechanized Corps meanwhile had almost its full complement of Komsomolets tractors in service. The situation varied greatly according to local circumstances, with much artillery in the summer of 1941 being towed by ZiS-5/6 and less powerful GAZ-AA/AAA trucks rather than artillery tractors. In July–August 1941 the combined Soviet Western Front had lost 46 artillery regiments with their artillery and tractors destroyed or abandoned in now occupied territory. In rear areas the situation was better, but still with an overall lack of artillery tractors. In late August 1941, the situation of the 16th Army remained typical: its tractor-park was at half-strength. The evacuation and repair of damaged vehicles was also problematical. In September 1941 armour repair bases Nos. 1, 2 and 8 combined had only 37 Komsomolets under repair. The Komsomolets saw extensive action in the defensive fighting in the summer and autumn of 1941 and subsequently served on all Fronts of the Great Patriotic War. The Komsomolets had been designed for towing anti-tank guns, latterly the 45mm M-1937 and M-1942 types, but in the absence of other tractors it was also used to tow heavier artillery systems, often small calibre anti-aircraft guns and divisional artillery. During the period of heavy defensive battles in the summer and autumn of 1941, the T-20, being armoured and with machine gun armament, was also used as a tankette against enemy infantry formations in the manner of the British Universal (Bren Gun) Carrier. In the mid-war years, the small tracked Komsomolets also proved to be an ideal vehicle for Soviet partisans, who used the vehicles on the forest roads of occupied territory. The use of standard truck mechanicals ensured the tractors could be easily maintained, with spare parts removed from damaged trucks.

Komsomolets tractor combat losses were high in comparison with other artillery tractors due to the nature of their front line anti-tank unit deployment, and losses grew incrementally. Red Army records show that on 1 January 1942, a total of 1,770 Komsomolets tractors remained in service, but that number reduced only slightly to 1,662 by 1 September 1942, with 1,048 remaining by

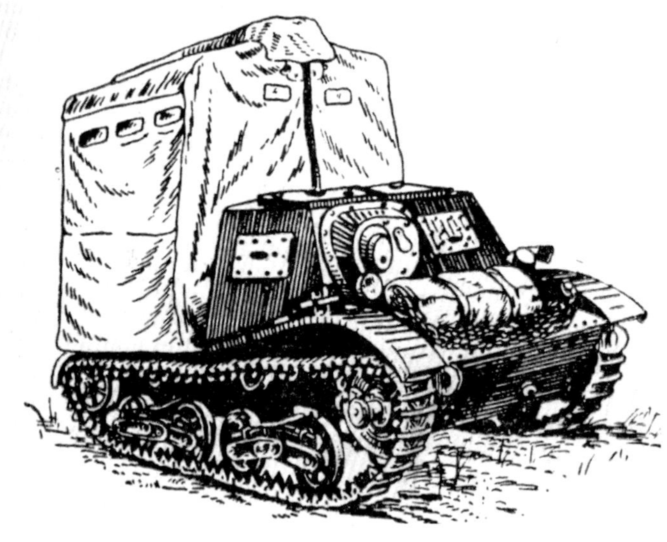

A drawing of the Komsomolets tractor from a Soviet technical manual.

1 January 1943, reflecting the change from desperate defensive to offensive operations. The Komsomolets continued in operational service until the very end of the war, with standard automotive components and plentiful standard spare parts keeping the tractors in service more easily than some other types. Due to a general lack of artillery tractors, the Komsomolets was used to tow 37mm M-1939 anti-aircraft guns and, as noted, divisional artillery, and with the gun crew seats inverted, the Komsomolets was also used as an ammunition supply vehicle and for transporting general cargo.

At the end of the war in Europe, fewer than 100 Komsomolets tractors remained in service on the Soviet Western Front. However, large numbers (apparently far more than left in the European theatre) of Komsomolets tractors continued in service in the Far Eastern and Baikal Military Districts, where they survived the war intact before being put into strategic storage, with a small number converted to civil use such as firefighting vehicles. On 25 December 1945, the 'tyl' reserve forces had only 18 Komsomolets tractors in service, located with the 8th and 23rd Reserve Regiments.

T-20 KOMSOMOLETS TELE-TANK

From the early 1930s, the USSR began to actively develop remote control tanks, at that time called 'teleupravlyaemye mashini' – remote-controlled machines. A number of series production armoured vehicles equipped with what were called telemechanical control systems were developed and tested in development trials, with a view to equipping telemechanical groups equipped with remotely controlled T-38, T-26 and BT-7 tanks; and from late 1939 work also progressed based on the T-20 Komsomolets artillery tractor. A telemechanical group consisting of two T-20 tractors was extensively tested in early 1940. A tele-tank system consisted of a TU (Tank Upravlenya – control tank) tractor acting as a command control machine, with a second TT (tele-tank) tractor equipped with a radio control receiver system. The TT vehicle weighed the same as a standard T-20 tractor at 3,640kg, the TU command vehicle with its larger 12v generator nominally more at 3,660kg.

A T-20 TT (tele-tank) set during trials. A (left) is the TU command tank, B (right) is the TT tele-tank slave unit.

The 'Groza' remote control complex mounted within the vehicles was developed at the NII-20 Research Institute NKAP, with the radio signal operated controls being electro-pneumatic. The radio-controlled tractor was armed with a 7.62mm DT machine gun with one 63 round magazine, a KS-61T flamethrower placed in the frontal plate (cylinder capacity – 45 litres) and an explosive charge for use as a 'land torpedo' against enemy DOTs. The system used 13.5 litre accumulator air tanks for air pressure, similar in operation to the pneumatic back-up starting system used on some tanks for cold weather starting.

The tele-tractor could accept and perform up to 12 commands (versus 15 on the T-26) for engine start, adjust engine revs, right and left turn, gear change, brake and engine shut down. The weapons were also remotely controlled, receiving commands for preparation to fire, fire from the machine gun or KS-61T flamethrower, smoke or chemical laying and weapon operation, preparation for charge detonation, charge detonation and system shut down. The flamethrower could fire 15–16 bursts to a range of 28–40m, lay a smoke screen (via rear mounted dispenser tubes) to a distance of up to 175m in favourable weather conditions, or dispense contaminating chemicals to the ground at 25–30g/cm^2). A modified KS-25 flamethrower installation was also conceived. The remote-controlled TT tele-tank had a maximum operating range of 2,500m.

Telemechanical battalions equipped with such vehicles were intended to conduct front line reconnaissance, attack enemy anti-tank defences, and destroy DOT fortifications by placing charges. The system was operationally tested using a TT-26 tele-tank mounted on the T-26 chassis during the 1939–40 Soviet–Finnish Winter War, but the results were not encouraging, as in close fighting in lightly wooded terrain the TU command vehicle operator had difficulty maintaining line of sight with the TT slave vehicle, and combat losses were very high relative to results. Trials nevertheless continued with the T-20 Komsomolets, albeit the tractor with its machine gun armament was more suited to reconnaissance, and this proved difficult as at a distance the TU operator could, once again, not observe the overall operational situation in which the slave vehicle was engaged. Further to the final trials using the Komsomolets based TU-20/TT-20 conducted in August–September 1940, no further wartime development was undertaken, with the subject being revived post-war.

TRACKED LOUDSPEAKER BROADCAST VEHICLE

An unusual variant of the T-20 Komsomolets mounted the MGU-1500 loudspeaker broadcast system,* which broadcast messages or 'disinformation' recordings from celluloid tape. The latter included pre-recorded tank engine, aircraft and military engineering sounds. Following on from the operational use of earlier ZiS-5 and ZiS-6 mounted variants used against the Japanese at Khalkin Gol and the Finns in the Karelian Isthmus, the decision was made to develop an improved model, the MGU-1500, which was built at the Leningrad Radio Broadcast Institute and mounted on both the Komsomolets tractor and the T-26 light tank. The system had a 70-watt output and a broadcast range of 1–2km. In January 1940, two tracked systems were dispatched to each of the 7th, 8th and 13th Armies, and a single vehicle to the 9th Army for operational trials, primarily in the Karelian Isthmus. How many of these vehicles were specifically mounted on the T-20 or the T-26 chassis is not known. The system was operationally deployed, with the ultimate decision that the Komsomolets tractor was not the optimal chassis for mounting such a system.

SHITIKOV ARMOURED TRACTOR

The limited production Pioner and the series production Komsomolets are well known, but the Komsomolets was the final result of a series of development prototypes, some of which remained design projects, with others being produced in metal.

One such alternative to mainstream design was a prototype developed by the design engineer I.P. Shitikov at Plant No. 37 in Moscow in 1936. Shitikov developed several design initiatives while working at the plant, including a redesign of the T-37A amphibious light tank designated T-37B and the '010'

* MGU-1500 Zvukoveshatelny Stantsiya – Loudspeaker Broadcast Station.

The Shitikov tractor was developed by P. Shitikov at Plant No. 37 in Moscow in 1936 as a low profile armoured artillery tractor alternative to the T-20 Komsomolets. Though extensively tested, it was not ultimately accepted for service.

prototype for the T-40 amphibious reconnaissance tank. Shitikov also developed to prototype stage as an initiative project a small, low profile armoured light artillery tractor for towing anti-tank guns in forward areas. The tractor featured a highly faceted armoured cab for the vehicle crew, a DT machine gun for local defence, and rear gun crew seats similar to the Komsomolets, all incorporated into a sleek design. The prototype design, known as the Shitikov artillery tractor, was completed in October 1936 and extensively tested, but not ultimately adopted for service with the Red Army.

The official test report on the Shitikov tractor noted the 2,600kg tractor as being powered by the GAZ-AA engine developing 40hp, linked to a four-speed gearbox, with a maximum road speed of 40km/h, a road range of 220km, 4–9mm armour, a crew of two and 7.62mm DT machine gun armament. The tractor was 2.35m in length, 2.33m wide and particularly low profile at 1.47m in height.

ABOVE The T-26T during evaluation trials. The T-26T, designed to tow regimental and divisional artillery in forward areas, featured a fully enclosed armoured casemate for the five-man gun crew.

T-26T

The T-26T (T-Tyagach tractor) armoured artillery tractor was developed at the KB of the Voroshilov plant (Plant No. 174) in Leningrad, with the prototype submitted for Red Army evaluation at the end of 1933 based on the T-26 M-1931 tank chassis. The T-26T was accepted for service in January 1934, and was assembled in a small series at the same plant from 1934 to 1936, with a total of 183 T-26T tractors built. The tractor, with an armoured casemate structure in lieu of the standard T-26 M-1931/M-1933 turret(s) was designed to tow artillery pieces such as divisional guns. In practice it was used to tow artillery such as the 76mm M-1936 (F-22) and M-1939 USV divisional guns and the 122mm M-1909/30 howitzer at convoy speeds of 7–11km/h, with a maximum speed of 15–20km/h. It could also be used as an armoured recovery vehicle (ARV) for light tank recovery. The T-26T crew consisted of a driver-mechanic and five gun crew located within the armoured casemate hull.

T-26T tractors were used during the Red Army invasion of Poland in September 1939, with a T-26T paraded alongside T-26 tanks in Brest on

(A) T-26 tractors towing 76.2mm M-1936 (F-22 USV/GRAU Index 52-P-363A) divisional guns through Red Square, Moscow, 1 May 1937. **(B)** A close up of the same T-26T artillery tractor. **(C)** T-26T tractors towing 76.2mm M-1936 (F-22 USV) divisional guns through Red Square towards St Basil's Cathedral during the same 1 May 1937 parade. Photographer: Kinelovsky. **(D)** A T-26T destroyed during the Continuation War against Finland, Rautalahti, 23 August 1941. (SA-Kuva) **(E)** This appears to be the same T-26 tractor, also recorded at Rautalahti, 23 August 1941. (SA-Kuva) **(F)** A T-26T captured by the Wehrmacht operating in an Axis ammunition storage yard.

This view of a destroyed T-26T being inspected by Axis forces clearly shows the twin roof hatch layout used by all crew except the driver-mechanic.

22 September 1941. In June 1941, the Red Army listed 211 T-26T tractors (the number included the T-26T and T-26T2) in operational service. Most of these tractors were lost in action within weeks of the outbreak of war, with a small number captured and used by Axis forces. A small number of T-26T tractors located in the Soviet Far East were used operationally against the Japanese in Manchuria, and survived the war.

T-26T2

The T-26T2 was developed at the KB of Plant No. 174 (the Voroshilov plant) in 1933 concurrently with the T26T, on the basis of a project initiated at the Bolshevik plant. Similar in design and concept to the T-26T, the T-26T2 differed primarily in having a canvas upper superstructure rather than an armoured compartment for the gun crew. The T-26T2 prototype was tested at the NIBT (NIABP) polygon between September 1933 and February 1934. The T-26T2 was accepted for service with the Red Army and a small number, 173,* were produced at the Voroshilov plant between 1934 and 1936, with another 28 early

* Some original Russian sources state that 48 T-26T2 semi-armoured tractors were delivered in September 1933 and a further 44 in October. The Red Army received 163 tractors based on T-26 chassis to the end of 1933. Data for the T-26T transport tractor are conflated, but the numbers built were nevertheless small. Some Russian primary sources state that the T-26T and T-26T2 were produced only in 1933.

The T-26T2 during evaluation trials. The T-26T2 served the same role as the T-26T and had an almost identical layout, but with a canvas superstructure rather than being fully armoured.

LEFT An abandoned T-26T2.

This captured T-26T2 in Wehrmacht service would seem to have been modified with a sheet steel (or perhaps wood) covering structure in place of the standard Soviet canvas screens.

production T-26s being converted to T-26T2 tractors in 1937–39. The T-26T2 had a single driver-mechanic for vehicle crew, with an artillery crew of four. The T-26T2, which was unarmed, could travel at 28km/h independently, and was used to tow the same artillery pieces as the T-26T.

AT-42

With development of the A-34 prototype medium tank being close to completion at Plant No. 183 in Kharkov, on 30 October 1939 the plant director Ya.E. Maksarov, together with plant chief designer M.I. Koshkin and plant chief engineer S.N. Makhonin, sent to the chief of Glavspetsmash (G.S. Surenyan), the Deputy Commissar of NKSM (A.A. Goreglyad) and the chief of ABTU (D.G. Pavlov) Letter No. S06415, which confirmed that Plant No. 183 was ready to put the A-34 tank into mass production in 1940 as the T-34 medium tank. The letter included commentary that the plant was also prepared for series production of an artillery tractor on the A-34 chassis, which later received the index A-42. The plant was at the time lacking the capacity to rapidly expand production, however, as it produced a large number of steam locomotives (the primary output of KhPZ, as the plant was named before 1936) and artillery tractors. In 1939, the plant had assembled 288 'SO' steam locomotives, 117 locomotive coal tenders, 467 'Komintern' medium artillery tractors, and 67 'Voroshilovets' heavy artillery tractors while preparing for series production of the T-34. The armoured AT-42 was nevertheless developed at the KB of Plant

LEFT An artist's impression of the AT-42 artillery tractor.

BELOW Technical Project drawings of the 'Machine 42' (AT-42).

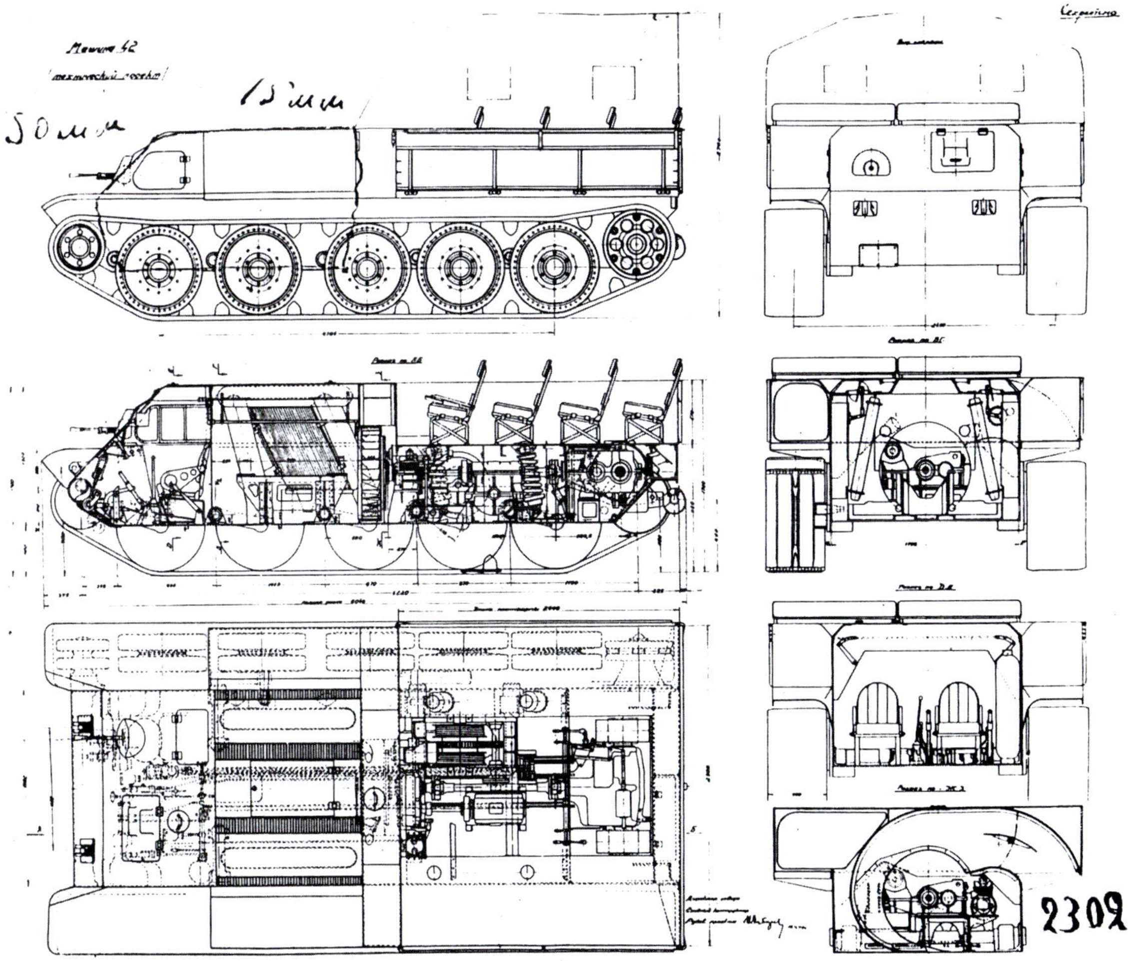

An AT-42 side view.

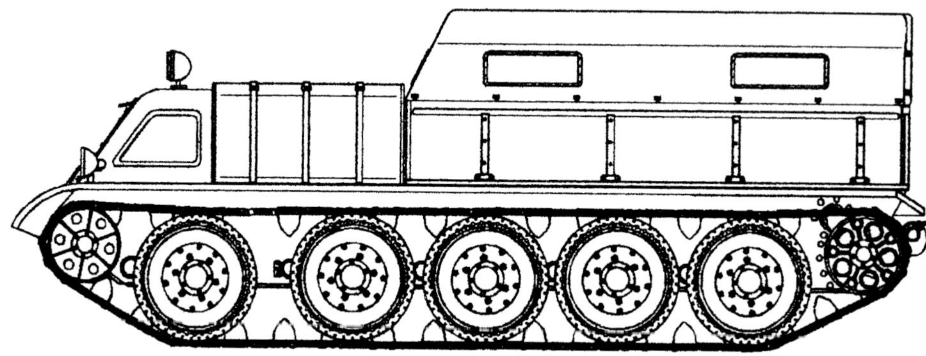

No. 183 on the chassis of the T-34 medium tank from April 1940 under the designation Obiekt-42. The armoured tractor had an armour basis of 15–50mm, a combat weight of 17 tonnes, a tow capacity of 15,000kg and a load capacity of 3,000kg. The AT-42 was to be fitted with the standard V-2 diesel engine developing 500hp as installed in the T-34, providing a 34km/h maximum road speed. The tractor had a planned crew of two and a 7.62mm DT machine gun for defensive armament.

Prototype plant trials conducted in December 1940 were generally successful, but with noted defects relating to the gearbox, track and winch system. The prototype was reworked and resubmitted for further trials, but with no further work undertaken beyond production and testing of the two prototypes. This seemingly leisurely approach to AT-42 development was primarily due to the main priority at the plant being output of the new T-34 medium tank.

ARMOURED VOROSHILOVETS TRACTORS

The idea of modifying the Plant No. 183 produced 'Voroshilovets' tractor with an armoured cab had been considered at ChKZ in late 1941, with the intention of producing an SAU in Chelyabinsk armed with an 85mm M-1939 anti-aircraft gun. Meanwhile, in Leningrad during the siege, an armoured cab and engine compartment were developed for the Voroshilovets tractor. Developed as an evacuation tractor from 1941 for use by the 52nd Army, with at least one such vehicle built in early 1942, the armour set, providing protection against small arms fire and shrapnel, added 1,750kg to the vehicle weight. The purpose was to allow the Voroshilovets to be used as an ARV to evacuate tanks from the battlefield under fire. In the summer of 1942, an armoured Voroshilets was used by the 43rd Army and a successful T-34 recovery under fire was documented near the River Ugra. The limited documentation available to date on this conversion includes the cab conversion blueprints and a single photograph of such a tractor next to a conventional Voroshilovets tractor on the streets of Leningrad. The standard Voroshilovets was vulnerable while recovering tanks in forward areas, which had been a major factor in the development of the subsequently abandoned AT-42 armoured tractor based on the T-34 chassis.

ChKZ ARMOURED HEAVY TRACTOR

By 1942, ChKZ in Chelyabinsk was focused on heavy KV-1 heavy tank production, having assimilated the tooling evacuated from LKZ in Leningrad and stopped S-65 and S-2 production to accommodate heavy (and later medium) tank production. The plant KB continued however to investigate potential new tractor designs, having in the spring of 1942 developed to prototype stage the S-10 tracked tractor on a modified S-2 chassis. Slightly later, on 5 June 1942, the TTTs were prepared for a new semi-armoured artillery transport tractor (tyagach) for towing corps artillery, capable of towing a minimum 13,000kg load, with a maximum road speed of 35km/h, as well as a rear load area with seating for 12 gun crew. The project did not progress beyond the initial design stage.

ATP-1

The ATP-1 armoured light artillery tractor was developed by the KB at Plant No. 40 at Mytischi in the northern suburbs of Moscow in late 1944 as a potential replacement for the pre-war Komsomolets and for towing larger calibre and heavier anti-tank guns such as the 100mm BS-3. The ATP-1 was a complete redesign of the earlier tractor, with modified mechanicals and running gear, and increased and highly faceted frontal armour providing better frontal protection for the seated gun crew. The vehicle crew remained as before, with side access doors for safer egress, and a sponson mounted DT machine gun for defence as on the Komsomolets. Production of a prototype was approved, but this was not built due to Plant No. 40 concurrently receiving orders to prepare for series assembly of the Ya-12 and Ya-13F artillery tractors (later built as the slightly modified M-12A and M-13A) as the Soviet Union reorganized tracked tractor production to compensate for a longstanding dearth in artillery tractors. Plant No. 40 (post-war renamed MMZ) and N.A. Astrov as chief design engineer returned to the subject in 1951 with a new design, given the plant index '561', which entered service with the Soviet Army in 1951 as the AT-P armoured light artillery tractor.

CHAPTER 6

HALF-TRACK ARTILLERY TRACTORS

This NATI-3 half-track undergoing trials in Moscow in 1933 was only one of numerous half-track designs developed in the late 1920s and early 1930s.

The Imperial Russian Army had used imported vehicles such as Holt and Allis-Chalmers half-track tractors for towing heavy artillery during World War I. Indigenous Soviet tractor development began after the end of the civil war, in 1923, when various imported tractors and domestic developments were considered for military service, as were a number of half-track designs such as Citroen-Kegresse, with several different prototypes being tested on different imported chassis. Development of half-tracks intended for series production in the Soviet Union began at the NAMI motor vehicle design institute from 1928 under the direction of A.S. Kuzin. In 1928 NAMI built a half-track prototype based on NAMI-1 vehicle components and with a 22hp NAMI engine, which underwent trials in 1929 as the first indigenous Soviet half-track design.

In the autumn and winter of 1932, NATI tested the similar NATI-2 half-track on which development work had begun in 1931, based on a Ford-AA 4x2 chassis, powered by a 40hp engine and fitted with rubber tracks.* The 2,800kg vehicle could travel at 25km/h and had a low ground pressure of 0.127kg/cm^2. Fuel consumption was however a significant 55–60 litres/100km – as would become the bane of all half-tracks. Prototype testing was undertaken in the Moscow region and in severe terrain conditions including the Karakum desert. While work continued on NATI prototypes, many alternatives were tested in parallel. For example, an AMO-2 Somua half-track design was tested for Red Army service at the Kubinka proving grounds in the autumn of 1931, including artillery tractor application trials towing a 107mm M-1910 corps gun. Slightly later, the YaZ-Somua half-track (YaSP) was developed to prototype stage at the Bolshevik plant in Leningrad in 1934. There were at the time many other prototype half-track developments, with the NATI-5 and GAZ-AA Kegresse being just two of myriad other examples. Early Citroen-Kegresse half-track prototypes were also extensively tested, performance proving excellent on desert sand but less so in snow.

Meanwhile at NATI, the NATI-2 was further developed as the NATI-3 (NATI-V3), again tested in the Karakum desert, and in remote Chukhotka, with the design being ultimately split into two

* NAMI was renamed NATI in 1931.

development paths, one based on the GAZ-AA chassis and the other on the heavier ZiS-5 chassis, which would ultimately lead to the GAZ-60 and ZiS-22/42 half-track families. The divergence in design began from 1934, initially at GAZ from 1934 to 1935 based on the GAZ-AA chassis, and slightly later from 1936 to 1938 at ZiS based on the ZiS-5 chassis. The concept was designated NATI-V (Vezdekhod – all-terrain vehicle) with GAZ and ZiS design paths developed in parallel.* The variant developed in collaboration with engineers from GAZ for series production at the plant on the basis of the GAZ-AA was initially known as the NATI-V, more fully as the NATI-VG (Vezdekhod GAZ), or sometimes simply abbreviated to 'V'. During trials, the NATI-3 (V3) travelled 5,000km on tracks with good reliability. The NATI-3 (V3) design was further refined via the GAZ-V (VG) into the later series production GAZ-60, which would not fare so well in operational conditions. Meantime NATI in collaboration with ZiS developed the NATI-3 concept into the similarly named NATI-VZ (Vezdekhod-ZiS), which was based on the heavier ZiS-5 chassis and would be developed via several prototypes and the ZiS-22 into the wartime series production ZiS-42/42M.

At the beginning of the 1930s, the engineer G.A. Sonkin at NATI meanwhile developed to prototype stage the Ford-A Kegresse half-track, based on an early Ford-A supplied by GAZ at Nizhny Novgorod, fitted with a Kegresse half-track assembly. The prototype, with its four-cylinder 40hp engine petrol, heavyweight rubber tracks and double (i.e dual on each side) front wheels was intended as a command vehicle for seven personnel. It was extensively tested as a vehicle capable of overcoming snow and marshland, and operating in all seasons and conditions including the infamous Russian 'Rasputitsa' (literally 'roadless') rain and thaw periods. The vehicle was further developed as the GAZ-A Kegresse from 1933 to 1934, based on the now series production GAZ-AA, proving reliable during trials, but with many mechanical defects that required considerable rework, hence the project was abandoned. The prototype was however one of several half-track designs the testing of which in time resulted in the larger and heavier series production GAZ-60 and ZiS-22/42 half-tracks.

GAZ-60

Further development at NATI resulted in the NATI-3 half-track based on the GAZ-AA chassis, the final NATI-V variant of which, developed to prototype stage in 1933, and powered by a 50hp engine, resolved most of the defects found

* The designations of the early GAZ and ZiS prototypes (the NATI-V3 and NATI-VZ) are sometimes conflated in English as the written number 3 and Z (З) in Cyrillic look almost identical in the original Cyrillic printed text.

The GAZ-NATI prototype would be developed via the GAZ-V to become the series production GAZ-60.

during trials of the earlier prototypes. The machine was prepared for series production, initially as the NATI-V (it would later be known as the GAZ-V). In 1934 engineers at GAZ began work on the GAZ-60 on the basis of the earlier NATI prototypes. Like the ZiS-42, the GAZ-60 would be used as an artillery tractor, but was significantly more limited in the role than the more powerful ZiS-42. The track mechanism used on what was to become the future GAZ-60 was developed by V.K. Rubtsov.

On 15 January 1938, in accordance with NKSM Resolution No. 12/s, GAZ began to prepare parts for the assembly of a pre-series batch of 12 prototype V (GAZ-V) half-tracks at the Leningrad (Military) Vehicle Repair Plant No. 1 (Leningradsky Voenny Avtomobilny Remontny Zavod No. 1 – LARZ-1) for operational evaluation trials. In the summer of 1938, parts were gathered under NATI supervision to build the pre-series batch of GAZ 'V' half-tracks, also known as the 'VG' (Vezdekhod–GAZ), while GAZ prepared tooling for series production of the new half-track. The GAZ-V was tested at the tank proving grounds at Kubinka together with the ZiS 'VZ' (VZ–Vezdekhod ZiS) between 17 July and 13 August 1938, the GAZ 'V' covering a driven distance of 2,660km, proving adequate performance with a typical 1.2-tonne load. With trials still underway, NKSM ordered GAZ to complete 100 GAZ-60 half-tracks by the end of that month and prepare to build a total of 2,000 vehicles.

The GAZ-60 was a further moderate development of the GAZ-V half-track based on the chassis of the GAZ-AA and taking into account lessons learned in trials of the GAZ-V. Powered by a GAZ-M engine developing 50hp coupled to

The GAZ-60 was used by the Red Army as an all-terrain transport, but its role as an artillery tractor was limited.

a four-speed gearbox, the GAZ-60 provided adequate all-terrain performance but because of its less powerful chassis it was not in the same league as the contemporary ZiS-22 and later series production 42 half-tracks. The GAZ-60 had a maximum road speed of 35km/h but during trials returned a fuel consumption of 57 litres/100km, only marginally better than the ZiS-22.

The working drawings for the series production GAZ-60 were drawn up from November 1938 to February 1939; the prototype was completed in October 1938 and trials were undertaken from October 1938 until March 1939. Meanwhile the machine tooling was installed at GAZ between January and May 1939, and the assembly process configured between December 1938 and March 1939. As was often the norm in the Soviet Union, while official acceptance trials continued, GAZ had begun series assembly of the GAZ-60 in Gorky, with 238 GAZ-60 half-tracks completed by 12 December 1938 before the workshops were complete, with a production plan to complete 691 GAZ-60 half-tracks in 1939. Production was later disrupted by the politically driven requirement to produce the GAZ-65 conversion of the GAZ-MM, fitted with a stowable track drive mechanism and removable tracks for road operation.

The GAZ-60 was deployed during the Soviet–Finnish 1939–40 Winter War, with vehicles also sent to other, often remote locations such as the Island of Ehzel (later Saaremaa, Estonia). Red Army operational feedback from the Winter War was scathing, and G.A. Sonkin was personally sent to investigate the root causes of the problems noted. The tracks, manufactured by the 'Rezinotekhnichesky Izdelye' plant lasted at best only 2,500–3,000km (which considering the huge vehicle losses during the short war was not the greatest of operational problems encountered) before the reinforced rubber tracks disintegrated. A GAZ-60 (No. MB 02-15) was delivered to the NII 'Rezinovo Promishlennosty' institute (NIEhIRP) where a new track design with reduced slack increased track life to 10,000km. The new tracks were ready for trials by 13 December 1939 and were to be tested by January 1940 but other priorities at GAZ, not least production of track sets for the GAZ-65, delayed their introduction.

In 1940, with early production GAZ-60s having been operationally tested in the Winter War, GAZ completed only 205 GAZ-60 half-tracks against a planned 250 production target for the year, together with 60 sets of spares, whereafter production was terminated. A total of 152 vehicles were delivered to the ABTU KA (for the Red Army), 50 to NKVD combat units, ten to the NKVMF (i.e. the navy) and six to NKSM.

The GAZ-60 was used by the Red Army as an all-terrain transport, but its role as an artillery tractor was limited.

The track drive for the GAZ-60 and ZiS-22 originally shared a common design origin, with the ZiS half-track system being entirely modified for the later ZiS-42.

In service specific to artillery tractor duties, the GAZ-60 was used by the Red Army for towing light field guns, and by air defence units for towing light anti-aircraft guns. The GAZ-60 was apparently capricious in service, with frequent mechanical breakdowns, and difficult to operate and repair.

Operational experience with the GAZ-60 during the 1939–40 Winter War prompted a return to the philosophy of full-time half-tracks rather than GAZ-65, ZiS-33 and ZiS-35 conversion sets, as being simpler to operate even allowing for the high fuel consumption, lower road speed and wear. In April 1940, I.A. Likhachev at NKSM ordered a modified and improved GAZ-60 (the GAZ-60P) to be developed, taking into account operational experience and feedback from the Red Army, and to be put into series production at a rate of 500 vehicles a year. The GAZ-60P had detail changes to improve mobility and reliability, most noticeably the use of steel drive and return wheels replacing the original truck-type large rubber tyres on the original GAZ-60. The suffix was rarely used and the later GAZ-60 not distinguished in practice from the original. The GAZ-60P, which rectified the defects revealed during operational use of the GAZ-60 and had much improved road speed and all-terrain capability, underwent state trials from 3 to 28 September 1940. The Red Army had planned to order the production of 2,000 modernized GAZ-60P and ZiS-22 half-tracks for delivery over a two-year period, but plans were disrupted by the outbreak of war. The GAZ-60 continued in series production until 1942, with an estimated total of 2,015 built (documented information is to date incomplete), nearly all of which were delivered to front line Red Army units.

ZiS-22

The ZiS development of earlier NATI-V half-track concepts was undertaken slightly later than at GAZ, over the period 1936–38, resulting in the ZiS-22 half-track, based on the ZiS-5 chassis, which was developed to prototype stage in 1938 as an all-terrain load carrier and light artillery tractor. Development from the earlier NATI developed NATI-V3 was under the direction of G.A. Sonkin, with half-track development at the ZiS plant under the direction of lead designer B.M. Fitterman, who had worked at NATI before moving to ZiS in Moscow. The ZiS half-track development path had taken shape in 1936 as the NATI-VZ (Vezdekhod-ZiS) or 'VZ'. The prototype as built and tested was 1,560kg heavier than the ZiS-5, for a total vehicle weight of 4,660kg, but powered by the standard ZiS-5 engine developing 73hp. The fuel tank capacity was increased from 60 litres on the ZiS-5 to 120 litres to compensate for the high fuel consumption, with the load platform raised 135mm to accommodate the track mechanism.

The NATI-VZ prototype for the ZiS-22.

The NATI-VZ underwent trials from 17 July to 13 August 1938, during which the prototype covered 2,190km on roads and cross country. The 4,660kg vehicle could transport a 2,250kg load in most terrain conditions, reducing to 1,750kg in snow. The vehicle had a maximum tested road speed of 35.5km/h but with high fuel consumption, ranging from 60–73 litres/100km even on made roads to 90–100 litres/100km on dirt roads and up to 200 litres/100km cross-country. The original 60 litre ZiS-5 fuel tank located under the driver's seat was insufficient to provide adequate range, so an additional three 60 litre tanks were subsequently added to the design for a total of 300 litres of fuel, which provided a dirt road range of approximately 300km. All-terrain performance was however excellent, and ground pressure on the 390mm wide tracks was only 0.27kg/cm^2 (which could be reduced further to 0.085kg/cm^2 with the use of ski-floats on the front wheels).

The ZiS-5 derived variant of the NATI-V (V3) began to be assembled in September 1938 at the same LARZ-1 repair plant that assembled the pre-series batch of GAZ-60 half-tracks. Series production was in 1939 transferred to ZiS in Moscow where it was further modified and received the ZiS index ZiS-22. ZiS plant archives indicate that around 200 ZiS-22 half-tracks would subsequently be built at ZiS in Moscow to the summer of 1940, at which point operational feedback regarding slow speed, reliability and high maintenance requirement issues became apparent. Meanwhile the ZiS-22-50 and ZiS-22-52 prototypes were tested, towing the 76.2mm M-1936 (F-22) divisional gun and 122mm M-1938 (M-30) howitzer.

ABOVE A ZiS-22 in 1940.

ABOVE RIGHT ZiS-22 half-tracks with 76mm M-1902/30 field guns on parade in Kishinyev, Bessarabia, 3 July 1940.

In the last days of 1939, the ZiS-22 took part in a demonstration at the NATI test polygon near Moscow in front of the assembled leadership of ABTU KA including D.G. Pavlov. The ZiS-22 had acceptable performance, but had difficulty with traction on ice roads and in snow 0.5m deep. On 26 December 1939, 50 ZiS-22 half-tracks were ordered to be sent to the 2nd Special Red Banner Army at the Zavitaya railway station (now Zavitinsk) in the Amur region of eastern Siberia.

The combat debut of the ZiS-22 resembled that of the GAZ-60 during the 1939–40 Soviet–Finnish Winter War where a small number of 'VZ' and pre-series ZiS-22 half-tracks were tested in operational conditions, used as a tracked artillery tractor and all-terrain load carrier in the light forests and deep snow of winter Karelia. Trials revealed that although the machine provided the expected all-terrain capability in most circumstances, deep snow over 0.5m in depth and soft mud tended to build up in the running gear. Like the GAZ-60, the ZiS-22 suffered from limited track endurance, and a lack of spares and trained and experienced maintenance technicians, such that vehicles often had to be abandoned after breakdown.

On 27 December 1939, in response to a formal Red Army complaint recorded in Act No. 8285 about the service history of VZ No. 364358, Chassis No. 286917 (and complaints also regarding GAZ half-tracks), G.A. Sonkin personally visited the Finnish front line with a team of mechanics to make repairs and evaluate the situation. The Red Army made great use of the Soviet–Finnish Winter War to evaluate the performance of new designs under combat conditions, including the ZiS-22 (VZ) and the GAZ-60 (VG). The endurance of the reinforced rubber tracks, maintenance difficulties and welding cracks were the key issues raised.

In January 1940, in severe winter conditions, the NATI-VZ, ZiS-22 and GAZ-60 half-track prototypes were tested at the NATI polygon together with new 4x4 and 6x6 wheeled prototypes in the presence of a commission headed by GABTU chief D.G. Pavlov. Sonkin, as head of NATI, on 26 January 1940 wrote to the Head of ABTU, Commissar Pavlov, advising of the required remedial work required on ZiS-22 (VZ) and GAZ-60 (VG) half-tracks. The response from ABTU was in Letter No. 1996375 from Pavlov's deputy, Engineer 1st Rank Datsyuk. The roads in Karelia had shown up the design flaws in the ZiS-22 (and GAZ-60) half-tracks, and in the case of ZiS, the 'simpler' ZiS-33 half-track conversion was considered a better design solution for all-terrain travel. Already on 26 December 1939, 50 ZiS-22s (25 per cent of all vehicles built to that date) had been delivered to Zavitaya (railway) Station (today Zavitinsk) in the Amur region to join the 2nd Special Red Banner Army, where their subsequent fate is unrecorded. It is noteworthy how many half-tracks were delivered to the Soviet Far East even as war raged against a neighbouring country in Europe.

On 3 March 1940, Letter No. 047 was sent to the Chief of ABTU Leningrad Military District by the headquarters of 17th Tank Regiment signed off by the regiment commander, Captain Lukashin, the regimental commissar, Senior Lieutenant Abramov, and the deputy regimental commander, Military Engineer 3rd Rank Belov. The letter, acknowledged by the recipient, ABTU Leningrad Military District, on 31 March 1940, concerned two half-tracks, with serial numbers 285634 and 285713, which had been tested in Karelia in operational conditions. The claims were related to the low all-terrain load

Despite the short production life of the ZiS-22 and the small numbers produced, specialized versions were produced, including this vehicle, apparently an ammunition resupply vehicle.

capacity of the ZiS-22, but also noted a lack of traction between the drive wheels and the track, with track slippage significantly increasing engine and clutch wear and with all-terrain load capacity actually less than the wheeled 4x2 ZiS-5 in most circumstances. Letter No. 047 requested permission to convert the two semi-tracked vehicles back to ZiS-5 wheeled specification. Early operational experience with the ZiS-22 was, as with the GAZ-60, not entirely encouraging. Meanwhile, a small number of completed ZiS-22s continued to be delivered to other units of the Red Army. The final batch of 19 series production ZiS-22s was accepted for service by the Red Army on 10 April 1940 at Military Warehouse No. 60 (Bryansk).

At a meeting between representatives of ZiS and the Red Army held on 19 April 1940, it was decided to modernize the ZiS-22. Modification of the original ZiS-22 as the ZiS-22M (the future ZiS-42) started the following month, with the TTTs, detailing modifications to the track drive mechanism and the track, confirmed in writing on 11 May 1940. The final 'series production' ZiS-22M was in fact the result of a considerable period of additional prototype building and evaluation rather than a single vehicle. On 4 May 1940, Resolution No. 396 issued by the Regional Economic Council of the SNK determined the production of 250 modified ZiS-22 (ZiS-22M) half-tracks. The total number of original production model ZiS-22 half-tracks built is unclear due to all the changes in production involved, but was under 200. The main distinguishing feature of the ZiS-22 that differentiated it from the later ZiS-42 was that it retained the steel cab of the ZiS-5, whereas the later ZiS-42/42M had wooden cabs.

On 20 May 1940, the Deputy Commissar of NKSM (Eliseev) sent the Director of ZiS (Volkhov) and the Director of NATI (Tolkunov) a letter requesting a prototype ZiS-22 fitted with new, steel tracks with riveted track shoes to be readied for testing by ABTU KA for Red Army service at the Kubinka polygon by 1 August 1940. The immensely experienced head of ABTU, General D.G. Pavlov, who was also concurrently head of the GVS (the Main Military Council) of the Red Army, was directly involved in the testing and redesign of the ZiS-22. NATI and ZiS collaboratively developed the modified half-track, later known as the ZiS-22M, fitted with new drive wheels and a new track, which was tested from 3 to 30 September 1940. Meantime, in accordance with Letter No. 17284 from Minister Likhachev, ZiS was ordered to halt production of the ZiS-22 'M-1940' and to concentrate on standard 4x2 ZiS-5 production. Other prototypes in the prolonged ZiS-22 to ZiS-42 development path included the ZiS-22-50 (NATI-VZ-50 or NATI-50), also with a simplified track drive mechanism, and the ZiS-22-52 (NATI-VZ-52 or NATI-52), also with a new track drive and track but powered by a ZiS-16 engine developing 83–85hp.

The latter was tested at the NATI polygon and found to be the best suited for Red Army service, primarily as an artillery tractor. The prototype was accepted for service with the Red Army and 2,000 were contracted for production at ZiS beginning from mid-1941 subject to testing of the final pre-series production prototype with earlier faults eliminated. As ZiS prepared the tooling for series production, the final prototype, which would later be designated as the ZiS-22M, was prepared for trials; however, these were conducted only in July 1941, by which time the country was at war. To the summer of 1941, only three prototype ZiS-22M half-tracks were built.

With the outbreak of war, the engineering group working on half-tracks at NATI under G.A. Sonkin, which included G.I. Pral, A.F. Andronov and D.D. Melman, were transferred from NATI to the ZiS plant in Moscow, in order to prepare the technical documentation for ZiS-22M series production. According to differing sources, an additional 20–30 pre-series production ZiS-22M vehicles may have been assembled at ZiS before the plant was evacuated in the autumn of 1941. There was a hiatus as ZiS production was re-established in Miass far to the east of Moscow, with ZiS-22M development continuing only in the spring of 1942. Sonkin received the Stalin Prize for his work on these half-track developments. The ZiS-22M underwent further trials for Red Army approval under NKO General-Colonel Voronov on 27 April 1942, with the testing commission led by the Deputy Chief of Artillery KA (GAU), General Lieutenant Tikhonov. The vehicle tested for Red Army service acceptance was the same ZiS-22M powered by a ZiS-16 engine developing 83hp as tested in July 1941.

The ZiS-22M used a new track mechanism, as also fitted on the later ZiS-42 and ZiS-42M.

However, the vehicle, which was accepted for production and Red Army service, was now given a new designation, namely ZiS-42; initially produced intermittently, it would remain in production as the later ZiS-42M until 1946.

The small number of ZiS-22 half-tracks in Red Army service were usually used at regimental level as artillery tractor and all-terrain ammunition load carrier vehicles, but the ZiS-22's weight meant that it had less cargo capacity than the ZiS-5 in most circumstances. In service the ZiS-22 was often still referred to in internal correspondence as the 'VZ' or ZiS all-terrain vehicle. The ZiS-22 is known to have been deployed during the defence of Moscow in the autumn and winter of 1941, and the vehicle was used in support of aerosan units operating NKL-26 raider aerosans during the same fateful winter, particularly in the region of Volokolamsk, on the front line in that direction 120km west of Moscow.

ZiS-33

Half-tracks by their very design were in the Soviet Union as elsewhere a compromise engineering solution for providing all-terrain transport logistics. Half-tracks were far more adept off-road than wheeled transport vehicles, but were slower on long road marches, with higher fuel consumption and maintenance requirements. Initial deployment of both the GAZ-60 and the ZiS-22 in Red Army service had also shown a tendency towards rapid track wear. Designers at GAZ and ZiS thereby developed hybrid half-track variants of the GAZ-MM and ZiS-5 as the GAZ-65 and ZiS-33 respectively, both mounting auxiliary track drive mechanisms to modified standard 4x2 trucks, with stowable drive assemblies and demountable tracks, such that the trucks could operate on wheels during road marches, with the tracks being mounted only as required for all-terrain operation.

As a result of early difficulties with the ZiS-22 full half-track, the ZiS-33 'ersatz vezdekhod' (ersatz all-terrain vehicle) was in the autumn of 1939 developed under the direction of B.M. Fitterman as a 'simpler' alternative, modified from an otherwise standard ZiS-5 4x2 truck. The ZiS-33 was developed as a conversion set, with drive, a deployable bogie set and demountable light tracks allowing occasional use as a half-track. The tracks could be quickly mounted, with the vehicle otherwise operating on roads as a conventional 4x2 ZiS-5. The system was effective in mud, and marginally less so in deep snow, but the track drive system and track added 1,322kg to the vehicle weight, which accordingly limited the load and towing capacity. The standard six-cylinder ZiS-5 engine, developing 73hp, provided a maximum road speed of 45km/h.

TOP LEFT A ZiS-33 half-track conversion during trials. The ZiS-33 was developed to combine the road performance of a standard ZiS-5V with the ability to mount tracks on soft ground or snow only as needed.

BELOW LEFT A restored ZiS-33 towing a 57mm ZiS-2 anti-tank gun leaving Red Square during a historical parade rehearsal, 1 November 2011.

The ZiS-33 had a particularly rapid development, not least because the tutelage of TsK member and member of the Politburo N.S. Khrushchev who was at the time in charge of the Communist Party in Ukraine with much influence in the development of vehicles suitable in agrarian regions, but had recent history in assisting Stalin's purges in the Moscow region. Neither ZiS nor GAZ were enthusiastic as regards the 'ersatz' half-tracks, but despite the overtones, development continued.

The ZiS-33 system was tested in the winter of 1939, followed by the rapid completion of a pre-series evaluation batch on 18 January 1940, some of these vehicles being immediately dispatched for operational trials during the final weeks of the Soviet–Finnish Winter War. The results of the operational trials showed the ZiS-33 to have a load capacity of 2,250kg, but with fuel consumption of 55–200 litres/100km (putting it on a par with the ZiS-22), an all-terrain range of only 50–60km and overall mobility not significantly better than that of the ZiS-5. The system proved over-complex for military application, and after a few weeks of operational service the vehicles were returned from the fighting in the Karelian Isthmus, decommissioned from Red Army service and given over for use in agriculture on state farms. The ZiS-33 was dropped in favour of the ZiS-22M and later ZiS-42, and also in lieu of all-wheel-drive vehicles in development such as the ZiS-32 4x4 truck. Statistics on the ZiS-33 are conflicting. Some sources state that 1,800 ZiS-35 conversion sets were built, others that 3,595 sets were built in 1940, but with only 16 sets remaining in Red Army service by 1942. The modified ZiS-35 system met a similar fate.

GAZ-65

The GAZ-65 was a GAZ equivalent to the ZiS-33 and ZiS-35 half-track conversions, with removable tracks for operation on roads. The order to develop and produce a removable track system at GAZ was given slightly later than for ZiS, arriving in early 1940. GAZ developed the GAZ-65 to prototype stage, but the work significantly disrupted series production of the existing production GAZ-60 which had its own development issues, and the GAZ-65 was apparently regarded by chief designer V.A. Grachev at GAZ as something of a tangential irritant. The GAZ-65 was almost simultaneously dropped in the spring of 1940 as the plant concentrated on existing production.

ZiS-42

The best-known Red Army half-track was the ZiS-42, produced, initially intermittently, from 1941 to 1944, designed to transport loads across all terrain particularly in the spring, autumn and winter seasons, and to tow divisional artillery with a travel order weight of up to 3,000kg. The ZiS-42 and later ZiS-42M were designed by a group led by chief engineer G.I. Pral, with A.F. Andronov, D.D. Melman, E.B. Armand and A.N. Makarenko, all of whom received a state prize for development of the ZiS-42.

The prototype for the ZiS-42 was the pre-war ZiS-22M, which completed trials immediately after the outbreak of war in the summer of 1941 and continued to be intermittently refined by engineers transferred to ZiS in Moscow from NATI. However, as noted, the ZiS-22M did not enter full series production, primarily due to the evacuation of the ZiS plant from Moscow.

A modified ZiS-22M prototype, effectively the same vehicle as tested the previous year but simplified for wartime production, with a wooden cab, angular wheel guards, no front brakes and other changes, underwent acceptance trials for the Red Army on 27 April 1942, powered by the standard ZiS-5 engine developing 73hp rather than the more powerful engine options as tested earlier,

(A) A ZiS-42 prototype during factory trials. Note the track drive system taken from the ZiS-22M, the radiator and the wooden cab with narrow cab planking replacing the steel cab of its predecessor. (Sergei Popsuevich) **(B)** This photograph is archived as a ZiS-42 though it is a ZiS-22M, with steel cab and intricate radiator grille and light protection. The differences between the evolving ZiS-22, ZiS-22M, ZiS-42 and ZiS-42 are nuanced. **(C)** The later ZiS-42M is most readily distinguished by the large combined radiator and light grille. This vehicle has narrow wood planking, but some later vehicles had wider planking. (Sergei Popsuevich) **(D)** A typical ZiS-42M configuration. Note the raised height of the cargo body compared with the 4x2 ZiS-5 truck. **(E)** A well-loaded ZiS-42M and 122mm M-1938 (M-30) howitzer on a pontoon barge. (Sergei Popsuevich) **(F)** A ZiS-42 towing a winter camouflaged 122mm M-1938 (M-30) howitzer at Nevsky Pyatachok on the River Neva, where the Siege of Leningrad was broken.

TOP RIGHT A ZiS-42 with 37mm M-1939 (K-61) anti-aircraft gun, Belorussia, May 1944 or River Dvina crossing, 1st Baltic Front, 3 June 1944 according to different sources.

RIGHT A ZiS-42M being assisted by Red Army soldiers in typically difficult 'Rasputitsa' (literally 'roadless' mud season) conditions.

FAR RIGHT Welder-Sapper Smirnov welding BM-13 MRS launch rails with a ZiS-42 in the background, 29 April 1945.

and was accepted for service, now renamed ZiS-42. The production ZiS-42 inherited the modified track drive mechanism and running gear from the ZiS-22M. The flexible two-section drive mechanism consisted of drive wheel, idler, four road wheel rollers and a single support roller. The idler was identical to the drive wheel but without the central track drive teeth. The rubber-metal tracks were now slightly wider – 415mm versus 380mm for ZiS-22.

After the ZiS plant evacuation, when Axis forces had been held and pushed back from taking Moscow, the decision was taken in early 1942 to re-establish ZiS-5 manufacture at the original site in Moscow, with existing and some returned tooling. The ZiS-42 entered production at re-established production workshops at ZiS in Moscow from the autumn of 1942 in response to an urgent Red Army requirement for artillery tractors and all-terrain vehicles. Like the ZiS-22M prototype, the original ZiS-42 was based on the simplified wartime production ZiS-5V, with no front brakes, a wooden cab and angular wheel guards, and powered by a standard ZiS-5 six-cylinder petrol engine developing 73hp. The first nine ZiS-42 half-tracks were built in September 1942, with series production rapidly ramping up to seven vehicles a day. The first ZiS-42 half-tracks produced were sent to the Stalingrad Front, where they were used to transport divisional artillery and ammunition.

To the end of 1942, 752 ZiS-42s were completed, with an additional 2,115 being completed in 1943. Some Russian sources distinguish M-1942 and M-1943 production models of the original ZiS-42, with minor differences, both based on the ZiS-5V chassis. The later ZiS-42M is in the same references referred to as the ZiS-42 M-1944. Overall production data between the ZiS-42/42M remains conflated, but approximately 5,900 ZiS-42 series half-tracks of early and late models were built in total.

The ZiS-42 cab was, like that of the ZiS-5V, fabricated from wooden planking fitted over a metal frame, with the planking on the later ZiS-42M being wider than on the earlier ZiS-42. Some ZiS-42s were fitted with a higher pre-war load platform (ZiS-5A/5U), with all subsequent ZiS-42Ms being fitted with the standard ZiS-5V load platform. The load platform was raised 130mm to allow for track clearance. As the tested dirt-road laden fuel consumption was 150 litres/100km, the standard 60-litre ZiS-5V fuel tank was complemented by an additional 120-litre fuel tank mounted above the frame behind the cab, on the later ZiS-42M increased to 300 litres capacity. From the winter of 1943, ZiS-42 half-tracks assembled at Miass began to be fitted with the ZiS-5M engine developing 76hp. The ZiS-42 and ZiS-42M could both be fitted with float skis on the front road wheels in winter to prevent the front axle from becoming embedded in deep snow, the vehicle length with skis fitted increasing to 6.75m. In winter ZiS-42/42M half-tracks were fitted with float skis mounted on the front road wheels.

ZiS-42M half-tracks with 85mm (52-K) anti-aircraft guns, Kreschatik, Kiev, 7 November 1945.

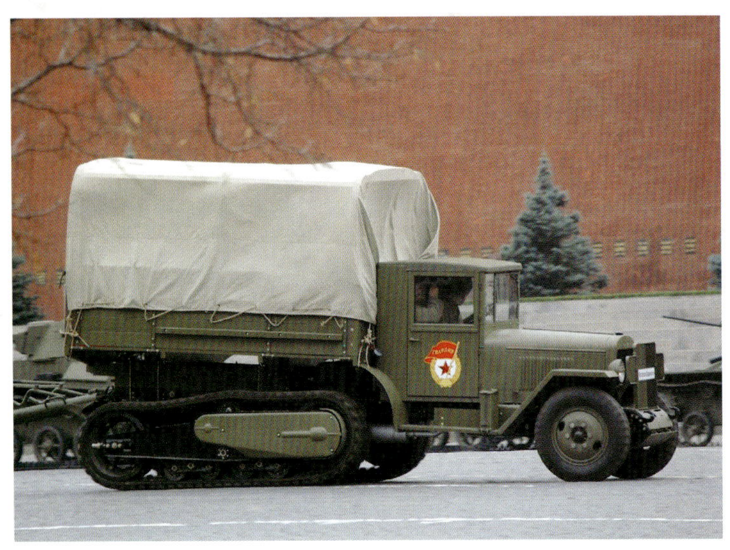

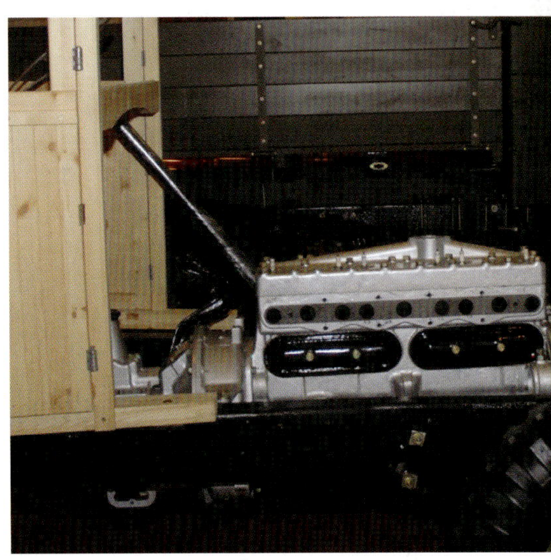

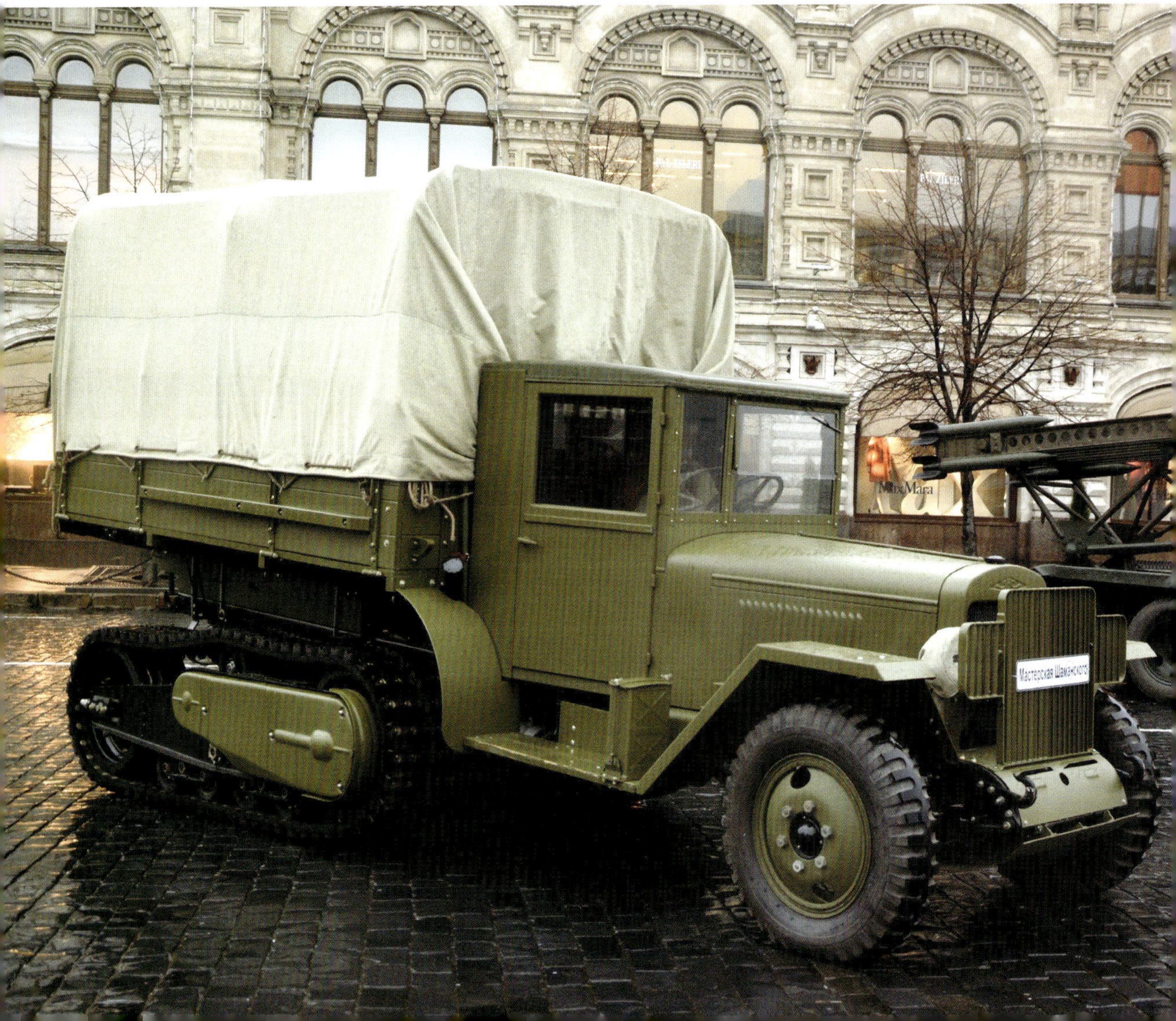
Мастерская Шаманского
MaxMara

The combat debut of the series production ZiS-42 was in November 1942. Feedback from Red Army service remarked on the high fuel consumption, relative slowness compared to the GAZ-AAA and ZiS-6 6x4 trucks on road marches (the half-track vehicles compromising overall convoy speed in mixed columns) and the short engine endurance before requiring capital repair.

OPPOSITE
TOP LEFT A restored ZiS-42M on Red Square during a memorial parade rehearsal, 3 November 2011.

TOP RIGHT A ZiS-42M during restoration, showing the location of the standard ZiS-5V engine. (Andrey Aksenov)

BELOW The same ZiS-42M parked outside the GUM department store on Red Square, 7 November 2013.

ZiS-42M

In 1943, due to a combination of combat losses and truck and tractor plants having converted to essential tank assembly, there remained a shortage of all-terrain vehicles in Red Army service. With factories having been re-established in geographically safer locations and tank assembly resolved, pre-war all-terrain projects were revisited at both GAZ and ZiS. Work on a new design to replace the ZiS-42 began at ZiS under the direction of G.A. Sonkin at NATI who had headed development of the original ZiS-22 from the NATI-V3. The resulting ZiS-42M (M – Modernizirovanny, modernized) was a modification of the original ZiS-42, developed from the late autumn of 1943, reflecting wartime experience and conditions, based on the ZiS-5V chassis and powered by an uprated ZiS-5M engine (as also used in the Ya-13 artillery tractor) developing 76hp at 2,400rpm depending on fuel quality. Like the ZiS-42, the ZiS-42M was developed primarily as a half-track artillery tractor with a 2,250kg all-terrain load capacity, with secondary use as an ammunition and general cargo load carrier capable of travelling at up to 42km/h on roads. The ZiS-42M prototype was successfully tested in the Moscow suburbs from 25 October to 26 December 1943. Series production was however delayed in part because by this time in the war Lend-Lease trucks such as the Studebaker US6 now fulfilled much of the need for divisional level artillery transport, and the ZiS-42M was not an urgent production priority.

Recognizing operational experience with the ZiS-42, the ZiS-42M had an enlarged (300-litre) fuel tank capacity, with a single 120-litre tank and three 60-litre tanks for a total of 300 litres of fuel, with the additional fuel tanks mounted on the chassis under the rear cargo body deck being refilled from within the cargo area. Fuel consumption remained high, typically well over 100 litres/100km when driving off-road, and as with all half-tracks the fuel consumption was noted by operational units, but as a T-34 tank could consume 270 litres/100km, the fuel consumption for a half-track supporting frontal units was relative. The ZiS-42M was 227kg heavier than the ZiS-42, with a towing capacity of 2,750kg (some sources state 4,380kg) and had a plant guarantee of 6,000km but this was never operationally achieved.

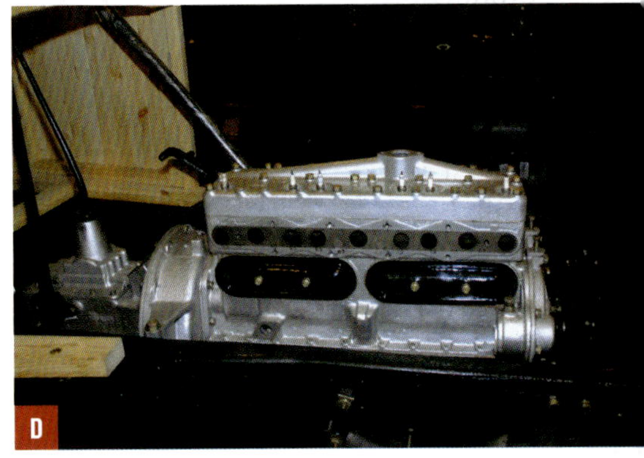

(A) The driver's instrument panel on the ZiS-42M, Museum of Russian Military History, Padikovo, near Moscow.
(B) The rudimentary ZiS-42M cab interior.
(C) The track mechanism on the ZiS-42M with bonded rubberized fabric track and metal and rubber track blocks.
(D) The ZiS-42M was powered in most series production vehicles by the 6-cylinder ZiS-5M engine. (Andrey Aksenov)

The major visual difference between the ZiS-42 and the ZiS-42M was that the later vehicle featured a modified cab built of wider wooden planking, with a new combined grille for the enlarged radiator protecting the radiator and headlights, and a modified rear cargo area. The ZiS-42M was also fitted with smaller-diameter headlights replacing the larger diameter pre-war ZiS type headlight. The ZiS-42M also had no brakes on the front wheels.

The ZiS-5MF engine was also experimentally mounted in the ZiS-42M, but production priority was given to the Ya-13F tractor built in Yaroslavl. Two ZiS-42M prototypes were also built with a ZiS-16 engine developing 85hp, and an engine taken from a Studebaker US6 truck, hence the more powerful engine power outputs often quoted for the ZiS-42M. The ZiS-42M used 25–29mm fabric-reinforced rubber tracks with individual metal links.

The ZiS-42 and later ZiS-42M were built at ZiS in Moscow and UralZiS at Miass in the Urals, with the interrupted production being a function of evacuation of the plant, other assembly priorities, and the re-establishment of specialist transport vehicle production only towards the end of the war. A total of 2,334 ZiS-42Ms were built in 1944, and a further 1,102 in 1945. The ZiS-42 and ZiS-42M were used primarily as artillery tractors, with approximately 5,200

ZiS-42/ZiS-42M half-tracks in service with the Red Army in the final months of the war. The ZiS-42M was used by the Red Army in the Volkov and Karelian Fronts, primarily as a tractor vehicle for 76–122mm calibre artillery pieces. Red Army records show 1,942 ZiS-42M half-tracks recorded as in operational service as of May 1945. A small number of ZiS-42M half-tracks were used during the assault on Berlin in the final days of the war.

A ZiS-41 with a 3-tonne ammunition load and a 122mm M-1938 (M-30) howitzer and limber, 1942.

Post-war, production continued into 1946, with 69 built that year before production ceased. Some final production post-war vehicles were powered by the ZiS-120 engine developing 90hp. G.A. Sonkin received a state prize for development of the ZiS-42/42M between 1942 and 1944, with 5,931 of both types built during the war years. The official numbers, though conflated, would suggest that approximately 2,426 ZiS-42 and 3,505 ZiS-42M half-tracks were built for a total of 5,931 ZiS-42 series half-tracks produced. Other original sources state that 6,372 ZiS-42/ZiS-42M half-tracks were built, including post-war 1945 and into 1946, but the records and data are slightly conflated between the models, reflecting the chaotic background in which they were developed and produced. The ZiS-42M remained in service for the post-war Soviet Army, being used in second echelon units, for towing anti-aircraft guns, in training units and also for geological expeditions. Soviet Army air defence units used the ZiS-42M until as late as 1951. A number of ZiS-42Ms were converted post-war to PMZ series fire engines. A single surviving ZiS-42M was preserved at the NIII-21 Museum at Bronnitsy until scrapped in 1967. The fate of a surviving example kept at the ZiS plant is unknown.

In 1941–43, the Gorky Artillery Plant (Plant No. 92) (ZiS) developed the ZiS-41 and ZiS-43 armoured half-tracks on the ZiS-22 (later ZiS-42) chassis, armed with a 57mm ZiS-4 tank and 37mm M-1939 (61K) anti-aircraft guns respectively. A small number were built and tested but not accepted for service.

AT-3

The 'AT' (Artilleriisky Tyagach – Artillery Tractor) series of half-track artillery tractors was developed in parallel with ongoing production of the ZiS-42M at the relocated ZiS plant in Miass. The AT-3 (Artillery Tractor – 3,000kg towing capacity) was developed at ZiS in the summer of 1943 under the direction of B.M. Fitterman on the basis of the ZiS-5V as a potential replacement for the original production ZiS-42. The AT-3 prototype half-track borrowed much of the running gear, and 300mm wide track from the SU-76M and T-70M

An AT-3 half-track artillery tractor on Podolskoye Shosse south of Moscow, during trials in October 1943.

self-propelled gun/tank chassis, hence a more standard track drive system than the 'bespoke' ZiS-42 arrangement. The AT-3 had a combat weight of 5,508kg and was powered by a ZiS-5M engine developing 80hp, providing a maximum unladen weight of 37km/h. The half-track had a towing capacity of 2,750kg and load capacity of 3,000kg.

The prototype AT-3 was completed in August 1943 and immediately subjected to trials towing the 122mm M-1938 (M-30) howitzer which had a travel order weight of 2,750kg. Towing the 122mm M-1938 (M-30) howitzer the AT-3 during these trials achieved a mean speed of 37km/h, only 2km more than the ZiS-42, with a medium convoy speed of 27km/h (ZiS-42M – 26km/h), the dirt road speed reducing to 9.1km/h (ZiS-42M – 10.1km/h) and the all-terrain towing speed during trials being a recorded 3.64km/h.

The AT-3 was a powerful and refined machine, with proven and reliable running gear, as noted, taken from the SU-76M/T-70M, but offered no particular advantage over the ZiS-42/42M, and so was not accepted for series production for the Red Army during wartime conditions. However, a pre-production lot of AT-3 half-track tractors was built and issued to operational Red Army artillery units in front line locations for evaluation purposes.

The concept of using tank/self-propelled gun running gear for half-tracks had been proven, and Fitterman considered the concept viable for further development. At the beginning of 1944, the B-3 half-track armoured personnel carrier (BTR) prototype was built on an AT-3 chassis.

AT-8 AND AT-14

The heavier capacity AT-8 and AT-14 were also developed at ZiS as part of a national programme to develop new artillery tractors, of which there was a general shortage by 1942. Development work began under the direction of B.M. Fitterman and continued until September 1943, with the AT-8 and AT-14 half-track artillery tractors developed and tested by ZiS earlier than the AT-3, from December 1942 to September 1943.

The AT-8 (Artillery Tractor – 8,000kg towing capacity) was powered by parallel ZiS-5M engines developing 77hp. ZiS later developed to prototype stage a twin ZiS-5MF engine installation for the AT-8/AT-14 tractors, with a total power output of 150–190hp. The AT-14 (Artillery Tractor – 14,000kg towing capacity) was a heavier duty variant of the AT-8, powered by parallel ZiS-16 engines developing 92hp, and designed to tow artillery up to 14,000kg in travelling order. Both tractors had parallel engines coupled to twin gearboxes, with each powertrain driving the tracks on one side of the vehicle, the same arrangement as installed in the SU-12 (SU-76) self-propelled gun which resulted in significant synchronization problems for the driver-mechanic. The distinctive wide engine compartment and cab distinguished the AT-8 and AT-14 from the AT-3.

The AT-8 used torsion bar suspension, with most of the running gear and the track also taken from the SU-76M/T-70M, and could operate in snow 30–40cm deep.

In 1943, a prototype AT-14 was tested by a state committee under the direction of Tyl RKKA (rear services of the Red Army), General-Colonel A.V. Khrulev. Ten AT-14 tractors were built for operational trials purposes, but ultimately the AT-8 and AT-14 were not accepted for service as, at the time of the proving trials, artillery tractor needs were being met by the Ya-12, built by YaAZ in Yaroslavl, and by 6x6 Lend-Lease vehicles such as the Studebaker US6.

Post-war half-track development continued at both ZiS and GAZ, with the development to prototype stage of the ZiS-153 (1948) and the GAZ-41 (1949).

BELOW The AT-8 and AT-14 half-tracks used the same chassis and track mechanisms as the AT-3, but with more powerful dual engine/gearbox installations; with twin ZiS-5M engines in the AT-8 and twin ZiS-16 engines in the AT-14. The engine compartment and cab were substantially widened accordingly. A pre-series batch of ten AT-14 half-tracks were built for operational trials in 1943.

CHAPTER 7

WHEELED ARTILLERY TRACTORS

An STZ-1 (STZ-15/30) in use on a Soviet airfield as a tow tractor for aircraft.

In the mid-1920s, as the STZ plant was being considered as a new facility specifically for tractor production, the Soviet hierarchy concluded based on long term evaluation that tracked tractors were as previously related often more suitable than wheeled types for the soil and climatic conditions found in the most fertile regions of the Soviet Union. Work was thereby undertaken to rapidly develop tracked tractors primarily for agricultural use, and to build manufacturing plants in which to assemble them on a massive scale. The production tooling and technology required was however not available for immediate implementation, and so as an interim measure the Soviet State, as noted previously, looked to foreign wheeled tractors as prototypes for beginning mass wheeled tractor production. Following on from the Fordson-Putilovets produced in moderate numbers in Leningrad, the American McCormick-Deering tractor type was chosen as the first mass-production prototype; a modified version was produced from 1930 at the Stalingrad Tractor Plant (STZ) as the STZ-1 (STZ-15/30) and from 1931 at the Kharkov Tractor Plant (KhTZ) as the KhTZ-1 (KhTZ-15/30). The 1930s became the era of mass industrialization in the Soviet Union, and also that of the mass production of wheeled and later tracked tractors for agricultural and military use.

Soviet development of wheeled vehicles suitable as artillery tractors was as in other countries dictated by the development of all-wheel drive vehicles. At the time of the outbreak of war in 1941 such vehicles were in the Soviet Union only just on the verge of being brought into service as potential replacements for existing Soviet tracked and half-track artillery tractors developed in the 1930s. In the Soviet Union, the origins of wheeled artillery tractors harked back to the early days of Soviet agricultural tractor development, which provided the technology, the mass production expertise and experience that begat the subsequent development of tracked – and later wheeled – artillery tractors. The utilitarian farm tractor was the starting point for the mechanization of the agricultural – and thereafter military – capability of the Soviet Union, providing as it did the experience of industrial mass production from which all future tractor production in the Soviet Union – both civil and military – ultimately stemmed.

ABOVE An STZ-1 (STZ-15/30) during military evaluation of domestic and imported tractors.

ABOVE RIGHT STZ-1 (STZ-15/30) tractors leaving the production line in Stalingrad.

SKhTZ-15/30 (SKhTZ-NATI) (STZ-1/KhTZ-1)

The SKhTZ-15/30 (SKhTZ-NATI) agricultural tractor was developed at the NATI tractor institute in Moscow for series production at both KhTZ in Kharkov and STZ in Stalingrad (hence the combined generic designation).* The SKhTZ-15/30 was a Soviet development of the American McCormick-Deering International-15/30 design, powered by a 32.5hp engine linked to a three-speed gearbox, the tractor being designed to tow agricultural implements such as ploughs at 3.5–7.5km/h.

The first SKhTZ-15/30 wheeled tractor left the production line at STZ in Stalingrad on 17 June 1930 at precisely 15:00 hours, designated STZ-1 and also known as the STZ-15/30, with a relatively small number of 53 STZ-15/30s being completed in 1930 as the plant geared up for mass production. In 1931, with full production underway, STZ by comparison produced 17,536 tractors, with the plant producing 144 tractors a day by 1932. The same SKhTZ-15/30 design entered production at KhTZ in Kharkov on 1 October 1931 as the KhTZ-1 or KhTZ-15/30, with 977 tractors completed that year, and 16,333 produced in 1932 as mass production also ramped up at KhTZ. The last SKhTZ-15/30 wheeled tractor left the production line at STZ on 15 May 1937, being replaced by the tracked STZ-3.

The SKhTZ-15/30 was an agricultural tractor; however in 1932 NATI developed a 'road tractor' version under the direction of V.Ya. Slominsky, with improved suspension and pneumatic tyres, better suited for military purposes than the standard steel-wheeled agricultural tractor. The prototype was tested for service with the Red Army, but not accepted. A half-track variant of the

* 15/30 – 15hp on the tow hook, 30hp on the output shaft (for driving mechanized farm equipment).

TOP LEFT A wheeled tractor towing an M-1902 field gun, Moscow Military District, 1932.

BELOW LEFT Axis soldiers posing for a photograph with a destroyed KhTZ-1 (KhTZ-15/30) tractor.

BELOW A KhTZ-1 (KhTZ-15/30) tractor in use as a tow vehicle.

SKhTZ-15/30 was also developed as a potential artillery tractor for the Red Army, but likewise did not progress beyond prototype stage.

The SKhTZ-15/30 tractor was not specifically designed for military use, but in the absence of other options it was for some years used as such, being used by the Red Army for up to 40 per cent of general transport requirements; a smaller number were specifically built as artillery tractors and used by the Red Army to tow regimental level artillery and so were recorded in Red Army records. The SKhTZ-15/30 was generally recorded in inventory as 'other type' rather than as 'artillery tractor'. The SKhTZ-15/30 was however intended for use as an artillery tractor in the event of mobilization, to be deployed where specialized artillery tractors were not available. The SKhTZ-15/30 was regularly used as an artillery tractor during peacetime military exercises, such as in August 1934, when operational trials recorded a typical medium artillery piece towing speed of 4–5km/h and an endurance of seven to eight hours before refueling. Large numbers of SKhTZ-15/30 wheeled tractors were drafted into Red Army service

A KhTZ-1 (SKhTZ-NATI using the original NATI generic designation for the type built at both STZ and KhTZ) at the (now relocated) Great Patriot War Museum in Minsk, Belarus.

with the outbreak of war in June 1941, due to their availability for mobilization in huge numbers, hence their ubiquitous presence on the battlefields of the early part of World War II.

The SKhTZ-15/30 was the most common wheeled tractor produced by the Soviet Union in the 1930s, with 344,600 in agricultural service on 1 January 1941, not including tractors in military service. Distribution of SKhTZ-15/30 tractors in military service was spread over all ministries – for example, 73 were in service with NKSM and 32 with NKTM on this date. As of 1 January 1941, there were in total 552,400 wheeled tractors of all types in civilian (primarily agricultural) service. By 22 January 1942, that number had reduced to 362,800.

WHEELED AGRICULTURAL TRACTORS IN PERSPECTIVE

As noted in Chapter 1, the Soviet Union imported a significant range of tractors from the United States, Great Britain and Europe in the 1920s with a view to mass production in the Soviet Union, whether by licence-production and technology transfer, or by local adoption of the best elements of tested foreign designs for use in Soviet manufacturing and operational conditions. The SKhTZ-15/30 is particularly significant within the context of Red Army artillery tractors in that its production at KhTZ in Kharkov and STZ in Stalingrad in the early 1930s gave both plants the manufacturing experience to later develop and build the next generation of (now tracked) tractors from the mid-1930s that formed a large part of the overall Red Army artillery park in the years leading up to war in 1941. Other mass production early wheeled artillery tractors such as the Fordson-Putilovets, built at the Krasny Putilovets plant (later LKZ) in

Leningrad, and the later NATI designed Universal-2 tractor, based on imported US Farmall tractor technology and modified for use in Soviet manufacturing and operational conditions, were also relevant, but without the direct link to future tracked artillery transporter developments. Some of these agricultural wheeled tractors were also used in small numbers as light artillery tractors, and drafted into Red Army service in 1941 on the basis that they were available in quantity and needed to replace more specialized tractors lost in combat.

While the transition from wheeled to tracked agricultural and tracked military tractors unfolded in the 1930s, parallel work continued on the development of half-tracks as potential artillery tractors, with a significant number of half-track designs developed in the Soviet Union by the mid-1930s. But the compromises inherent in half-track design, particularly road performance, maintenance, reliability and fuel consumption, remained less than optimal for military vehicle use. The successful development of all-wheel-drive military vehicles in the mid- to late 1930s now also provided the potential deployment of all-terrain wheeled artillery tractors that had not been available at the beginning of the decade. The development of multi-axle drive technology in the Soviet Union had been no slower than abroad (the 8x8 YaAG-12 was developed to prototype stage as early as 1932 with 6x4 GAZ, ZiS and YaAG trucks concurrently introduced into series production) but work on all-wheel-drive light and medium vehicles matured slowly over the decade, with the result that all-terrain vehicles based on chassis suitable for mass production such as the GAZ-61-416 and GAZ-63 matured only on the eve of total war. With the outbreak of war these fledgling designs were abandoned in lieu of more urgent production priorities; consequently the mass production of all-wheel-drive all-terrain vehicles, including for use as artillery tractors, matured in the Soviet Union only in the immediate post-war era.

GAZ-TK

An early all-terrain wheeled vehicle developed in 1934 for service in the Red Army was the 6x4 GAZ-TK (TK – three-axle–Kurchevsky) designed by I. Zhabotinsky (chassis) and the artillery engineer L.V. Kurchevsky (armament). The vehicle was intended primarily for mounting or towing the 'K' series recoilless guns developed by the latter engineer, specifically the 76.2mm BPK battalion gun, but was also considered as a wheeled tractor for other light artillery. The GAZ-TK was based on the GAZ-A powered by its standard 40hp GAZ-A engine, providing a maximum road speed of 63km/h. During Red Army acceptance trials there were claims against the GAZ-TK, mainly related to the vehicle being mechanically underpowered for its role. It was nevertheless

TOP A 6x4 GAZ-TK configured as an artillery tractor with six-man gun crew.

BOTTOM A 6x4 GAZ-TK being tested as a tractor for a 76.2mm 'K' (Kurchevsky) BPK recoilless gun.

accepted for service, by order of M.N. Tukhachevsky (from 1935 Marshal of the Soviet Union) who was at the time driving many of the changes in Red Army structure, particularly its mass mechanization. The GAZ-TK was assembled from 1934 to 1937 at the Gudok Oktyabrskaya (October Klaxon) plant in Gorky, the bus assembly filial of GAZ, with a total of 247 being built. Only 23 vehicles were fitted with the 76.2mm 'K' recoilless gun, the SAU version being designated SU-4 in the Red Army. The great majority of the other GAZ-TK vehicles were used as light artillery tractors for anti-tank guns, fitted with GAZ-4 'pikap' bodywork. The GAZ-TK was used as an artillery tractor during the Khalkin Gol campaign against Japan in 1939.

GAZ-21

The 6x4 GAZ-21 was developed by V.A. Grachev at GAZ in Gorky from late 1936 as a further development of the GAZ-TK and similar GAZ-AAAA (4A) designs. The GAZ-21 was developed specifically as a potential wheeled tractor for anti-tank guns, based on a modified GAZ-M1 chassis and powered by a GAZ-M engine coupled to a four-speed gearbox taken from the GAZ-AA 4x2 truck. The prototype was tested in the summer of 1937.

The prototype, with a two-seat cab borrowed from the GAZ-AA, 950kg rear load platform capacity and an impressive unladen maximum road speed of 76–87km/h, underwent 18 months of extensive trials in central Russia and the Caucasus in 1937–38, covering 10,000km overall. Although the 1,730kg combat weight GAZ-21 was well received by the commission testing the vehicle for the Red Army, the vehicle nevertheless did not enter series production, due to a cardinal change in technical policy at GAZ, namely a decision to concentrate on all-wheel-drive technology then maturing on vehicles such as the GAZ-61 for all-terrain military purposes.

The chassis of the GAZ-21 prototype was later used in the development of the BA-21 armoured car, developed at the Vyksunsky plant near Leningrad in 1939. The BA-21 design was also abandoned as a direct result of the decision not to proceed with the 6x4 GAZ-21 chassis on which the armoured car project depended.

ABOVE A GAZ-21 during evaluation trials. The 6x4 GAZ-21 was a further development of the automotive side of the GAZ-TK project.

GAZ-61-416

In parallel with development of the 6x4 GAZ-21, designers at GAZ under the direction of V.A. Grachev worked on a 4x4 all-terrain version of the GAZ-M1 powered by a six-cylinder GAZ-11 petrol engine developing 85hp, for use primarily as a Red Army command vehicle, but also as a light artillery tractor. The prototype of the resulting 4x4 GAZ-61, based on the modification of the existing 4x2 GAZ-11-40 and GAZ-11-73 designs, was built and tested in 1938 and accepted for production by a state resolution dated 19 December 1939. Series production was initially to commence at the end of 1940, but technical difficulties related to preparing elements of the Soviet Union's first 4x4 vehicle for series production led to significant delays. Several versions of the GAZ-61 were developed, namely the GAZ-61-73 closed sedan, the GAZ-61-40 phaeton (cabriolet), the GAZ-61-415 'pikap' and from the latter the more specialized GAZ-61-416 wheeled artillery tractor, both tractor variants having a two-seat cab and rear cargo area.

BELOW The GAZ-61 4x4 sedan vehicle series was used in the Red Army as an officer transport vehicle. (Sergei Popsuevich)

The GAZ-61 series had increased ground clearance compared to the GAZ-11 and the GAZ-M1 from which it was derived, all-wheel drive, and was powered

(A) A GAZ-61-40 during trials as an anti-tank gun tractor at the Kubinka polygon in early 1941. **(B)** A GAZ-61-415 'pikap' during trials, towing a 37mm M-1939 (61-K) anti-aircraft gun. Note the windscreen. **(C)** A GAZ-61-73 restored by the Shamansky Workshops at an exhibition in Moscow in 2021.

(D) (E) A GAZ-61-416 'pikap' during trials. The GAZ-61-416 resembled the GAZ-61-415 but had a specialized cargo area with pull-out storage racking for 57mm ammunition. It also used the windscreen from the GAZ-64. **(F)** A GAZ-41-416, apparently the only surviving wartime vehicle, providing entertainment for children.

LEFT AND BELOW LEFT A restored GAZ-61-416 at a military gathering near Moscow. (Andrey Aksenov)

BELOW A GAZ-61-416 at the Urals Military Glory Museum, Verkhnyayay Pyshma (Ekaterinburg). (John Ham)

(A) A GAZ-64 towing a 45mm M-1932 anti-tank gun across a stream during evaluation trials.
(B) A GAZ-67 towing a 76.2mm M-1942 (ZiS-3) during factory trials of the GAZ-67 at GAZ in Gorky.
(C) Columns of GAZ-67 vehicles towing 57mm M-1941 (ZiS-2) anti-tank guns at a parade on Kreschatik, Kiev, in 1948.
(D) A GAZ-67 and 76.2mm ZiS-3 dual-purpose gun exit a YaK-14 transport glider.

by a 3,480cm^3 six-cylinder in line GAZ-11 engine developing 76hp at 3,400rpm (85hp at 3,600rpm), providing significantly increased performance and a wheeled chassis with a more powerful engine than the armoured Komsomolets tracked artillery tractor. The GAZ-11 was in modified form designated GAZ-11 Model 202; it was therefore the same engine, better known as the GAZ-202, that was installed in several Red Army light tanks and SAUs.

The GAZ-61 series could travel at up to 100km/h on made roads, with the base chassis providing the possibility of a wheeled artillery tractor variant with reasonable towing performance relative to the tracked Komsomolets, better road speed (an optimistic 98km/h unladen when fitted with road rather than all-terrain tyres) and much lower fuel consumption with correspondingly improved road range.

The first version to be developed for planned series production was the GAZ-61-40 cabriolet, which was tested for service in the summer of 1940. In December 1940 the GAZ-61-40 was tested at the NIABP polygon at Kubinka as a potential wheeled artillery tractor for 45mm anti-tank guns. The GAZ-61-73 sedan developed in 1940–41 was meantime evaluated as a staff and command transport vehicle, being used in service by senior officers including G.K. Zhukov and I.S. Konev. Only six GAZ-61–40 vehicles were built in 1939–40.

The 4x4 ZiS-32 was developed pre-war but with series production curtailed by the outbreak of war, plant evacuation and subsequent other production priorities at ZiS. (Sergei Popsuevich)

The venerable ZiS-5 4x2 truck was a staple artillery tractor widely used by the Red Army, such as this column of ZiS-5 trucks towing 76.2mm M-1942 dual-purpose guns. Photographer: Arkady Shaiket.

In 1940, two prototype GAZ-61-415 4x4 'pikap' (pick-up) versions of the GAZ-61 series were built and evaluated as a wheeled tractor for towing light anti-tank and anti-aircraft artillery pieces with a travel order weight of up to 750kg, with a 400kg capacity load platform for crew and ammunition. The GAZ-61-415 closely resembled the later GAZ-61-416, with the standard GAZ windscreen on the former being the primary distinguishing feature. The GAZ-61-415 was not accepted for production, with only the two prototypes built.

The GAZ-61-416 was developed on the basis of the earlier GAZ-415 on the very eve of war in May 1941 as a more specialized 4x4 artillery tractor, developed as a potential wheeled successor to the tracked Komsomolets for towing 57mm ZiS-2 and earlier 45mm towed anti-tank guns, particularly in rear areas.* The GAZ-61-416, the first prototype of which was completed on 25 June 1941, could tow a 57mm ZiS-2 anti-tank weapon and accommodate ammunition and

* Russian original sources often conflate the GAZ-415, GAZ-416 and GAZ-417. The GAZ-61-416 has in more recent years been designated GAZ-61-417 even by collections and museums due to a small research mistake made decades ago and repeated ever since. GAZ-61-416 was the wartime designation used by GAZ and in internal correspondence between GAZ and their client, GAU KA.

five crew. It was equipped with fitted slide-out loading trays designed for 57mm ammunition, with a load capacity of 250kg (GAZ states 750kg) and could tow ordnance with a travel order weight of 1,650kg. The GAZ-61-416 used some components from the GAZ-64 including the distinctive folding windshield.

Series production of the 4x4 GAZ-61-73 sedan began on 9 July 1941, with the country plunged into a war of survival, with 158 built in 1941, more than half of which were built in September, with very small numbers built sporadically thereafter, for a total of 194 assembled. The GAZ-61-416 wheeled artillery tractor was meanwhile tested for Red Army service and was accepted for series production, with a specific role envisaged for the vehicle. The GAZ-61 (GAZ-61-416) was detailed in GKO Resolution Nos 252/ss and 255/ss dated 23 and 27 July 1941 respectively, both signed by Stalin personally as the chief of GKO, which instructed Commissar Ustinov at the Ministry of Armaments (NKV) and Commissar Malyshev at the Ministry of Medium Machine Building (NKSM) to assemble the 'first' batch of 100 Komsomolets tractor based ZiS-30 tracked SAUs armed with the 57mm anti-tank gun. The same resolution obliged NKV from 10 August 1941 to produce 57mm ZiS-2 anti-tank guns – for which the GAZ-61 (GAZ-61-416) was to be the tractor – and NKSM to provide Plant No. 92 with sufficient GAZ-61 (the resolution did not specify further) wheeled tractors to complete the production programme – i.e. to make up complete sets of anti-tank guns and wheeled tractors for supply to the Red Army. In October of 1941, the bus assembly workshop filial of GAZ (which assembled small production lots of non-mainstream vehicles such as the earlier GAZ-TK) assembled 36 GAZ-61-416 wheeled artillery tractors which were delivered to the Red Army in October and November 1941. The bus division records also note that 50 'simplified pikaps' were also produced in 1941, 14 of which were fitted with the four-cylinder GAZ-M engine. Production was thereafter curtailed primarily due to a lack of GAZ-11 engines and the changing priorities of a country at war.

In Red Army service the GAZ-61-416 was used as light wheeled artillery tractor for transporting 45mm and per design 57mm ZiS-2 anti-tank guns together with their gun crews and ammunition. Nearly all GAZ-61-416 wheeled tractors were destroyed in the winter fighting of 1941–42.

During the war years, the GAZ-64 (GAZ-64-416) (as distinct from the larger GAZ-61-416) and later GAZ-67 were also used to tow 45mm and 57mm anti-tank guns, as were ZiS-5 and GAZ-AA/AAA trucks and a variety of wheeled Lend-Lease vehicles as operational needs dictated. The ZiS-5 could tow divisional artillery on roads without difficulty, but was restricted in operating off-road. American Lend-Lease Studebaker US6 and GMC CCKW trucks were also used in large numbers by the Red Army for towing artillery.

CHAPTER 8

SELF-PROPELLED ARTILLERY ON TRACTOR CHASSIS

In June 1916, Colonel of Artillery N.A. Gulkevich presented to the Main Artillery Directorate (GAU) his plans for an armoured all-terrain tracked vehicle to be based on an imported chassis such as Holt or Allis-Chalmers. A prototype developed in 1916–17 based on the latter option, armed with a 76.2mm gun, and originally named 'Akhtirets', was the first domestically designed self-propelled assault artillery weapon, which might equally lay claim to being the starting point of Russian tank history. Trials were successful, and a second prototype, named 'Ilya Muromets', was ordered.

Developments continued after the Russian Revolution and the ensuing civil war, but with self-propelled artillery such as existed in the early years of the Soviet Union being regarded as 'second echelon' rather than direct assault support for armoured vehicles. For such a support role, a slow tracked agricultural tractor chassis was considered adequate. In the years that followed, SAU developments mounted on tractor chassis were built and tested as new indigenous tracked tractor designs were introduced into Red Army service, but were not adopted due to the increasing availability of more suitable tank chassis. However, following a hiatus in the 1930s, tracked tractor chassis would again gain relevance as SAU mountings after the outbreak of war in 1941.

The SU-2, based on the Kommunar chassis, was the first Soviet SAU development.

SU-2

Development of an SAU based on a tracked tractor chassis was authorized in accordance with an RVS resolution dated 2 October 1930, which ordered the prototype workshop at the Bolshevik plant in Leningrad to develop a 'Second Echelon SAU' for artillery support. Over the winter of 1931–32 the Bolshevik plant in collaboration with workers at Storage Facility No. 60 in Bryansk duly completed a prototype self-propelled gun, mounted on a Kommunar 3-90 tracked tractor chassis, designated SU-2. In parallel, the same designers worked on a self-propelled air defence (ZSU) vehicle on the same chassis.

The SU-2 prototype mounted a 76.2mm M-1902/30 gun retaining the original gun shield in a semi-open mounting, with untreated 10mm plate steel armour protecting the engine and driver's compartments being welded and riveted to the tractor for trials purposes. The tractor chassis required significant modification for its new role, including to the driver's cab area and the armoured fuel tank location. The prototype was tested from 12 to 16 October 1931 near Storage Facility No. 60, travelling 35km with a crew of five on board and firing 39 rounds while static and one round while moving. For trials purposes, the SU-2 was loaded with 2,500kg of ballast in lieu of ammunition, and in such configuration achieved an average speed of 12km/h. Surviving documents suggest that a total of 12 Kommunar based SU-2 SAUs were built, with and without armour, for polygon and Red Army evaluation trials purposes.

The SU-2 was not accepted by UMM RKKA for production for the Red Army on the basis that although trials performance was satisfactory, tank derived chassis were deemed more appropriate for long term development. The SU-2 concept nevertheless continued with the SU-5 series of self-propelled guns based on the T-26 light tank chassis, with the SU-2 designation also re-appearing related to SAU project developments in 1941.

SU-5

The Kommunar chassis was also developed to prototype stage as a ZSU air defence mounting for the 76.2mm M-1915/28 anti-aircraft gun. The 10-tonne combat weight unarmoured prototype, with a flat platform gun mounting and four stabilizer jacks, was operated by a six-man crew. Prototype trials were successful, with ten (some sources state 12) ZSUs ordered for more extensive operational evaluation trials with the Red Army. However, this project too was terminated, due to a concurrent decision to standardize on the new 76.2mm M-1931 anti-aircraft gun. The Kommunar tractor chassis was considered too narrow with too high a centre of gravity to provide a stable firing platform for the more powerful weapon, while the obsolescent 76mm M-1915/28 was to be removed from operational service. This closed the subject of SAU mountings on the Kommunar chassis; the subject of tracked tractor mounted SAUs remained dormant for some years, and was revived exactly a decade later under wartime conditions. The SU-5 SAU designation would however continue, with developments to build a 'triplex' of SAU variants on the T-26 light tank chassis then being prepared for series production.

ZiS-30

In the late summer of 1941, at a time of severe self-propelled artillery (SAU) mounting shortages, the T-20 Komsomolets tractor was used as the chassis for the ZiS-30 tracked self-propelled anti-tank gun. With the outbreak of war, GABTU KA had in late June 1941 met to consider the re-armament of worn-out T-26 and BT-5 tanks as SAUs; the adaption of tracked tractors, specifically the STZ-5, was also considered.

A resolution issued by the People's Commissar of Armaments, D.F. Ustinov, on 1 July 1941 ordered several plants to urgently consider the development of various SAUs specifically for anti-tank purposes. Within the text, Clause 3 instructed Plant No. 92 to prepare three prototype SAU options for mounting the 57mm ZiS-2 anti-tank gun. In response, a special design group was on 4 July assembled under the direction of P.F. Muravev; five days later it presented several SAU design options to chief designer V.G. Grabin, who had initiated the project:

A Red Army ZiS-30 in action.

A ZiS-30 in standard Red Army three-colour summer camouflage.

3.1 SU-2-1 mounted on the Komsomolets armoured tractor chassis
3.2 SU-2-2 mounted on the STZ-5 tracked tractor chassis
3.3 SU-2-3 mounted on a GAZ or ZiS wheeled chassis.

The SU-2-2 variant based on the STZ-5 chassis was rejected almost immediately, but the SU-2-1 (later ZiS-30), for mounting on the T-20 Komsomolets, and the SU-2-3 (ZiS-31), to be based on a ZiS-5 or GAZ-AAA truck chassis, were developed further at Plant No. 92. At the end of July two prototypes were completed, the SU-2-1 (ZiS-30) mounted on the Komsomolets chassis, and the SU-2-3 (ZiS-31), mounted on a GAZ-AAA chassis with an armoured cab. The two prototypes, both mounting the 57mm M-1941 (ZiS-29) modification of the ZiS-2 anti-tank gun with shield, were competitively tested in July–August 1941. The rapidly expedited trials indicated that the SU-2-1 (ZiS-30) had significant flaws. The relatively small Komsomolets tractor chassis, being short and narrow with a high centre of gravity and related significant firing height, was not ideal with regard to firing accuracy, while the overloaded engine frequently overheated. The armament was however a known quantity and the compromise accepted in the dire circumstances of the time. The truck mounted SU-2-3

A German soldier poses by an abandoned ZiS-30 in the winter of 1941–42. The SAU as with most machines, is still painted in the summer three-colour camouflage.

LEFT Another abandoned ZiS-30 in 1941, also in the standard three-colour camouflage scheme. Most if not all ZiS-30 SAUs were built on 4th Series production Komsomolets tractors.

BELOW Another destroyed or abandoned ZiS-30 based on a 4th Series production model Komsomolets tractor and in summer three-colour camouflage.

(ZiS-31) actually performed better during the trials, being a more stable firing platform, but the testing commission preferred the tracked prototype as it was more rigid, had better all-terrain mobility and was armoured, which considering its envisaged intended close-range anti-tank role was not inconsequential.

The SU-2-1, now better known by its plant designation ZiS-30, was further tested in the presence of Marshal G.I. Kulik, with mixed results. The firing platform was, as noted, not ideal, but wartime needs nevertheless resulted in the ZiS-30 with its known design compromises being accepted for service with the Red Army.

The ZiS-30 retained the DT machine gun of the standard Komsomolets chassis for local defence and the standard gun shield from the ZiS-2. The ammunition complement was 20 57mm and 756 7.62mm rounds. Mechanically, the ZiS-30 was identical to the standard T-20 Komsomolets on which it was based, being powered by a standard GAZ-M (GAZ-MM 6002) four-cylinder petrol engine developing 50hp, providing a maximum road speed of 50km/h and road range of 250km. The ZiS-30 had a combat weight of 4,760kg and a crew of five.

OPPOSITE A restored ZiS-30 at the Urals Military Glory Museum in Verkhnyaya Pyshma, Ekaterinburg. The restoration is based on a recovered 4th Series production Komsomolets. (All photographs John Ham)

Development work on the ZiS-30 remained only one of many directives at the time issued to production plants. When competitive testing of the ZiS-30 prototype had just begun, GKO Resolution No. GKO-252/ss dated 23 July 1941, signed by Stalin, was issued obliging Ustinov as the NKV Commissar to develop the 'first' batch of 100 'improved' 57mm anti-tank guns on the Komsomolets chassis. In parallel, Malyshev as the Commissar at NKSM was to ensure that Plant No. 92 built 100 ZiS-30 SAUs armed with the 57mm anti-tank gun with an unachievable deadline of 10 August 1941. Meanwhile, reflecting the recent technical availability of 4x4 wheeled vehicles, NKV and NKSM were in parallel ordered to build dedicated 57mm ZiS-2 anti-tank gun/wheeled tractor combinations, for which the 4x4 GAZ-61 (GAZ-61-416) was to be the wheeled artillery tractor. The same resolution terminated the SU-2-3 (ZiS-31) based on the GAZ-AAA chassis. Ustinov instructed Plant No. 92 to prepare for series production of these wheeled tractor/anti-tank gun combinations to commence on 1 September 1941, which due to delays in ZiS-30 production would be undertaken in parallel with assembly of Komsomolets based SAUs.

The delay in ZiS-30 assembly was due to difficulties with obtaining the Komsomolets chassis. Supply of the 57mm ZiS-2 was within the plant's control as the weapons were produced there, but Plant No. 37 in Moscow had ceased production of the Komsomolets tractor the previous month as it prepared for evacuation (the relocated plant would subsequently produce T-60 small tanks) so there were no available new production Komsomolets chassis on which to mount the armament from Plant No. 92. There was no shortage of anti-tank guns in the summer of 1941, but rather of tractors to move them around, and the Red Army was not inclined to easily give up operational tractors. A special group from NKSM scoured locations including operational service units to sequester Komsomolets tractors, and recover and repair damaged tractors for delivery to Plant No. 92 for conversion to ZiS-30 SAUs. Plant No. 92 was ordered to begin series production of the hybrid SAU also from 1 September 1941 in line with the GKO Resolution No. GKO-252/ss, with the majority of ZiS-30s built from ex-service rather than new tractors. Actual production started on 21 September and was terminated on 15 October, during which three weeks

101 ZiS-30s were produced (including the first prototype) armed with 57mm armament, and a single ZiS-30 armed with a 45mm M-1938 (20-K) tank gun, or per differing sources a 45mm BM (high power) tank gun – likely an early 45mm M-1942.

The first ZiS-30s produced entered combat at the end of September 1941, literally a few days after series production had begun. The combat history of the ZiS-30 is intertwined with the towed 57mm ZiS-2, usually described as the '57mm Gun PTO', and sometimes noted as the 57mm SAU or as the '57mm gun on tractor chassis'.

In service the ZiS-30 proved to be a highly effective tank killer, but suffered from a higher than standard number of mechanical failures, such that many machines were abandoned rather than destroyed. Immediately after the combat debut of the ZiS-30, a plenum of ArtKom GAU held on 1 October 1941 under the direction of Eh.A. Satel reviewed the performance of the new machine as having been successful, being a proven and now mobile anti-tank weapon. Records indicate that 72 of these SAUs within 20 separate tank brigades partook in the battles around Moscow in November–December 1941, and were integral to PTO (anti-tank) batteries that operated on the Western, Bryansk and South Western Fronts during 1941–42. After a winter of defensive combat experience, ArtKom GAU on 15 April 1942 reviewed the performance of several weapons systems, including the ZiS-30. The feedback from combat units indicated known and some additional deficiencies. The firing height and chassis stability were accepted design compromises, with lack of ammunition stowage, insufficient armour protection for the engine compartment and limited operational range being additionally noted. The ZiS-30 had by the early summer served its stopgap role, however, and few vehicles had survived the decisive winter of the war that held Axis forces, with the Red Army now beginning the turn to offensive operations.

Soviet-era sources indicated that all ZiS-30s were lost in the Battle for Moscow in the early winter of 1941, but based on recent access to formerly closed archive records a small number (less than 20) appear to have remained in service as late as April 1942, with the last documented survivor being recorded as in inventory in early 1944.

In the spring of 1942, a group of engineers under the direction of Muravev built a ZiS-30 variant armed with a 76.2mm ZiS-3 dual-purpose gun, however plant trials were unsuccessful and the project was terminated. The 57mm ZiS-2 was also mounted on the ZiS-22 half-track chassis and tested for service in November 1941. The future of 57mm calibre anti-tank weapons was however by that time already under question, and the ZiS-22 chassis not available in any quantity due to the evacuation of the ZiS plant from Moscow.

SU-S2

A later project to build a self-propelled gun on a tracked tractor chassis was the SU-S2, developed to prototype stage at ChTZ in Chelyabinsk on the chassis of the Stalinets-2 tractor. The principle design idea was to utilize weapons and equipment produced in the Urals region. The only available tractor chassis suitable for a self-propelled installation was the Stalinets-2 (S-2 or ST-2) transport tractor. The S-2 had been delivered to operational units only after the outbreak of war, and in service had proven to be slow and not particularly reliable, but it was in the late summer of 1941 the only chassis available at ChTZ. The tractor suspension and running gear was however considered too short and unstable for a self-propelled gun mounting and so it was radically modified. ChTZ designers developed an elongated chassis, in which only the drive wheel and track support rollers remained from the running gear of the S-2. The suspension was changed to torsion bar type, with modified road wheels and return rollers taken from the KV-1 tank then entering production at ChTZ.

The SU-S2 was developed to prototype stage at ChTZ in Chelyabinsk based on the Stalinets-2 tractor with entirely rebuilt running gear and a casemate hull mounting a 122mm M-1938 (M-30) howitzer, the same armament as the UZTM built later in the war. The prototype was completed in October 1941 but series production was not undertaken, not least because the S-2 was removed from production to make way for KV tank assembly.

A combined casemate armoured control and fighting compartment was installed on the modified chassis. The driver's position remained as before but with a single seat and the driver being more restricted in movement. The rear of the fighting compartment accommodated the gun crew and ammunition. The SU-S2 was armed with a 122mm M-1938 (M-30) howitzer as later used on the T-34 based SU-122 self-propelled assault gun due to the fact that the weapon was produced at UZTM in 'nearby' Sverdlovsk (today Ekaterinburg), where its chief designer, F.F. Petrov, was at the time also based. The M-30 was the only gun system mass-produced in the Urals region at that time (hence also the reasoning behind development of the SU-122 on the T-34 chassis).

According to limited surviving documentation, the single SU-S2 prototype was completed in October 1941, with plant trials undertaken immediately thereafter. The SU-S2 was one of several Soviet medium SAU designs developed on the basis of tractor chassis at the time, but the only design to be have been developed to prototype stage. The limitations of such a hybrid SAU were clear, and series production would have been relatively complex. The main factor that determined the fate of the SU-S2 was however unrelated to the design itself. With the LKZ plant in Leningrad in the process of evacuation to Chelyabinsk, the ChTZ plant there was by the autumn of 1941 preparing for KV heavy tank production. With tank rather than tractor assembly now the priority at ChTZ, S-65 and S-2 tractor production was terminated and the SU-S2 project cancelled due to lack of available chassis.

STZ-5 BM-13 'KATYUSHA' MRS

At the beginning of the war, the Moscow Kompressor plant had just begun in collaboration with sub-contractor plants in Moscow and the region to build 132mm BM-13 'Katyusha' multiple rocket launchers (MRS) on the wheeled 6x4 ZiS-6 chassis, based on technical documentation provided by the Komintern plant in Voronezh. On 4 July 1941, Soviet Minister P.I. Parshin ordered 210 BM-13 MRS be built at the plant in July and August. This quantity was on 2 August increased to 339, with an expectation that 456 BM-13 MRS be

An STZ-5 based BM-13 'Katyusha' MRS in winter camouflage firing a salvo near Stalingrad, December 1942.

assembled on the ZiS-6 chassis by 1 November 1941, representing the remaining ZiS-6 chassis inventory located at ZiS in Moscow. ZiS-6 assembly was curtailed at the ZiS plant in October 1941 as machine tooling and personnel began to be evacuated by rail to Miass, located safely beyond the Ural mountains. As the ZiS-6 was at the time the main chassis on which the BM-13 'Katyusha' MRS was mounted, the Kompressor plant had no available chassis on which to mount BM-13 PU (Puskovaya Ustanovka – launcher mounting) vehicles; and alternative chassis were required to mount the system as an interim measure.

ABOVE LEFT A destroyed STZ-5 BM-13. Note the rubber rimmed road wheels, road track and the opening windscreen windows. (Sergei Popsuevich)

ABOVE A Russian drawing of the STZ-5 BM-13.

LEFT This destroyed STZ-5 BM-13 has the all-steel road wheels usually associated with the STZ-NATI 1TA (STZ-3) tractor.

ABOVE The STZ-5 BM-13 recovered from the Shatskoye reservoir near Novomoskovsk as it appeared when landed on the shore.

ABOVE RIGHT The STZ-5 BM-13 recovered from the Shatskoye reservoir near Novomoskovsk after initial restoration.

RIGHT The same STZ-5 BM-13 at a local museum in Novomoskovsk. (Sergei Popsuevich)

In light of an upcoming deficit of wheeled chassis, the Defence Committee (KO) in early September 1941 ordered designers at NATI and the Kompressor plant to develop a combat vehicle for the BM-13 rocket launcher based on the tracked STZ-5 artillery tractor chassis. The Special (rocket system) Design Bureau (SKB) directed by V.P. Barmin responsible for BM-8 and BM-13 'Katyusha' production was instructed to develop a BM-8-24 PU for the 82mm BM-8 rocket launcher on the T-40 and or T-60 tank chassis, with a similar modification for the larger calibre 16-rail 132mm BM-13 system to be based on the STZ-5 chassis. Design engineers at the Kompressor plant under the direction of lead designer A.N. Vasiliev developed the high mobility all-terrain variants per KO instructions in collaboration with NATI engineers including N.I. Korotonoshko, E.G. Popov and B.N. Tikhomirov. A BM-8 prototype was per instruction duly mounted on a light tank chassis and a BM-13 variant on the STZ-5 NATI (as designated in plant documentation) tractor chassis.

Development of the BM-13 PU vehicle mounted on the STZ-5 chassis was undertaken by the Barmin SKB under the direction of Vasiliev in collaboration with the Komintern plant in Voronezh. Barmin argued that the STZ-5 represented a relatively powerful tracked chassis with better mobility than a truck, and without the weight of unnecessary armour that applied to the T-40 and T-60 chassis. The STZ-5 mounted BM-13 MRS received the SKB index KS-75, with the GAU index used by the Red Army being 52-TR-492. The tractor was referred to in internal documents as the STZ-NATI rather than by its full designation STZ-NATI 2TV.

The first four prototypes were completed at the Kompressor plant at the end of September 1941. Polygon trials conducted in the first days of October showed the 8,200kg vehicle to have better all-terrain mobility than the ZiS-6 chassis, with a slower but adequate road speed of 21.5km/h, an all-terrain speed moving between firing positions of 10–14km/h and a road range of 200km. The STZ-5 based BM-13 could fire a full salvo of any M-13 rocket type in eight to ten seconds, with reload taking eight to ten minutes. The BM-13 had a maximum firing range of 8,470m. The new STZ-5 mounted BM-13, now formally designated KS-75, was officially accepted for service on 13 October 1941, with the production drawings having in the meantime been sent to the Komintern plant in Voronezh to establish series production there.

Obtaining the STZ-5 chassis required for series production proved difficult, due to the perennial deficit of artillery tractors, with the Red Army – as with the requisitioning of Komsomolets tractors for the ZiS-30 SAU – not being unduly inclined to give them up, and few STZ-5 chassis in civil service that could be requisitioned. A small series of STZ-5 BM-13 MRS was nevertheless manufactured in Voronezh from November 1941 and delivered to newly formed rocket artillery units. Production continued until the spring of 1942 when Voronezh came under threat from advancing Axis forces.

In service the STZ-5 BM-13 PU combination proved a stable and highly mobile launch platform, but with a relatively slow road speed compared to the wheeled ZiS-6 chassis, and considerably reduced range, a design compromise that had been accepted from the outset. The slow travel speed resulted in many STZ-BM-13 vehicles being destroyed while in transit between fire positions, hence such moves were often taken at night. The STZ-5 tractor based BM-13 'Katyusha' rocket launchers were used in the

The STZ-5 BM-13 as photographed by the author in Novomoskovsk. The restored machine was built on a modified STZ-5 chassis, with the BM-13 launcher, cab blast shields and rear stabilizers, and used standard STZ-5 rubber rimmed road wheels and road track.

defence of Moscow in the early winter of 1941–42, with the majority of STZ-5 mounted BM-13 MRS lost in combat that winter. Immediately after the Red Square parade of 7 November 1941, STZ-5 based BM-13 PU vehicles of the 12th Separate Guards Mortar (Rocket Artillery) Division formed in Alabino on 9 November 1941 were deployed on the front line near the city of Kashira, and were later used near the town of Stalinogorsk (today Novomoskovsk) near Tula. On 11 December 1942, four STZ mounted BM-13s launched salvoes against Axis forces located at Maklets (some sources state Uzlovaya) railway station. On the night of 14 December the division relocated to a new fire position on the south side of the Shatskoye water reservoir north of the town by driving across the ice of the frozen reservoir. Three vehicles completed the move, but the fourth, the 3rd Launcher Unit of the 1st Battery of the 12th Guards Mortar Division, was lost when it broke through the ice and sank in the reservoir. Nearly half a century later, in 1988, it was located, restored locally to running condition and ceremoniously plinth-mounted outside the regional museum in the town where it remains to the present day. The few surviving STZ-5 based BM-13 systems continued in service, with the system also used in the defence of Stalingrad the following year.

VOROSHILOV BASED SAU PROJECTS

With the T-34 medium tank in series production at Plant No. 183, development work had been undertaken at the plant on potential artillery tractors based on the T-34 chassis, with the aforementioned AT-42 armoured tractor being developed to prototype stage in June 1940 and several T-34 based SAU projects being developed to varying stages of completion before June 1941. On the outbreak of war, tank assembly took immediate priority over all other production, with T-34 chassis being only reluctantly provided for potential SAU developments. The Voroshilovets tractor chassis as previously rejected by GABTU KA remained available at the plant however. At the end of June 1941, the factory KB on its own initiative developed a technical design for installing an 85mm gun on a tractor chassis, while design work was concurrently begun on another combat vehicle on the Voroshilovets chassis. On 27 August 1941, a technical meeting was held at Plant No. 183, to review self-propelled gun projects. Among them was the A-46, an 85mm SAU based on the T-34 chassis which had been in development since 1940, and two SAUs based on the Voroshilovets heavy artillery tractor. Articles 1–3 of the written protocol (meeting minutes) concerned SAUs on the T-34 tank chassis, while points 4–6 noted:

4. Planned production by the plant during October–November – 25 pcs. SAU should be approved on condition that the specified number of SAUs will be in addition to the number of Voroshilovets tractors ordered by the NKO.
5. The first SAU prototype to be submitted for testing to the NKO-NKSM Commission, and according to the test results with necessary corrections introduced into series production.
6. In order to increase the armament capability of the Voroshilovets armoured tractor, the plant, together with GAU and Plant No. 8, should determine the possibility of installing on this SAU an 85mm anti-aircraft gun provided by Plant No. 8.

In the event, the ongoing concentration on T-34 tank production at Plant No. 183 curtailed the Voroshilovets based developments. The tractor remained under development however at Artillery Plant No. 8 in Kaliningrad (later Korolev) near Moscow. During the period when it was being evacuated to Ekaterinburg, and perhaps as a follow-on from work related to the developments outlined above, Artillery Plant No. 8 developed the designs for an 85mm M-1939 (52-K*) anti-aircraft gun – the main weapon built at the plant – mounted on the Voroshilovets chassis. Development was curtailed with the evacuation of the plant.

152-SG (SG-152)

The last documented wartime instance of a medium SAU being developed on the chassis of an artillery tractor was the 152-SG, designed at Plant No. 592 in the spring of 1942 under the direction of E.V. Sinilshikov and S.G. Pererushev as a prototype SAU mounted on the Komintern artillery tractor chassis. The priority at the plant was at the time the 122-SG (also known as the SG-122) based on captured German Sturmgeschütz (StuG-III) chassis. The designers nevertheless continued to consider domestic chassis options, including the 152-SG, to be armed with a 152mm M-1909/30 howitzer and specifically intended for destroying DZOT bunkers in the manner of the KV-2 heavy tank. The 152-SG (the designation of which was also transposed as SG-152 in some drawings) had a crew of five and a projected combat weight of 18.5 tonnes. The design envisaged a highly faceted armoured casemate with an armour basis of 15mm: deemed sufficient to protect the crew from 12.7mm DShK heavy machine gun (or rather Axis equivalent) rounds fired from a range of 200m. Another variant envisaged an

* K – Kalinin (the Kalinin Plant, Kaliningrad).

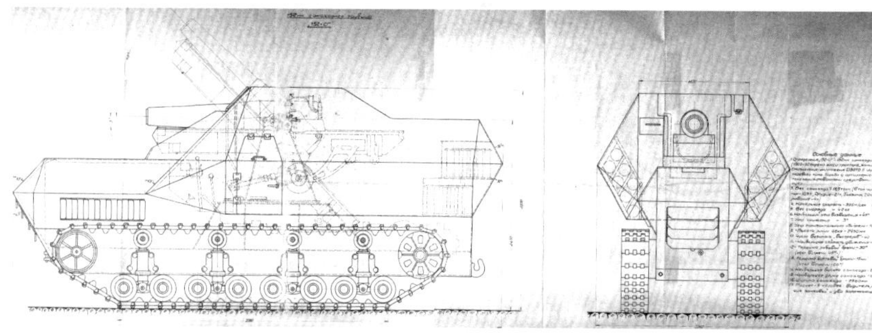

SAU with an increased 30mm armour basis. Although the 152-SG was potentially a powerful 'bunker buster' it did not progress beyond the design project stage, primarily because the Komintern artillery tractor on which it was based was already out of production and in short supply for its primary artillery tractor role, while the obsolescent 152mm M-1909/30 howitzer also proved scarcer than originally envisaged.

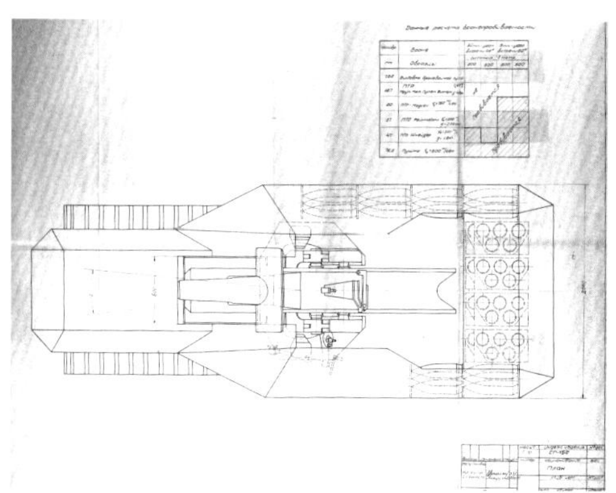

The 152mm SG-152 (also referred to as 152-SG) project envisaged a machine armed with 152mm M-1909/30 howitzer armament on the chassis of the Komintern tractor and intended primarily for destroying DZOT bunkers. The tractor design considered various alternative and secondary armament including a 12.7mm PTR (anti-tank rifle) and 37mm 'Rheinmetall' and 47mm 'Schneider' weapons, with the option of a 76.2mm tank gun.

A-46 SAU

In 1941, among several projects to create tank destroyers was the A-46 SAU, developed by the KB of Plant No. 183 based on the A-42 (AT-42) tractor developed pre-war on the T-34 chassis. Armament was to be the 105-K gun modified at Plant No. 8, which was to be mounted with a gun shield on the AT-42 chassis at the rear of the vehicle with a 360° traverse in a similar arrangement to the German semi-tracked 8.8cm Flak 18 (Sfl.) auf Zugkraftwagen 12t (Sd.Kfz.8). The exact appearance of the A-46 is to date unknown, albeit the layout is clear from written specifications. The A-46 was considered for production in September 1941 and a prototype was apparently tested at the plant the following month, but there was no further development as all plans to use the long-in-development AT-42 (A-42) chassis evaporated as the plant prepared for evacuation, and the project was not carried forward at the new plant location at Nizhny Tagil.

SU-45 (STZ-5) (PLANT No. 264)

With the outbreak of war and an urgent need for armoured vehicles of all types, Plant No. 264 at Krasnoarmeisk near Stalingrad considered a project to convert STZ-5 tractors produced in the city to tracked SAU vehicles, mounting a 45mm anti-tank gun in a casemate armoured hull. Plant No. 264 supplied the armour sets for (and latterly assembled) the T-60 small tank, and built the Project 1124 and 1125 gunboats fitted with T-34 turrets, so was well versed in such design work. This project too did not progress beyond initial drawing concept stage due to tank production priorities at STZ.

ChTZ STALINETS-2 (S-2) TANK DESTROYER

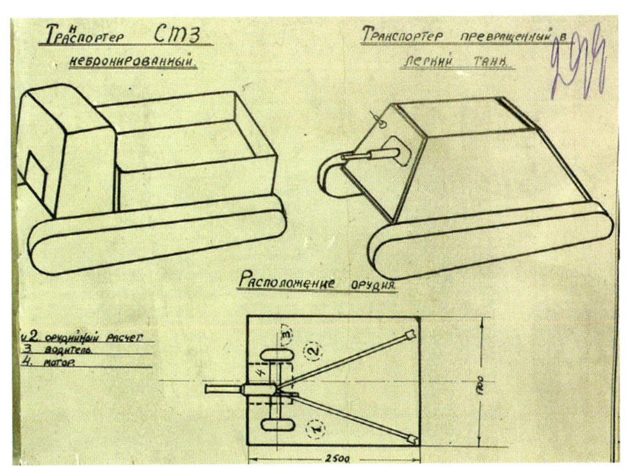

A Soviet concept diagram reviewing the potential conversion of STZ-5 tractors at Plant No. 264 to light tanks (as described) by means of armouring, and the installation of a 45mm anti-tank gun.

After the Stalinets-2 (S-2) had ceased production at ChTZ in favour of increased tank output, there remained a number of unassembled components at the plant. As one of several such projects at the time, engineers at ChTZ proposed building a fully armoured SAU on the basis of the S-2 chassis, armed with the 76.2mm ZiS-5 gun then being installed in the KV heavy tank at the same plant. The paper designs indicated a low profile (1.8m high) machine, with 25–32mm armour and a combat weight of under 7,000kg and a similarly theoretical speed of 40km/h. The project did not progress beyond the paper design initiative stage as it was clear the S-2 would not re-enter production at ChTZ and so there was no chassis available to realize the design in metal.

SU-57 AND SU-76 PROTOTYPES

In the early summer of 1943, a NATI initiative headed by V.Ya. Slominsky developed an SAU powered by two parallel GAZ-M (MM) engines mounted in an armoured hull based on work undertaken developing the original Tyagach Type D prototype for the original Ya-11 and later series production Ya-12; intended to be armed with either the 57mm ZiS-4 or 76.2mm F-34 tank guns. Both prototypes were approved for development in accordance with GKO Resolution No. 3187ss dated 15 April 1943. In May, a GKO meeting to review the design was held at NATI, headed by V.M. Ryabikov (NKV) and attended by NKSM and NKV representatives. The two prototypes were approved for further development, which was undertaken by GAZ in Gorky under GAZ designations using components common to the T-70 tank and SU-76 SAU.

CHAPTER 9
IMPROVISED ARMOURED TRACTORS

The Dyrenkov D-10 (based on a Kommunar chassis) and very similar D-11 (based on a Caterpillar-60 chassis) during evaluation trials.

Tracked artillery tractors were integral to the early development of armoured vehicles in the years leading up to the Russian Revolution of 1917. Armoured cars such as the Austin-Putilovets and Fiat-Izhorsk built in Russia on imported chassis were widely used by the Imperial Russian Army during World War I, as were armoured cars built on half-track chassis. In 1915, Colonel of Artillery Gulkevich developed and patented the first Russian bronetraktor armoured tractor – also effectively a tank – on the basis that what a tracked tractor chassis sacrificed in road performance was made up for by all-terrain mobility. In 1916, a 'tankotraktor' based on an Allis-Chalmers chassis and named 'Ilya Muromets' left the gates of the Putilov plant in St Petersburg but only a very small number of such vehicles were built. The armoured tractor was duly replaced by the tank in the post-revolutionary Soviet Union as purpose designed tank chassis became available, and the concept of armoured tractors became dormant. At the beginning of the 1930s, prototype armoured tractors were again developed on tracked tractor chassis, ostensibly as a means of adding to the overall tank park in times of war rather than specifically orientated towards use as artillery tractors, but these tractors, which were development prototypes rather than improvised designs, also did not enter series production. The concept continued to be considered periodically in the years ahead, however, and would be revived in earnest during the darkest months of World War II in the late summer of 1941.

DYRENKOV ARMOURED TRACTORS

In 1930, the UMM RKKA approved a design initiative by its director, engineer N.I. Dyrenkov for a series of bronetraktor armoured tractor prototypes utilizing tracked tractor chassis then entering series production in the Soviet Union. Dyrenkov's design group duly developed four such armoured tractor prototypes, three based on the Kommunar 9GU chassis and one based on an imported Caterpillar-60 chassis, a modified variant of which would soon thereafter be mass produced at the newly constructed ChTZ plant in Chelyabinsk as the Stalinets-60 (S-60). The prototypes were assembled at the Mozherez plant (later renamed the Lyubinsk Casting-Metallurgical Plant) based on tractor chassis delivered to the plant.

The Dyrenkov D-10 was armed with a 76.2mm M-1927 regimental gun and two 7.62mm DT machine guns with four alternative ball mountings. It was tested for Red Army service at the Kubinka polygon in May 1931.

DYRENKOV D-10

The Dyrenkov D-10 prototype mounted a 76.2mm M-1927 regimental gun and two 7.62mm DT machine guns in an armoured casemate mounted on a Kommunar 9GU chassis, with four alternative ball mountings for the DT weapons. The prototype of what was effectively a close-support gun or 'SAU', as such vehicles would later be commonly known, was completed in February 1931.

DYRENKOV D-11

The Dyrenkov D-11 was nearly identical to the D-10, using an identical armoured casemate with the same 76.2mm M-1927 main armament and two DT machine guns with a four ball mounting secondary armament arrangement, but mounted on an imported Caterpillar-60 chassis. The prototype was completed in February 1931, with the D-10 and D-11 competitively tested at Kubinka in May of the same year.

The Dyrenkov D-14, based on a modified Kommunar chassis, was a tracked 'bronetransporter' (BTR) which also underwent trials in May 1931.

DYRENKOV D-14

The Dyrenkov D-14 was developed as a tracked 'bronetransporter' (BTR) or armoured personnel carrier for 15 'desant' infantry, also on a modified Kommunar chassis; the D-14 was also armed with two DT machine guns with four alternate ball mountings. The completed vehicle was handed over for trials in May 1931.

DYRENKOV D-15

The Dyrenkov D-15 was a chemical tank with two contaminating agent reservoirs with a combined capacity of 4,000 litres and two sets of dispersing apparatus for chemical ground contamination. The D-15 was armed with a single DT machine gun, with four alternative ball mount firing points in the casemate hull. Development of the D-15 was at a more leisurely pace than the other variants, with the prototype being incomplete in May 1931 at the time the other prototypes were evaluated for military service.

The D-10, D-11 and D-14 were tested at the NIABP UMM polygon at Kubinka in May 1931.The vehicles performed satisfactorily, but noted defects included engine overheating, lack of fume extraction with a build-up of toxic fumes in the fighting compartments, limited driver-mechanic visibility and not least the maximum speed of 5km/h in keeping with their base chassis being unacceptable for a military vehicle. Accordingly, none of the Dyrenkov designs were developed beyond prototype stage. The D-15 was completed slightly later, and remained at the Mozherez plant at the end of 1932.

KPD ARMOURED TRACTOR

The KPD (Katerpillar Podolsky Dieselny – Podolsk Caterpillar–Diesel) was an armoured tractor developed for use in forward Front areas. It was also a prototype development rather than an improvization, but with experience in armouring and arming tractors as combat vehicles dating from the early KPD development. The KPD was developed and built at the Podolsk plant near Moscow in 1931, based on an imported Caterpillar-60 tractor chassis. The KPD had separate armoured compartments for the engine and for the driver and machine gunner so as to reduce overall combat weight and maximize performance. The driver's armoured casemate was provided with a turret similar to the ancillary turrets used on the later T-28 medium and T-35 heavy tanks, armed with a DT machine gun.

The KPD was powered by a Soviet sourced and apparently capricious diesel (motor oil) engine developing 60–78hp, with low road speed as expected from the base chassis utilized. The KPD prototype was tested concurrently with a

The KPD armoured tractor, built in Podolsk near Moscow in 1931, was based on a Caterpillar-60 chassis and was designed for towing artillery in forward areas. The separate engine and fighting compartments were designed to save weight.

pre-series S-60 and several other tractors for towing artillery in forward areas, being described during trials both as 'bronnirovanny traktor' (armoured tractor) and 'artillerisky tyagach' (artillery tractor). Final trials began on 24 February 1932 and lasted for three weeks. In the period 1–16 March 1932 the KPD travelled 300km on road and 50km on dirt roads towing a 203mm B-4 tracked howitzer among other artillery pieces, and a road train consisting of two P-26 3-tonne load military trailers. The KPD performed per requirements, with the armour clearly being an advantage for its intended role, but the average speed was unsurprisingly a low 5.9km/h (albeit not much slower than the base tractor chassis), with poor traction on loose surfaces and difficulty in starting. The KPD was not accepted for service, but the prototype was later used at the Podolsk plant to evaluate potential engine and drivetrain arrangements; these included a diesel engine developing 60–78hp at 850rpm tested in 1933, providing a Stalinets-60 tractor with a 17.9km/h test speed as the Soviet Union worked to perfect diesel engine technology for tanks and artillery tractors.

As Soviet tank production expanded exponentially in the 1930s, the armouring of tractors became a dormant theme, but it was resurrected with the urgent need for armoured vehicles in the late summer of 1941 to replace horrendous battlefield losses, with plants in Kharkov, Odessa, Stalingrad and some other cities involved in the development of wartime armoured tractor designs.

On 20 July 1941, GKO Resolution No. 19 *About Screening Light Tanks and About Armoured Tractors* was issued, requiring tracked KhTZ tractors from

Kharkov and STZ tractors from Stalingrad to be armed with 45mm tank guns and used as SAUs, with overall development under the direction of NATI. The NATI KB worked on several such tractor conversion plans, including a project undertaken from June to October 1941 to install a 37mm M-1939 ZU anti-aircraft gun mounting on the chassis of the STZ-NATI (designated as the 1 TMB – either a KhTZ or STZ-3) tractor.

In June 1941, according to the NATI official history, engineers N.I. Korotonoshko and I.I. Trepenenkov in five days assembled two prototype armoured SAUs armed with a 76.2mm gun on the basis of the STZ-5 chassis modified by I.I. Drong, for which the Podolsk Machine Building Plant near Moscow (which had developed the KPD armoured tractor) was to produce the armoured hulls, with series production to be undertaken at KhTZ in Kharkov. The prototypes were tested at the NATI polygon and this project would appear to be an early development for what would become the KhT-16 as later built at KhTZ. In early August 1941, NATI built four prototype armoured tractor variants, all armed with a 45mm tank gun, on the basis of both the STZ-NATI 1TA (SKhTZ-NATI/STZ-3/KhTZ-3) agricultural and STZ-5 transport tractor chassis, of which a single prototype was evaluated at the Kubinka polygon for Red Army service. The production of armoured tractors was ultimately focused on the KhTZ-16 chassis assembled at KhTZ in Kharkov, but at the time various contingency measures were considered involving KhTZ, STZ and other plants. A separate bronetraktor production plan, signed off in August 1941, authorized the conversion of 2,000 STZ tractors at Plant No. 264 near Stalingrad, which produced armour hull and turret sets for the T-34 as assembled at STZ. These large scale production plans remained unfulfilled.

KhTZ-16 (KhT-16) 'KHARKOV TANK'

With the outbreak of war, designers at NATI in early July 1941 returned to the pre-war idea of utilizing tractor chassis to build bronetraktor armoured and armed tractors – i.e. makeshift tanks and SAUs – in the event of a major war. Contingency plans for production had already been initiated pre-war, and the speed of development in the summer of 1941 would suggest that much of the work undertaken at NATI and KhTZ in 1941 was based on existing plans.

The NATI armoured tractor design team was headed by V.Ya. Slonimsky, who had led the development of the SKhTZ-NATI into the production STZ-NATI 1TA (STZ-3/KhTZ-3), and E.G. Popov, who would later create the NATI-D prototype for the Ya-11 and later Ya-12. They were assisted by A.M. Cherepin and A.V. Sapozhnikov. By mid-July NATI had prepared the technical project for an armoured tractor on the basis of the STZ-NATI 1TA

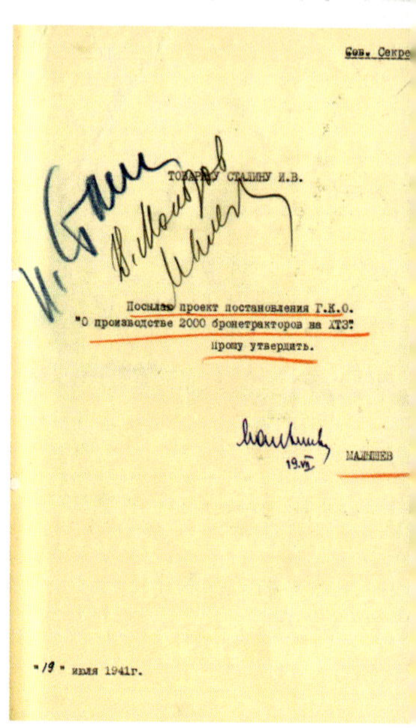

Сов. Секре

ТОВАРИЩУ СТАЛИНУ И.В.

Посылаю проект постановления Г.К.О.
"О производстве 2000 бронетракторов на ХТЗ"
Прошу утвердить.

МАЛЫШЕВ

"19" июля 1941г.

ABOVE The SKhTZ-NATI was an unarmoured artillery tractor design based on KhTZ-3 components, developed to prototype stage in June 1941, with the rubber rimmed road wheels and road track as used on the STZ-5. The machine was closely related to the armoured and armed KhT-16.

ABOVE RIGHT The signature page of the GKO draft resolution forwarded to Stalin by V.A. Malyshev (the People's Commissar at NKSM, the ministry responsible for tank production) for the production of 2,000 armoured tractors at KhTZ in Kharkov. Stalin's approval signature is in blue ink on the far left of the page.

(SKhTZ-NATI) and sent it to V.A. Malyshev, the People's Commissar for Medium Machine Building (NKSM). The NATI proposal was approved – with some reservations – and on 19 July 1941 Malyshev sent Stalin a draft resolution for approval requiring the assembly of 2,000 'KhTZ' combat vehicles by 1 September 1941. In addition to defining the base chassis as the SKhTZ-NATI (STZ-NATI 1TA), GKO Resolution No. 219/ss specified that the armament was to be a 45mm M-1938 (20-K) tank gun mounted in a casemate hull with a 75 round ammunition complement, with a co-axial 7.62mm DT machine gun and a crew of two – gunner/commander and driver-mechanic/machine gunner. The frontal armour was to be 30mm, with 13mm on the hull sides and 10mm roof armour. The tractor had an expected road speed of 18–20km/h, reducing to 10km/h on dirt roads. Production was initially considered for both KhTZ (producing the KhTZ-3) and STZ (producing the near identical STZ-3); however, GKO Resolution No. 219/ss, as signed by Stalin on 20 July 1941 and entitled *About the Organization of Production of Two Thousand Armoured Tractors*, designated that assembly of these armoured tractors be undertaken exclusively at KhTZ in Kharkov, with 50 to be assembled in the final days of July, rising rapidly to 850 in August and 1,100 in September.

The specific designation KhTZ-16 rather than the generic term 'bronetraktor' appears in formal correspondence at the beginning of August 1941, by which time engineers at NATI and KhTZ were already collaborating to introduce the new bronetraktor into series production. Plans to also assemble the KhTZ-16 at STZ remained unfulfilled, not least due to STZ being critically focused on T-34

A destroyed or abandoned KhTZ-16 with what appear to be Wehrmacht troops posing for staged photographs rather than the surrender of the Red Army crew.

tank and STZ-5 artillery tractor production. KhTZ-16 production was also considered by Plant No. 64. While the Kharkov designed KhTZ-16 was undergoing trials at Kubinka, the engineers Krasilshikov and Nemchinsky at Plant No. 264 in Stalingrad wrote a letter to Stalin and the NKSP (shipbuilding) Commissar, I.I. Nosenko, suggesting that Plant No. 264 could build armoured tractors using the Stalingrad-built STZ-5 artillery tractor chassis. The suggestion was declined, but even had it been approved, Plant No. 264 was loaded with building hull and turret sets and other components for T-34 assembly at STZ in Stalingrad, and had additionally received orders to begin assembly of the T-60 'small' tank (T-60s were at the time defined as 'small' rather than 'light' tanks). Plant No. 264 was not, therefore, in a position to also assemble KhTZ-16 type 'bronetraktori'. A lack of armoured casemate production capability for KhTZ-16 type armoured tractors would in any event have prevented the KhTZ-16 from being more widely assembled at Stalingrad and Plant No. 264.

ABOVE LEFT The majority of KhTZ-16 bronetraktori armoured tractors were destroyed in the fighting of late 1941.

ABOVE This KhTZ-16 has armour-piercing penetrations in the casemate superstructure armour. Note the combination of KhTZ-3 all-steel road wheels but STZ-5 type road tracks.

(A) An abandoned KhTZ-16. The 45mm M-1938 (20-K) tank gun was the same armament as fitted in the T-26, BT fast tank series and other Russian tanks, but the casemate structure near vertical and relatively thin armour was vulnerable. **(B)** This view of a destroyed KhTZ-16 clearly shows the main access crew hatch in the rear armour. There were a further two hatches in the superstructure roof, but these were not ideal for egress, especially in combat conditions. **(C) (D)** A KhTZ-16 in camouflage paintwork destroyed in the winter of 1941–42. **(E)** The same KhTZ-16 during summer months, the bronetraktor having been apparently left where destroyed for a long period of time. **(F)** A burned out KhTZ-16 in central Kharkov, November 1941. Note again the all-steel rather than rubber rimmed roadwheels. **(G)** Many KhTZ-16 bronetraktori such as this abandoned example were painted in an ad hoc camouflage scheme. **(H)** A reproduction KhTZ-16 at the Urals Military Glory Museum, Verkhnyaya Pyshma, Ekaterinburg. (John Ham)

An armoured STZ-3 bronetraktor believed to have been produced at the Izhorsk plant near Leningrad. This machine, with turret mounted 12.7mm DShK armament and faceted armour, is painted in the official standard pre-war three-colour summer camouflage scheme. Several cities built a small number of bronetraktori in addition to Kharkov and Odessa.

In the first days of August, in accordance with GKO Resolution No. 019 *About the Additional Armouring of Light Tanks and the Armouring of Tractors*, and the aforementioned Resolution No. 219/ss, designers at NATI including Popov, Sapozhnikov and Cherepin under the direction of Slonimsky, together with a design group at KhTZ under the direction of chief design engineer M.S. Sidelnikov, meanwhile worked to complete two prototypes for evaluation by 12 August. Only a single prototype was completed in time for Red Army trials at the NIABP proving grounds at Kubinka. Some sources indicate, as noted earlier, that four rather than two armoured tractors were developed to prototype stage in the first days of August, based on four different tracked chassis, the 1 TMB (based on the STZ-NATI 1TA), STZ-3 and SKhTZ-NATI 'agricultural' tractors and the STZ-5 transport tractor, all armed with a 45mm tank gun mounted in a limited traverse mantlet, with DT machine gun secondary armament. This may be a conflation of work being carried out at NATI and at KhTZ. Nevertheless, only a single armoured and armed prototype was sent to Kubinka for trials; it was based on the STZ-NATI 1TA chassis, had a casemate hull with an armour basis of 10–25mm and was fitted with the 'road track' of the STZ-5. The trials were deemed successful, and the bronetraktor armoured tractor or 'tractor tank' was approved for series production at KhTZ in Kharkov as the KhTZ-16.*

* The KhTZ-16 was sometimes abbreviated to KhT-16 (Kharkov Tank – 16) in official records.

The KhTZ-16 prototype was assembled from available components, with inevitable compromises. Due to the lack of 13.5mm steel plate, the prototype used 10mm plate on the hull sides, with the majority of the armour from non-hardened steel. The production KhTZ-16 had 10–20mm frontal armour, 10mm side armour and 25mm armour plate on the front 'rubka' of the casemate structure. By the time the prototype was released for testing, KhTZ was already completing chassis modifications for the new bronetraktor.

Historically it was always assumed that the Stalingrad-built STZ-3 and or even the STZ-5 was used as the chassis for the KhTZ-16, but recently uncovered wartime archive material indicates that this is not the case. The technical drawings for the KhTZ-16 clearly indicate that the chassis was based on existing design work for an unarmoured artillery tractor based on the Kharkov-built SKhTZ-NATI (KhTZ-3) version of the STZ-NATI 1TA tractor, albeit the STZ-3 was essentially the same NATI design built at another plant, with the base chassis being effectively interchangeable with some reconfiguration of the control mechanisms, such that either plant could have supplied chassis. The development inter-relationship between the designers and manufacturers of the STZ-3/KhTZ-3, STZ-5 and KhTZ-16 remains somewhat opaque. The majority of components were interchangeable among all the tractor variants, with the gearbox ratios allowing a higher road speed on the STZ-5 and KhTZ-16 tractors. All the tractor modifications originated at the NATI design bureau in Moscow and were further evolved for manufacturing at KhTZ and STZ, thereby considering the component interchangeability it would seem likely that optional control linkages for rear or forward control cab options and specialized variants were designed from the outset. The SKhTZ-NATI chassis required 27 significant engineering changes to make it suitable as the chassis for the KhTZ-16, inevitable since SKhTZ-NATI with its front mounted engine and rear cab did not immediately lend itself to providing good internal space for an armoured fighting vehicle. The four-cylinder kerosene fuel 1MA engine was slightly uprated from 52 to 58hp: a moderate increase, but with the KhTZ-16 adding 3,500kg of armour and armament onto the KhTZ-16 chassis (for a combat weight of 8,600kg – 7,800kg per different sources) any additional power output from the engine was critical. Due to the significantly increased and now 'combat' weight, and uprated engine, the transmission also had to be strengthened. For good measure, the chassis was extended, rubber rimmed 'road' wheels as used on the STZ-5 were fitted when available and the return rollers were moved forward slightly. The STZ-5 'road' track that replaced the agricultural track used on the SKhTZ-NATI (KhTZ-3) and STZ-3 was better suited for a combat vehicle, allowing higher road speed, with less vibration and extended track life in combined surface use. The fuel tank was moved to the left of the vehicle, and the driver-mechanic's position moved slightly forward and to the right to provide a better working layout within the fighting compartment for the commander and gunner/loader. The KhT-16 had a maximum road speed of 17km/h and a range of 119km.

Effectively armouring the diminutive SKhTZ-NATI chassis was a challenge. The base chassis was only 3.45m long, while the lengthened KhTZ-16 was 3.83m long and 1.87m wide, and 2.30m to the casemate superstructure roof. The 30mm glacis armour protecting the engine was sloped at 20°, and the fighting compartment increased in slope to 25°. The frontal elevations provided protection from large calibre machine guns and 20mm cannon fire, but the KhTZ-16 could not withstand fire from anti-tank guns. It was as well armoured as most contemporary Soviet light tanks, but with large near vertical armour surfaces. The armoured casemate was of welded construction, with the frontal glacis plate bolted on so as to allow engine access. Crew access hatches were confined to the vehicle's right side and rear, with visibility deemed acceptable. The 45mm tank gun was considered obsolescent by the autumn of 1941, but again compared not unfavourably with the armament of the majority of contemporary Soviet – and Axis – tanks.

PROTOTYPE TESTING AND EARLY PRODUCTION

Despite the urgency of the time, the prototype KhTZ-16 was subjected to extensive mobility and firing trials as would have been conducted with any pre-war tank design. During these trials, the KhTZ-16 travelled 470km, of which 139km was on made roads, 240km on cobbled roads, 69km on dirt roads and 22km on other surfaces. The KhTZ-16 managed an average road speed of 17km/h, reducing to approximately 9km/h when travelling across terrain. Range for the underpowered bronetraktor was limited, at 119km on roads and with an all-terrain range of 61km; however, as the vehicle was expected to participate in local defence, these figures were inconsequential. The uprated but overloaded engine ran very hot during testing, not aided by the fact that cooling air was drawn via the fighting compartment and that testing was conducted in summer temperatures of nearly 30°C. Other than minor track damage, the tests indicated no significant issues. Firing trials were also extensive, with 247 rounds fired of which 147 were armour-piercing rounds. Accuracy was observed as slightly below the standard firing table for 45mm armament, which was attributed to recoil forces affecting the weaker gun mounting. The calculated rate of fire was five rounds per minute. The armour around the rear of the gun mantlet was observed as inadequate, allowing small arms fire and shrapnel to penetrate when directed obliquely from behind the vehicle centreline.

The test results might be described as not untypical, particularly for an emergency hybrid tank designed under wartime conditions; however, the Red Army hierarchy was not impressed and dissenting opinion demanded the establishment of fully fledged (T-60) tank production at KhTZ in the shortest possible time. GKO Resolution No. 222 issued on 20 July 1941 instructed KhTZ to prepare for series production of the T-60 'small' tank, which might have terminated all further consideration of the KhTZ-16, but on 18 August as KhTZ was still receiving the production drawings and preparing machine tooling for T-60 assembly, there were 329 chassis for the KhTZ-16 then in various stages of final assembly at the plant, albeit with many lacking components such as electrical items and road track. By 30 August some 1,037 chassis had been completed – i.e. approximately 70 chassis a day were being built – but armoured hulls were not available in anything like the required quantities. Most KhTZ-16s were fitted with KhTZ-3 type all-steel road wheels, but a small number were fitted with rubber rimmed wheels from the STZ-5, with the smoother profile 'road tracks' of the STZ-5 fitted on all machines. Some components arriving for T-60 production, such as the observation devices, were purloined for the KhTZ-16.

The original plan had envisaged the assembly of as many as 750 KhTZ-16 conversions at KhTZ in August–September 1941, based on the STZ-3 or STZ-5 chassis (or rather NATI based tractor components)* with the welded casemate armoured hulls for the KhTZ-16 (and the T-60 armour sets also for KhTZ) to be provided by the Novo-Kramatorsk Machine Building Plant (Novokramatorsky Mashinostroitelny Zavod – NKMZ) and the Voroshilovgrad plant, with the armour plate provided by the Ilyich plant in Mariupol. Due largely to a lack of furnace capacity for heat treatment of the armour plate neither plant had by the end of August delivered a single armoured hull set to KhTZ. The situation being critical, the first 33 KhTZ-16s were assembled with hulls constructed of mild steel. The first KhTZ-16 to be completed, which in GABTU correspondence was also referred to as the T-16, passed through the KhTZ plant gates on 7 September 1941. KhTZ-16s had serial numbers beginning with No. 16 (i.e. No. 16-001, etc.); however the serial number was attached to the chassis rather than the completed bronetraktor, so completed bronetraktori had serial numbers

* The chassis for the KhT-16 is often referred to as being that of the STZ-5. But as the KhTZ-16 was built in Kharkov, with the STZ-NATI 1TA KhTZ-3 derivative native to Kharkov having a rear cab and control layout, it is more likely that the KhTZ-3 (using the plant designation) was the main chassis source, albeit with a mix of STZ-NATI components such as used on the NATI developed unarmoured transporter-tractor detailed separately. All tractors were essentially from the same STZ-NATI family and control linkages would not have been an insurmountable problem if using the STZ-5 chassis.

such as No. 16-1672, even though production of the KhTZ-16 never reached anything like this quantity. A week later, 36 KhTZ-16 bronetraktori had been delivered by 14 September, at which time a backlog of 1,528 assembled chassis had been accumulated at KhTZ, of which 717 were without tracks, 1,334 without fuel tanks and 1,304 without electrical equipment. The acute shortage of armoured casemate hulls was however the fatal bottleneck that prevented delivery of completed KhT-16s. Two days later, on 16 September, GKO Resolution No. 681 was issued, instructing the evacuation of the machine tooling from KhTZ to STZ in Stalingrad. The assembly of KhTZ-16 bronetraktori continued after this date, but the planned overall production of 2,000 such tractors was now out of the question. Only around 100 sets of armour were provided to KhTZ due to the ongoing evacuation of the NKMZ plant, which was completed on 9 October 1941, and not all the armour sets delivered were used by KhTZ as the situation in Kharkov was equally tenuous. KhTZ-16 production had begun at KhTZ only at the beginning of September, with evacuation of the plant beginning from 18 September. The city was captured at the end of the following month, with the loss of both the KhTZ and Plant No. 183 production facilities. The actual number of KhTZ-16 armoured tractors built in the autumn of 1941 is unknown, but estimated to be 55–60 machines (70 according to the NATI official history, with higher numbers of up to 142 sometimes cited), with 809 complete or near complete chassis left abandoned during evacuation according to plant records. Some conflicting sources indicate that as many as 1,500 KhTZ-16 chassis were at different stages of assembly at KhTZ before its evacuation; but that the smaller quoted number were completed as armoured tractors due to a lack of armoured casemate hulls, 33 of which were, as mentioned previously, welded from mild steel as armour parts became available from NKMZ only in mid-September, and only for a very short period.

COMBAT HISTORY

According to available plant documentation, the original batch of KhTZ-16 bronetraktor armoured tractors built with mild steel hulls was sent to training units, located not just in Kharkov but also in Ulyanovsk, Armavir and Stalingrad. The first KhTZ-16s produced with armoured steel hulls were delivered to the 12th Tank Brigade, which received 14 machines. The largest individual batch of KhTZ-16s was received by the 133rd Tank Brigade, which received 36 machines. Eight KhTZ-16s went to the 14th Tank Brigade, one to the 13th Tank Brigade, and five to the 7th Tank Brigade. Eight were received by the 47th Tank Division and eight by the 23rd Reserve Regiment. Documentation confirming despatch did not necessarily confirm receipt; for example, the 35th Tank Brigade formally received eight KhTZ-16s, but in reality they never arrived.

The combat debut of the KhTZ-16 was in and around the city of Kharkov where it was built, the KhTZ-16 bronetraktor being used by the Soviet 38th Army in the defence of the city from the German 6th Army in the autumn of 1941. The combat debut was during heavy fighting against Italian forces when on 22 September the 12th Tank Brigade was given the task to take Krasnograd in the Kharkov region. A few days later the 12th Tank Brigade including KhTZ-16 machines was engaged in heavy street fighting in the city suburbs. On 27 September Red Army units went on the defensive, and the brigade suffered heavy losses in tanks and personnel. One KhT-16 is documented in action on 24 October 1941 in support of militia troops near the TsUM (Central Department Store) in Kharkov, during which action it was destroyed and the crew killed. Kharkov fell to the German 6th Army the same day. The Red Army defensive action, with its eclectic mix of tanks and armoured vehicles including the KhTZ-16, had bought sufficient time to organize the evacuation of machine tooling and personnel from 70 military plants from Kharkov to other cities on 320 separate train loads. A small number of KhTZ-16 armoured tractors survived the combat engagements of 1941, with documented use of a handful of KhTZ-16s extending as late as May 1942, though Soviet records of the time are for obvious reasons minimal. The manufacturing documentation for the KhTZ-16 'Kharkov tank' was lost with the fall of the city to Axis forces.

KhT-16 – NEW OWNERSHIP AND NEW ROLES

The German 6th Army inherited a considerable amount of Red Army military equipment when it captured Kharkov, including a number of SKhTZ-NATI (STZ-3/KhTZ-3) tractors and a few KhTZ-16s which had survived intact but were of little operational use to the Wehrmacht. A number of incomplete KhT-16s and base chassis were also captured within the KhTZ plant. As the Wehrmacht was also lacking in mechanized transport, a number of captured KhTZ-16 chassis were modified as artillery tractors; with myriad variants based on component availability to make the tractors serviceable. Some were fitted with cabs, others were open, some had STZ-5 type 'road' tracks, and others were fitted with standard agricultural track. The Wehrmacht used most of these conversions as artillery and trailer 'road train' tractors.

STZ-16 'STALINGRAD TANK'

The original intent, or at least a consideration, had been to produce the KhTZ-16 at both KhTZ in Kharkov and STZ in Stalingrad, but with series production ultimately only undertaken at KhTZ. The machine tooling evacuated from KhTZ as Axis forces closed on Kharkov was partially evacuated to STZ in Stalingrad which received some of the KhT-16 production tooling in October

1941. In an attempt to continue production during a time of huge losses and plant evacuations, on 16 October 1941 NKTP Commissar V.A. Malyshev issued an order to produce 500 STZ-5 chassis, to be fitted with casemate hulls fabricated by Plant No. 264, which may have been inventory belatedly delivered from Novo-Kramatorsk. Delivery of armoured hulls was to commence by 1 November at the latest (i.e. within two weeks of the order being given) with daily production output to be initially ten machines, rapidly rising to 20. In reality, STZ and Plant No. 264 were both overloaded with other work (as noted, Plant No. 264 was tasked with T-60 small tank production and the ongoing delivery of T-34 medium tank hull and turret sets to STZ). A small number (believed to be fewer than 30) of KhT-16 (technically STZ-16) tractor-tanks were completed at STZ, and used in the immediate area until the spring of 1942.

NI-1 'ODESSA TANK'

The NI-1, known as the 'Odessa Tank' or by legend as the 'Na Ispug' (the frightener) was built from August 1941 in the Crimean Peninsula port city of Odessa (today Odesa) on the STZ-5 transport tractor chassis.* The NI-1 'Odessa' tank remains to this day one of the least documented armoured vehicles used by the Red Army, as such documentation as existed was destroyed when the city fell to Axis forces. In contrast with the KhTZ-16, which was built at Kharkov in compliance with a state order, the NI-1 'Odessa Tank' was built as a local emergency initiative, with little or no input from NATI, GABTU or any other state level authorities.

As German 11th Army and Romanian 4th Army forces closed on Odessa, the majority of manufacturing capability was evacuated from the city, with tooling being evacuated from July 1941 to cities including Kirov and Kurgan, but the decision was made to hold the city as it came under siege. Some machine tooling was left in situ in facilities such as the January Uprising (Yanvarets) Machine Building Plant, a former crane assembly plant, which during the siege repaired tanks in collaboration with other locations including the October Revolution and Red Guard plants, and the Odessa naval shipyards.

In mid-August 1941, P.K. Romanov, the chief engineer of the plant, working in collaboration with Engineer of Artillery Captain V.G. Kogan from the Soviet naval headquarters in the city proposed to manufacture ersatz tanks by armouring available STZ-5 tracked tractors with steel ship plate and installing light weapons.

* The terms 'NI', 'NI-1' and 'Tanki NI' were not used in any surviving official wartime document, the term 'Na Ispug' being introduced in later memoirs. Where wartime documentation exists, 'NI' tanks are referred to as 'armoured tractors' or 'tank-tractors'.

ABOVE One of the first NI-1 'Odessa Tanks' with a T-26 M-1931 turret and machine gun armament. Note the STZ-5 type configuration, with the driver at the front of the machine, rubber rimmed road wheels and road track.

ABOVE MIDDLE An early NI-1 bronetraktor during what would appear to be a field trial.

ABOVE RIGHT The three first NI-1 'Odessa Tanks' leaving the assembly workshops. These machines have all-steel roadwheels and 'agricultural' off-road track.

The proposal was accepted, and the plant was for this purpose allocated three 'STZ-NATI' (STZ-5) tractors, materials and weapons to build prototypes. The first prototype 'Odessa Tank' was completed within ten days, with another two completed a few days later.

During the Siege of Odessa, one of the former workshops within the January Uprising plant was converted as a tank repair workshop, which repaired BT tanks, built three armoured trains from trams, and slightly later would undertake final assembly of the (later designated) NI-1 armoured tractors, initially known as 'Yanvarets' tractors and later generically designated 'Odessa Tanks'.

The turret components were fabricated in the tram maintenance workshops and the armoured hulls at the October Revolution plant, with the final assembly of armoured tractors undertaken at the January Uprising tank repair workshop as the city came under siege. The NI 'Odessa Tank' was a local design (actually several designs), with final assembly at the January Uprising plant being undertaken with the collaboration of the Naval Repair Plant No. 1, the October Revolution and the Red Guards plants. Design and production of the armoured tractors was led by the January Uprising plant chief engineer, P.K. Romanov, military engineer I.A. Obednikov and artillery engineer Yu.G. Kogan from the headquarters of the Odessa Naval Base. Workers from the Odessa Ship Repair Plant (OSZ) also participated in the production of the NI-1 tractors. The STZ-5 tractors had the original cab and cargo area replaced by armoured casemate hulls.

As there was no ability to secure consistent supplies of armour plate in the city, the NI tanks were – according to the official report on the defence of Odessa dated 1943 – assembled at the January Uprising and October Revolution plants, being constructed of two layers of 6–12mm ship boiler plate steel with wood planking affixed internally, or with 14–20mm plate steel as available. The driver's position on the NI-1 remained at the front of the armoured tractor as on the STZ-5. Individual tanks varied in their armament, completion and appearance, based on available components.

ABOVE LEFT An NI-1 bronetraktor leaving the assembly workshops (the same machine as the photograph above). Contrast the rubber road wheels and road track indigenous to the STZ-5 chassis as compared to the other NI-1 machines pictured. The crew are naval infantry – marines.

ABOVE The only known photograph of an operational NI-1, taken from an archive film, of an STZ-5 based machine. The frontal armour and much else differs from the other machines pictured, with almost no two machines being identical.

The first two NI tanks were completed on the STZ-5 transporter-tractor chassis at the October Revolution plant under the supervision of N.G. Lutsenko* on 20 August 1941, at least one being fitted with the turret from the T-26 M-1931 and armed with two DT machine guns. One tank initially mounted a turret armed with a 37mm B-3 gun recovered from a combat damaged T-26 M-1932 tank, but the high centre of gravity did not provide a stable firing platform. The first three 'series' production tractors to be completed (two armed with machine guns and one armed with a 37mm B-3 gun) were manufactured within ten days, and on 20 August 1941 deployed to the southern sector of the city. The following armoured tractors were all equipped with a locally produced turret containing 7.62mm DT machine gun armament, usually with a secondary DT machine gun.

According to the post-war memoirs of Lutsenko, the two tanks which exited the gates of the October Revolution Plant on 20 August were marked 'смерть фашизму' (Death to Fascism). Assembly was complicated by almost nightly ariel bombardment of the plant, but careful blackout observance and concentrated anti-aircraft fire prevented major destruction. A total of 31 NI tanks had been completed by 14 September, with work continuing on a further series of 15 armoured vehicles, some if not all intended to be based on truck rather than tractor chassis. Two days later, the 157th Rifle Division under the command of D.I. Tomilov (later General-Major Tomilov) began to be ferried from Novorossisk on the 'mainland' to Odessa together with a contingent of 'Katyusha' multiple rocket launchers (MRS). NI tanks were incorporated within the 176th and 633rd Infantry Regiments, where they were at the time also referred to as armoured tractors. The 210th Tank Battalion was in late September 1941 organized under the command of Senior Lieutenant N.I. Yudin, and was initially equipped with 35 tanks, mainly NI types, plus rebuilt BT and T-26 tanks.

* N.G. Lutsenko directed the assembly of the NI tanks in Odessa. He was also Secretary of the Leninsky District Party.

An Axis forces soldier inspects two abandoned NI bronetraktori abandoned in Odessa during the siege.

Due to the loss of all documentation when the city fell to Axis forces, and with the assembly of wheeled armoured vehicles in the city also sometimes being conflated with tractor tank production, the quoted production numbers for the NI-1 remain only in the personal memoirs cited.

The NI tank had its combat debut during a counter-offensive by the 25th 'Chapaevsky' Infantry Division commanded by General-Major I. Petrov, in the region of the Dalny settlement. At this time, plans were being made to evacuate military assets from Odessa by sea, with a counter-offensive by the 25th 'Chapaevsky' Infantry Division, the 2nd Cavalry Division, and the 384th Regiment of the 157th Division, supported by BM 'Katyusha' MRS units being undertaken in the area of Dalny, intended to cover the evacuation operation in the southern sector of the city.

Under the command of Yudin, a tank platoon of one (T-26 or BT) tank and three armored tractors from the 210th Tank Battalion on 3 October 1941 led a successful counter-attack by the 25th 'Chapaevsky' Infantry Division against positions of the 4th Romanian Army in the area of Lenintal, resulting in a Romanian defeat, with 24 artillery pieces, mortars and machine guns captured. A total of six or seven NI armoured tractors were lost during the attack, hit by artillery fire or lost due to breakdown. Subsequent inspection of the armoured tractors indicated that the armour had resisted small arms fire and shrapnel, albeit one tank was penetrated by a 45mm round. The slow (maximum 7km/h) speed of the tanks was noted as inadequate, but sufficient in the context of an infantry support tank. The 'combat trial' was deemed successful, with the Military Council of the Odessa Defensive Region (OOP) ordering the assembly of a further 70 'Odessa Tanks'. This was unfulfilled due to insufficient parts and resources being available.

The Odessa garrison, including 19 tanks and armoured vehicles, 163 tractors, various other vehicles and 3,500 horses, was evacuated by sea to Sevastopol beginning on the night of 14 October. The following day, the last surviving armoured tractors covered the retreat and evacuation of the last military units defending Odessa. Having served their purpose,* the 'NI' tanks were abandoned within the city and environs, after being destroyed by their crews; some were apparently driven into the sea at Odessa naval docks, with the crews evacuated on the transport vessel *Volga*. Romanian troops entering Odessa 'captured' a few NI-1s, which were subsequently used for various purposes including as training tanks. As of 1 November 1942, some 14 NI-1 'Odessa Tanks' were still in service with Romanian forces as training tanks.

The NI-1 designation for these 'tractor-tanks' appeared later, the abbreviated term NI – 'Na Ispug' – meaning literally 'the frightener'. This has been attributed to the psychological effect their initial combat deployment had on Romanian forces, but is also related as being a commentary on the noise they made clanking through the cobbled streets of Odessa rather than their combat effectiveness. The term was not used in contemporary documentation, the description appearing in personal memoirs written after the event. According to the post-war memoirs of N.G. Lutsenko, 55 such tracked tractors were converted to NI-1 'Odessa Tanks' in the period 20 August to 15 October 1941, with other sources stating that as many as 69 may have been completed.

TRACTOR TANK CONVERSIONS IN OTHER CITIES

The NI-1 and KhT-16 armoured tractors were not the only 'tractor tanks' produced during the Great Patriotic War. In conditions of a shortage of armoured vehicles, similar ersatz armoured vehicles were built in other cities, but although there is photographic evidence of their existence their precise production history has yet to be uncovered. Besides Odessa and Kharkov, a small number of armoured tractors were built in the same time period in Leningrad. On 5 August 1941 the 2nd Rifle Division in the Leningrad region was recorded as having two T-26s, five BA-10 armoured cars, two KV-2s and five 'IZ medium tanks'. IZ refers to the armour plant at Izhorsk where an STZ tank similar to the KhT-16 was apparently built in small numbers, but what these tanks were is not to date clear from available archives.

* Although Odessa was captured, Axis forces lost 160,000 men and around 100 tanks (a small tank division) while taking the city.

CHAPTER 10

POST-WAR SERVICE

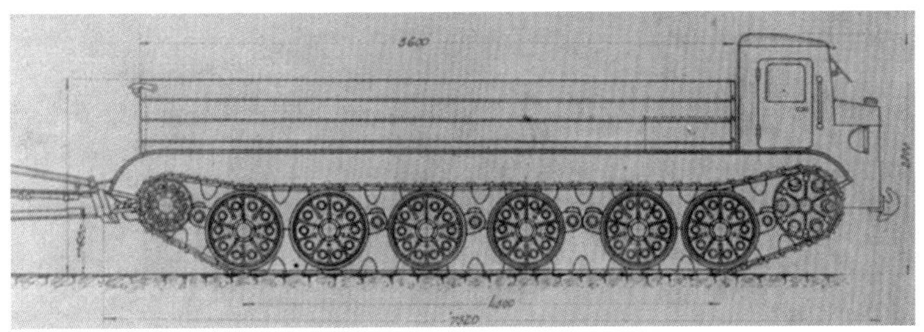

A drawing of an early 1945 Plant No. 183 initiative project for a heavy artillery transport tractor based on the (lengthened) chassis of the T-44 medium tank then being prepared for production at Plant No. 75 (Kharkov) and potentially Plant No. 264 (Stalingrad).

For decades, the received wisdom derived from books published outside the Soviet Union was that the majority of Red Army artillery tractors were destroyed during Operation *Barbarossa* in 1941. The Red Army indeed lost huge numbers of artillery tractors of both civil and military origin in the summer and autumn of 1941, estimated at more than half the entire military tractor park. The subsequent lack of artillery tractors was exacerbated due to a decline in tractor output as assembly plants such as ChTZ and Plant No. 37 were redirected towards tank and other primary weapon production, with the tractor plants in Kharkov and Stalingrad being evacuated to safety beyond the Ural mountains. The majority of artillery tractors that survived the ravages of 1941 and early 1942 had a particularly long service life, however. Large numbers of pre-war Red Army artillery tractors remained in service throughout the war, with the ostensibly 'civil' S-65 tracked tractor still being the standard tractor used to tow tracked heavy artillery such as the 203mm B-4 tracked howitzer as the Red Army approached Berlin in 1945. According to Soviet archives the number of tractors that remained in service with the Red Army at the end of the war in May 1945 were:

S-60 artillery tractors towing 280mm M-1939 (Br-5) heavy mortars along Kreschatik, Kiev, during the 1945 Victory Parade.

Stalinets-60, Stalinets-65 and Stalinets-2	16,132
STZ-3, STZ-5	9,781
Komintern	568
Voroshilovets	336
Other types and Lend-Lease	3,058

Production of the pre-war STZ-NATI 1TA (SKhTZ-NATI 1TA), assembled at Kharkov (as the KhTZ-3) and Stalingrad (as the STZ-3) until 1941 and 1942 respectively, was restarted at the Altai

(A) S-65 artillery tractors on parade on Kreschatik, Kiev, during the same 1945 Victory Parade.
(B) An S-65 levelling a Soviet Air Force (VVS) runway in the DDR (East Germany) in 1954, with an IL-4 aircraft in the background.
(C) S-80 tractors towing 152mm M-1935 (Br-2) heavy tracked howitzers through Red Square during a post-war parade.
(D) A Soviet Army S-80 towing a 152mm M-1937 (ML-20) gun-howitzer during an exercise in the DDR, 1954.

(E) (F) A 3rd production series Komsomolets armoured tractor converted to a fire tender, Bodaibo, Irkutsk Oblast, Siberia, 1948. **(G)** A 3rd production series Komsomolets tractor at a Pioneer youth camp, 1967. **(H)** All the surviving SKhTZ-NATI 1TA (STZ-NATI 1TA) variants, as built in Kharkov (KhTZ-3), Stalingrad (STZ-3) and the later ATZ-3 built in Rubtsovsk were used in military engineering roles in post-war civil service. This tractor has a modified split windscreen and additional view windows in the lower cab sides. (Sergei Popsuevich) **(I)** The wartime SKhTZ-NATI 1TA as produced at three Soviet production plants was modified post-war, as seen with this KhTZ example, and ultimately the design was replaced by the DT-54. Post-war these light tractors were not used in the artillery tractor role. (Sergei Popsuevich) **(J)** An STZ-5 in Soviet Army service in the post-war era.

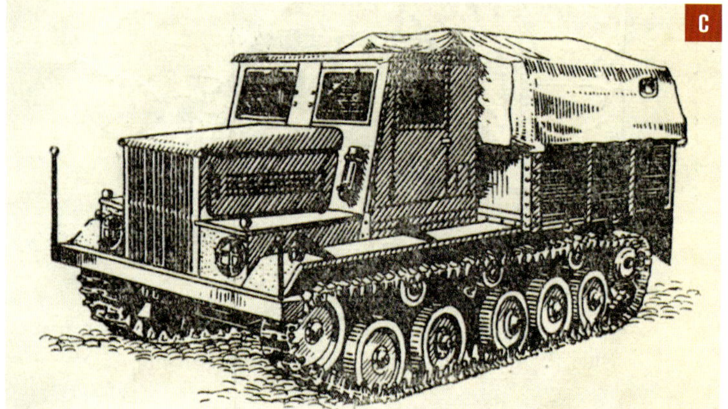

(A) A Ya-12 towing a 152mm D-1 howitzer, Belorussian SSSR, 1954. **(B)** The original Ya-12 design was incrementally modified post-war via the Mytischi-built M-12A and M-13A variants into the later and final tractor in the series, the M-2. This tractor in post-war Soviet Army service – archive labelled as an M-2 – has the original wooden cab planking sheathed in sheet metal. (Sergei Popsuevich) **(C)** A Soviet drawing of the M-2 from the Operator's Manual. Note the front bumper, integral headlights and higher cargo body than the Ya-12. The use of cab planking or sheet metal sheathed planking is undeterminable from the drawing. **(D)** Soviet Army M-2 artillery tractors towing 152mm M-1937 (ML-20) gun-howitzers through Red Square, 7 November 1950. Note the headlight locations. **(E)** This is ostensibly an M-2 tractor in Soviet Army post-war service. Note however the wooden planking on the cab, and the single driving light position with the 'standard' M-2 driving light locations blanked off, which is the standard configuration for the earlier M-12A produced at Mytischi in small batches before the M-2 entered full series production.

Tractor Plant (ATZ) from late 1942, and continued until 1952, with production also restarted in more moderate numbers at STZ and KhTZ from 1944.

The wartime S-65 produced at ChTZ until the autumn of 1941 was replaced in production post-war by the modernized S-80. The first pre-series S-80 was completed on 5 January 1946; full series production started on 12 July 1946, with the S-80 being paraded on Moscow's Red Square from that year. The S-80 was quickly replaced in the artillery tractor role by the purpose designed AT-T, with the S-65 and S-80 continuing to be used by the Soviet Army in engineering applications. The main external distinguishing feature of the S-80 was the new engine radiator assembly with curved frontal engine side covers.

The Ya-12 and later Ya-13 produced in Yaroslavl in the last two years of the war were replaced in the immediate post-war era by the Plant No. 40 (Mytischi) produced M-12A and M-13A modifications. The change of assembly plant and designation (Ya – Yaroslavl, M – Mytischi) was accompanied by design changes such as a modified load platform, a new front bumper beam, wooden cabs being sheathed in sheet metal and modified headlight arrangements. The M-12A and M-13A were duly replaced by the post-war M-2 artillery tractor, which resembled its predecessors but with significant revisions. Artillery tractor production resumed in Kharkov only in the immediate post-war era with the AT-L light and AT-T heavy tractors. The AT-45 initiated at Kharkov in the pre-war era was resurrected at the end of the war, and further developed into the post-war AT-T heavy artillery tractor, based on the T-44 medium tank chassis.

Post-war there was a general shortage of trucks and tractors for civil operation in the Soviet Union, and ex-military vehicles continued in use for as long as they remained serviceable. A significant number of Komsomolets tractors were used in the immediate post-war era in forestry and other roles, with some even being converted to fire tender vehicles. Some Komsomolets tractors were used from the 1950s by DOSAAF* youth training units, with the tractor evidenced as in use at a Pioneer youth camp as late as 1967. A number of ZiS-42M half-tracks were modified as PMZ-2 fire tenders in the immediate post-war period. Former Axis countries meantime continued to use captured tractors including the S-65 and STZ-5, which were employed in countries such as Czechoslovakia, Hungary and Romania, while Poland also used a significant number of ex-Red Army tractors.

* DOSAAF – Dobrovolnoe Obshestvo Sodeistvya Armii, Aviatsii i Floty SSSR (Volunteer Society for Assistance to the Army, Air Force and Navy of the Soviet Union).

CHAPTER 11

PRESERVED WORLD WAR II ARTILLERY TRACTORS

A fully restored and running S-65 tractor during an open day at the Motors of War Museum, Moscow, May 2024.

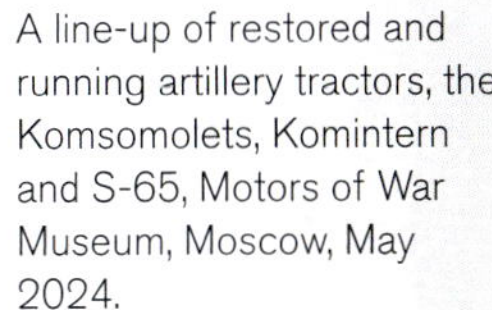

A line-up of restored and running artillery tractors, the Komsomolets, Komintern and S-65, Motors of War Museum, Moscow, May 2024.

A large number of Red Army artillery tractors survived the war, with many being used post-war in civil applications. As the tractors fell into disrepair they were abandoned or scrapped, there being for several decades no general interest in preserving such vehicles as historical artefacts.

The NIII-21 military vehicle institute collection at Bronnitsy near Moscow held a significant number of 1941–45-era Red Army artillery tractors, including two Voroshilovets types, a Kommunar and a Komintern, a Stalinets-2 (S-2), a Ya-12, Ya-13 and Ya-13F, an M-12A and a ZiS-42M half-track. The collection was however displayed outside, open to the ravages of the Russian climate. The collection was broken up in 1967, with all tractors believed to have been scrapped. A historical anomaly thereafter arose in that after the closed military NIII-21 Museum collection was scrapped there were in the Soviet era no surviving wartime artillery tractors to be found in any Soviet museum, whether public or closed military. A significant number of Komsomolets tractors were however preserved in Finland, where they had been captured during the 1939–40 Winter War (with 62 tractors originally repaired and returned to service) and the later Continuation War, with at one time as many as 200 Komsomolets tractors being in Finnish service. The tractor continued in service with the Finnish Army post-war, the last batch of ten tractors being decommissioned from military service as late as 1961.* The only known Soviet-era example of a surviving artillery

* As of 20 June 1944, Finland had 242 STZ-NATI (STZ-3), 123 'Stalinets' (S-60 and 65), 68 'HTZ' (KhTZ-3) and 38 STZ-5 tractors in inventory.

(A) The first wartime artillery tractor recovery in the post-Soviet Russian Federation was a Komsomolets. Sergey Kosenkov and colleagues of Club Iskatel in the Bryansk region in the early 1990s. **(B)** The 4th production series Komsomolets artillery tractor recovered from the Bryansk region after restoration, located at Park Pobedy (Victory Park), Moscow, May 1993. **(C)** A 3rd production series Komsomolets tractor restored by the Shamansky Workshops on display at an exhibition in Moscow in 2021. **(D)** A 3rd production series Komsomolets tractor located at the Museum of Russian Military History, Padikovo, near Moscow. **(E)** This 3rd production series Komsomolets tractor restored by the Shamansky Workshops is permanently located at the Motors of War Museum, Moscow. **(F)** This 3rd production series Komsomolets tractor is located at the Museum of Russian Military History, Padikovo, near Moscow. **(G)** The Museum of Russian Military History, Padikovo, has two Komsomolets tractors. **(H)** A 4th production series Komsomolets tractor located at the Urals Military Glory Museum, Verkhnyaya Pyshma, Ekaterinburg. (Aleksandr Koshchavtsev) **(I)** A 4th production series Komsomolets tractor located at the Urals Military Glory Museum, Verkhnyaya Pyshma, Ekaterinburg. (John Ham) **(J)** A 4th production series Komsomolets tractor located at the Motors of War Museum, Moscow. This tractor was captured and used by the Wehrmacht and later lost in action to the Red Army. (Andrey Aksenov) **(K)** **(L)** Front and rear views of the 3rd production series Komsomolets tractor located at the Motors of War Museum.

(M) A rare 2nd production series Komsomolets tractor belonging to the Muzei Tekhniki, Arkhangelskoe, Moscow region (the Vadim Zadorozhny Museum) during a commemorative display on Red Square in November 2023.

(N) A 3rd production series Komsomolets used by the Finnish Army as Ps756-82 (ex-R336) during an event at the Parola Armour Museum in June 2003. Note the numerous Finnish modifications including the clipped track guards and the armoured headlight cover. (Esa Muikku)

(A) The same Komsomolets tractor (Ps336) photographed earlier by the author.
(B) A 3rd production series Komsomolets (Ps756-67) formerly located near the Artillery Museum at Hameenlinna, Finland.
(C) A 3rd production series Komsomolets (Ps755-22) with typical Finnish modifications at Suomenlina, Helsinki, in 1990, now relocated.
(D) A 3rd production series Komsomolets tractor photographed in the 1980s when Finland possessed more Red Army artillery tractors in museum collections than the Soviet Union that manufactured them.

tractor was recovered from a reservoir as late as 1988, being an STZ-5 BM-13 'Katyusha' rocket launcher vehicle rather than a base artillery tractor.

There remained however many ex-military tractors in civilian service in the Soviet Union, such as in forestry, geological and oil and gas exploration, which in time would become available for restoration. A relatively large number of Komsomolets tractors survived the war; some were used in remote regions where all-terrain capability was required, with a small number being converted to specialist applications such as fire tenders in Siberia. The tractor was also used into the 1960s in DOSAAF training camps. A single Ya-12 tractor fitted with a YaAZ-204 engine was used within the YaMZ plant in Yaroslavl post-war before being plinth mounted in front of the plant administration buildings as a memorial.

The first wartime-era Red Army tractor to be restored in the post-Soviet Russian Federation was located in the early 1990s. The recovery was recorded by Sergei Kosenkov of the 'Iskatel' (search) group from Desnogorsk, which located the tractor in marshland 15km from the village of Igorevka in the Smolensk region. Due to its remote location, the tractor was airlifted out by Mi-8 helicopter, and thereafter restored by the workshops of the Kubinka Tank Museum before being displayed at Paklonnaya Gora (Victory Park) in Moscow from May

(E) A ZiS-33 restored by the Shamansky Workshops at the Motors of War Museum, Moscow.
(F) A ZiS-33 with ski floats for snow travel located at the Museum of Russian Military History, Padikovo, near Moscow.
(G) A ZiS-42M restored by the Shamansky Workshops at the Motors of War Museum, Moscow.
(H) A ZiS-42M located at the Museum of Russian Military History, Padikovo, near Moscow.
(I) (J) The ZiS-42M restored by the Shamansky Workshops during an outdoor exhibition in Moscow in 2021. The rear aspect gives a good view of the raised cargo body, additional fuel tanks and the technically intricate metal reinforced fabric and rubber track mechanism.

of 1993. The tractor became part of the official display in the newly opened Museum of the Great Patriotic War inaugurated at the same location on 9 May 1995. Subsequent research unveiled that the Komsomolets tractor had originally belonged to the 152nd Rifle Division which had operated in the area where it was located until mid-October 1941, at which point the region fell under Wehrmacht control before being retaken by Red Army forces in

(A) An inaccurate reproduction KhTZ-16 made some decades ago, at the National Museum of the History of Ukraine in World War II (formerly the Great Patriotic War Memorial Museum) in Kyiv, Ukraine. (John Ham) **(B)** An accurate modern-day reproduction of the KhTZ-16 at the Urals Military Glory Museum, Verkhnyaya Pyshma, Ekaterinburg. (John Ham) **(C) (D) (E)** A reproduction NI 'Odessa Tank' based on a mix of SKhTZ-NATI 1TA and post-war DT-54 chassis components at the 411th Battery Museum open air memorial exhibition in Odesa (formally Odessa), Ukraine. (Alexander Morzhitsky) **(F) (G)** A second reproduction NI 'Odessa Tank' plinth mounted as a memorial in Ordzhonikidze Street, Odesa. (Alexander Morzhitsky)

(H) (I) This Komintern restored by the Shamansky Workshops and located at the Motors of War Museum in Moscow was the first Komintern to be restored to running condition in the Russian Federation.
(J) (K) A Kommunar tractor under restoration at the Shamansky Workshops having been recovered from a long sojourn in the Soviet (and latterly Russian) Arctic.
(L) This Kommunar tractor, shown displayed at an exhibition of the Arctic in St Petersburg, is in remarkably complete condition. That such vehicles can still be found, and recovered, from the vast expanses in the remote regions of the Russian Federation, is in itself remarkable.

(A) An S-60 plinth mounted outside the administration offices of ChTZ in Chelyabinsk. (Alexander Morzhitsky) **(B)** A plinth mounted S-60 at Adzhimushkayskiye kamenolomni (Adjimushkai quarries, a hardened defensive position in World War II) near Kerch, Crimea. (Alexander Morzhitsky) **(C)** An S-60 located outside regional administration offices in the city of Sakha, Yakutia. **(D)** A restored S-60 painted in standard 4B0 military green, location believed to be near Nevsky Pyatachok. **(E)** Another of several restored S-60 tractors in the Russian Federation. **(F)** An S-60 under restoration at the Shamansky Workshops, Mytischi, Moscow in 2024. **(G)** An S-60 recovered from the River Nerussa in Bryansk Oblast in 2011 and now on display at the Partizanskaya Polyanna Memorial Complex near Bryansk.

(H) An S-65 tractor in the process of recovery from many decades sunk in a marsh, subsequently restored to running condition by the Shamansky Workshops in Mytischi. **(I)** The same recovered S-65 tractor on display at the Crocus City exhibition centre in 2008. (Andrey Aksenov) **(J)** An S-65 on display exposed to the elements at the Technical Museum, Toliatti. This tractor still retains the engine panels. (Andrey Aksenov) **(K)** Another S-65, location unknown, in the process of restoration. **(L)** An S-65 and 152mm M-1937 (ML-20) at the Urals Military Glory Museum, Verkhnyaya Pyshma, Ekaterinburg, in 2013. (Alexander Koshchavtsev) **(M)** The same S-65 tractor and 152mm M-1937 (ML-20) combination during a 9 May parade in 2013. **(N)** Another restored S-65 tractor, location unknown. **(O)** A plinth mounted S-65 memorial at Uryv Pokrovka, Voronezh Oblast.

(A) A fully restored S-65 with cab, located at the Russian Military History Museum, Padikovo, near Moscow.
(B) A restored S-65 with cab on display at a commemorative display on Red Square, Moscow, in November 2023.
(C) This S-65 with cab, in running order, as restored by the Shamansky Workshops and located at the Motors of War Museum in Moscow.
(D) These collected parts are the very beginning of an S-2 restoration which began at the Shamansky Workshops in 2024.
(E) The STZ-5 BM-13, which was recovered from the Shatskoye reservoir near Novomoskovsk, in the streets of the town before being installed on a plinth outside the regional museum.
(F) The STZ-5 BM-13 at the handover ceremony having been restored after being raised from the bed of the Shatskoye reservoir in 1988.

(G) The STZ-5 BM-13 at Novomoskovsk having been removed from its plinth mounting outside the regional museum, fettled, and paraded through the town on 9 May 2015 before being returned to its habitual location.
(H) The STZ-5 BM-13 in its usual location outside the regional museum in Novomoskovsk.
(I) A ZiS-30 SAU at the Urals Military Glory Museum at Verkhnyaya Pyshma, Ekaterinburg. (John Ham)

September 1943. A curious nuance discovered on inspecting the tractor was that the inner hatch roof was inscribed '*1942 – crew Ustinov V.M; Petrashov, A.S.*' i.e. during the period of German occupation. Komsomolets tractors were used by Soviet partisan forces, which perhaps explains the inscription, but as with all historical research, questions arising often outweigh answers obtained.

Today there are several other restored examples of Komsomolets tractors in Russian museums. Late 3rd Series examples restored to running condition are located at the Museum of Russian Military History at Padikovo near Moscow and the Motors of War Museum in Moscow. The latter example was captured and used by the Wehrmacht, fitted with a new towing mechanism, then destroyed by the Red Army as it crossed the River Dniepr. It was recovered by the Shamansky Workshops and first shown in public in Moscow in March 2012. Another Komsomolets is located at the Urals Miliary Glory Museum in Verkhnyaya Pyshma, Ekaterinburg.

(A) A SKhTZ-15/30 tractor restored by the Shamansky Workshops at an Oldtimer exhibition at Crocus City exhibition centre in 2013.
(B) A restored GAZ-61-416 at a military gathering in Chernogolovka near Moscow. (Andrey Aksenov)
(C) The recovered wreck of a GAZ-61-416 at the Shamansky Workshops at Mytischi awaiting restoration.
(D) A restored GAZ-61-416 at the Urals Military Glory Museum at Verkhnyaya Pyshma, Ekaterinburg. (John Ham)
(E) A SKhTZ-NATI 1TA (specifically the STZ produced STZ-3 variant) restored by the Shamansky Workshops at the Oldtimer exhibition in Moscow in 2013.

(F) A SKhTZ-NATI 1TA (a Stalingrad produced STZ-3) at the Urals Military Glory Museum, Verkhnyaya Pyshma, Ekaterinburg. (John Ham)
(G) The STZ-5 restored by the Shamansky Workshops at the Motors of War Museum, Moscow.
(H) A recovered STZ-5 cab and road wheels at the Shamansky Workshops, Mytischi.
(I) A collection of recovered STZ-5 driver control panels at the Shamansky Workshops. No two of them are identical, indicating several suppliers even for an artillery tractor produced as a single model at a single plant.
(J) A Ya-12 artillery tractor outside the YaMZ (formerly YaAZ) plant in Yaroslavl.

STZ-5 BM-13 – AN 'ARTILLERY TRACTOR' WITH A KNOWN HISTORY

Due to their functional role, the majority of artillery tractors were not particularly documented within Red Army unit combat histories except as an occasional footnote as to the numbers and types deployed in any given operation. The history of one unique artillery tractor conversion is however well documented. The STZ-5 based BM-13, the 3rd Launcher Unit of the 1st Battery of the 12th Guards Mortar Division, as described earlier in the book, was lost in action when it broke through the ice on the Shatskoye reservoir near Stalinogorsk (today Novomoskovsk) on 14 December 1941 while moving to a new fire position. The wreck was discovered in 1988 by DOSAAF divers. After a failed attempt the previous week, the wreck was recovered from the reservoir by several tracked tractors on 25 November of the same year. It was subsequently restored to running condition and mounted on a plinth outside the local history museum in Novomoskovsk where it remained for almost two decades. In 2015, the unique original STZ-5 BM-13 was again restored to running condition and paraded through the town during the Victory Day commemorations held on 9 May 2015, before being returned back to its habitual plinth location.

In recent years there have been many expeditions in Russia to locate and recover the remains of wartime vehicles including artillery tractors, some of which have resulted in historical relics once lost to time being restored for future generations. As but one of many examples, in the summer of 2002 an expedition led by the National Automobile Museum in St Petersburg located the remains of two GAZ-60 half-tracks deep in woods in the Novgorod region, lost during a battle fought in 1942.

In recent years, the recovery and restoration of wartime and even pre-war artillery tractors has increased exponentially in the Russian Federation. Several S-65 tractors have been recovered and restored to running condition, as have examples of the Komintern, STZ-5 and the ZiS-42M half-track, with reproductions built of other tractor-based vehicles such as the KhT-16 and ZiS-30.

At the time of writing, examples of the Kommunar, S-60 and S-2 tractors were in the final stages of restoration by the Shamansky Workshops in Mytischi in the suburbs of Moscow, with two other Komintern tractors under restoration in the country.

Three final production model Kommunar tractors were also recently recovered from the Island of Vaygach in the Arctic Pechora Sea, with around ten such tractors surviving in the countries of the former Soviet Union as patriotic-minded Russians recover, rebuild and put on public display rare and in some cases previously lost to history Soviet artillery and general service tractors.

RED ARMY ARTILLERY TRACTORS IN MUSEUMS

Belarus	
KhTZ-1	Belorussian Great Patriotic War Memorial Museum, Minsk

Finland	
Komsomolets M-1938 (Ps756-67)	Located near (but not part of) the Military Museum (ex-Artillery Museum), Hameenlinna
Komsomolets M-1940 (Ps756-35)	Winter War Museum, Kuhmo
Komsomolets M-1939 (Ps756-99)	Infantry Museum, Mikkeli
Komsomolets M-1938 (Ps755-38)	Parola Armour Museum, Parola
Komsomolets M-1939 (Ps756-82)	Parola Armour Museum, Parola (not on permanent display)
Komsomolets M-1940 (Ps756-100)	Parola Armour Museum, Parola (not on permanent display)
Komsomolets M-1937 (Ps755-22)	Not on public display as of 2025 (ex-Suomenlinna Island, Helsinki)

Russian Federation	
GAZ-61-416	Urals Military Glory Museum, Verkhnyaya Pyshma, Ekaterinburg
GAZ-64-416	Shamansky Workshops (awaiting restoration)
GAZ-V (GAZ-60)	Motors of War Museum, Moscow (Shamansky Collection). Running order
Kommunar	Shamansky Workshops, Mytischi, Moscow region (under restoration)
Kommunar	Arctic Museum Exhibition Centre, St Petersburg. Recovered from the Arctic Island of Vaygach
Komsomolets	Motors of War Museum, Moscow (Shamansky Collection). Running order
Komsomolets	Motors of War Museum, Moscow. Static display
Komsomolets	Museum of Russian Military History, Padikovo, Moscow (ex-Finland – Ps756-40). Running order
Komsomolets	Vadim Zadorozhny Museum, Arkhangelskoe, Moscow region
Komsomolets	Paklonnaya Gora (Victory Park), Kutuzovsky Prospect, Moscow
Komsomolets	Urals Military Glory Museum, Verkhnyaya Pyshma, Ekaterinburg
KhT-16	Urals Military Glory Museum, Verkhnyaya Pyshma, Ekaterinburg
KhT-16	A reproduction film-prop vehicle held at the Kubinka Tank Museum, Moscow region
Komintern	Motors of War Museum, Moscow (Shamansky Collection). Running order
M5 Medium Fast Tractor (Lend-Lease)	Urals Military Glory Museum, Verkhnyaya Pyshma, Ekaterinburg
S-2	Shamansky Workshops, Mytischi, Moscow region (under restoration)
S-60	Chelyabinsk, plinth mounted outside ChTZ plant
S-60	Kerch, plinth mounted at the Partisan Memorial Complex
S-60	Shamansky Workshops, Mytischi, Moscow region (under restoration)
S-65	Partizanskaya Polyanna Memorial Complex, Bryansk. Restored by Bryansky Arsenal
S-65	Motors of War Museum, Moscow (Shamansky Collection). Running order
S-65	Museum of Russian Military History, Padikovo, Moscow. Running order
S-65	Muzei Tekhniki, Arkhangelskoe, Moscow region. Running order
S-65	Museum of Combat and Labour Glory, Saratov. Static exhibit
S-65	Park Complex of Technical History (AvtoVAZ), Toliatti
S-65	Urals Military Glory Museum, Verkhnyaya Pyshma, Ekaterinburg. Running order
STZ-3	Shamansky Workshops, Mytischi, Moscow region.
STZ-3	Urals Military Glory Museum, Verkhnyaya Pyshma, Ekaterinburg
STZ-5	Motors of War Museum, Moscow (Shamansky Collection). Running order
STZ-5	Urals Military Glory Museum, Verkhnyaya Pyshma, Ekaterinburg
STZ-5, STZ-5 BM-13 (KS-75)	Novomoskovsk, Tula Oblast. Running order
STZ-15/30 (STZ-1)	Muzei Tekhniki, Chernogolovka
Ya-12	Yaroslavl, plinth mounted outside former YaAZ plant
ZiS-30	Urals Military Glory Museum, Verkhnyaya Pyshma, Ekaterinburg
ZiS-33	Motors of War Museum, Moscow (Shamansky Collection). Running order
ZiS-33	Museum of Russian Military History, Padikovo, Moscow
ZiS-42M	Motors of War Museum, Moscow (Shamansky Collection). Running order
ZIS-42M	Museum of Russian Military History, Padikovo, Moscow

Ukraine	
NI Tank	Ordzhonikidze Ulitsa, Odesa
NI Tank	411th Battery Memorial Exhibition to the Defence of Odessa (Odesa)
NI Tank	Location unknown
KhT16	Great Patriotic War Memorial Museum, Kyiv. Reproduction labelled as an NI tank

CHAPTER 12
WALKAROUNDS

In recent years, a significant number of wartime Red Army artillery tractors have been recovered, or rebuilt from recovered parts, and restored to running condition in the Russian Federation, such that for the first time since the end of World War II it is possible to view such tractors, including examples that for decades were to all intents and purposes extinct. These recent restorations have been undertaken with increasingly meticulous attention to originality and detail. A few examples of such restorations are shown in the following pages.

S-65 TRACTOR – TYPICAL 'CIVIL' VERSION AS PRESSED INTO RED ARMY SERVICE

An S-65 located at Partizanskaya Polyanna, Bryansk, Russian Federation. Recovered in 2011 from the River Nerussa, Bryansk Oblast, having sunk in the river during the retreat of the 13th Army.

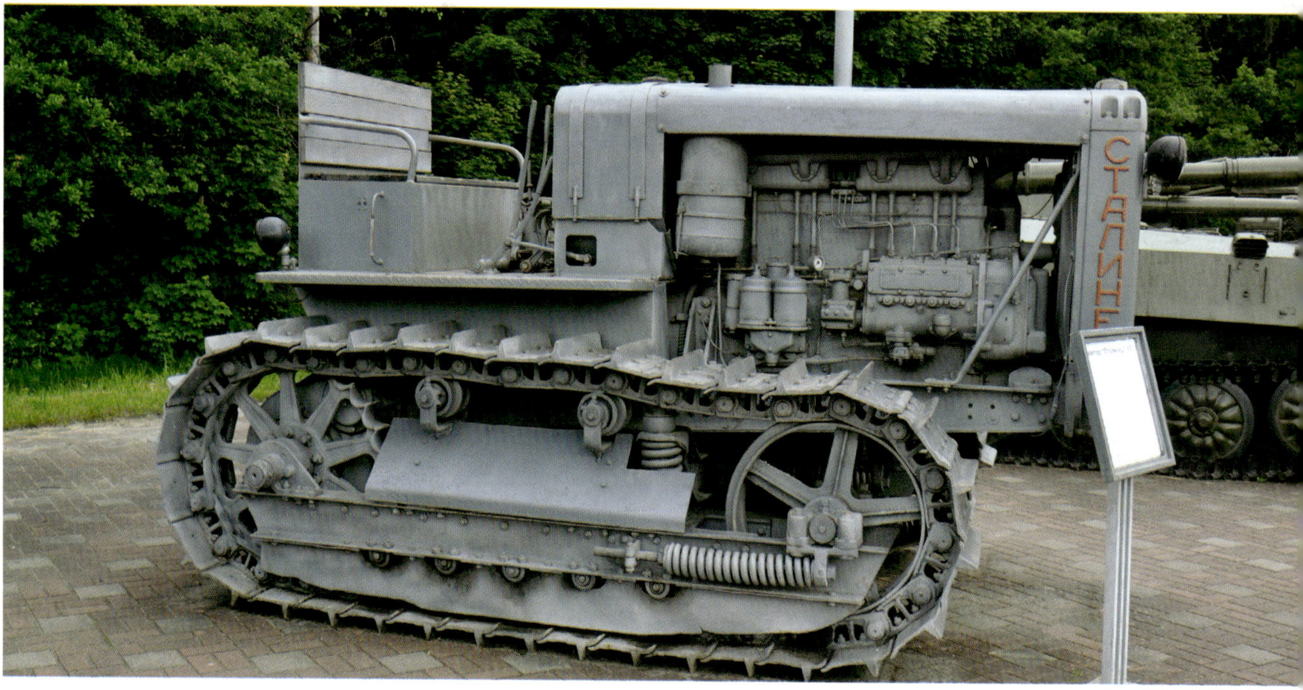

СТАЛИНЕЦ
ДИЗЕЛЬ

СТАЛИНЕЦ

СТАЛИНЕЦ

ИЗЕЛЬ

ДИЗЕЛЬ

S-65 TRACTOR – TYPICAL 'MILITARY' VERSION AS USED BY THE RED ARMY

S-65 tractors located at the Museum of Russian Military History, Padikovo, and the Shamansky Collection at the Motors of War Museum, Moscow, Russian Federation.

СТАЛИНЕЦ
ДИЗЕЛЬ

СТАЛИНЕЦ

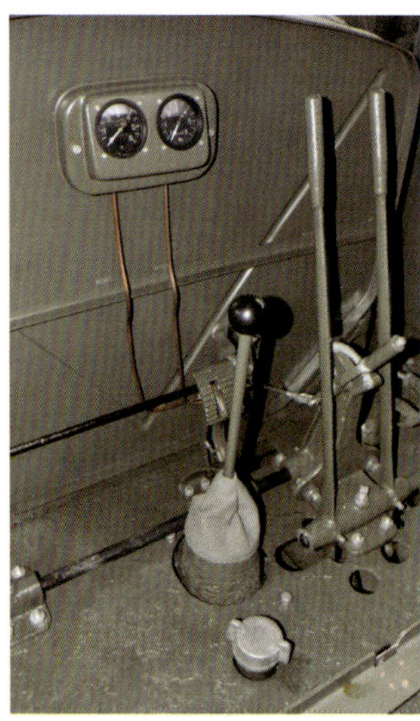

СТАЛИНЕЦ

ЧЕЛЯБИНСКИЙ ТРАКТОРНЫЙ ЗАВОД
СТАЛИНА

СТАЛИНЕЦ
СТАЛИНЕЦ
ЧТЗ
ДИЗЕЛЬ

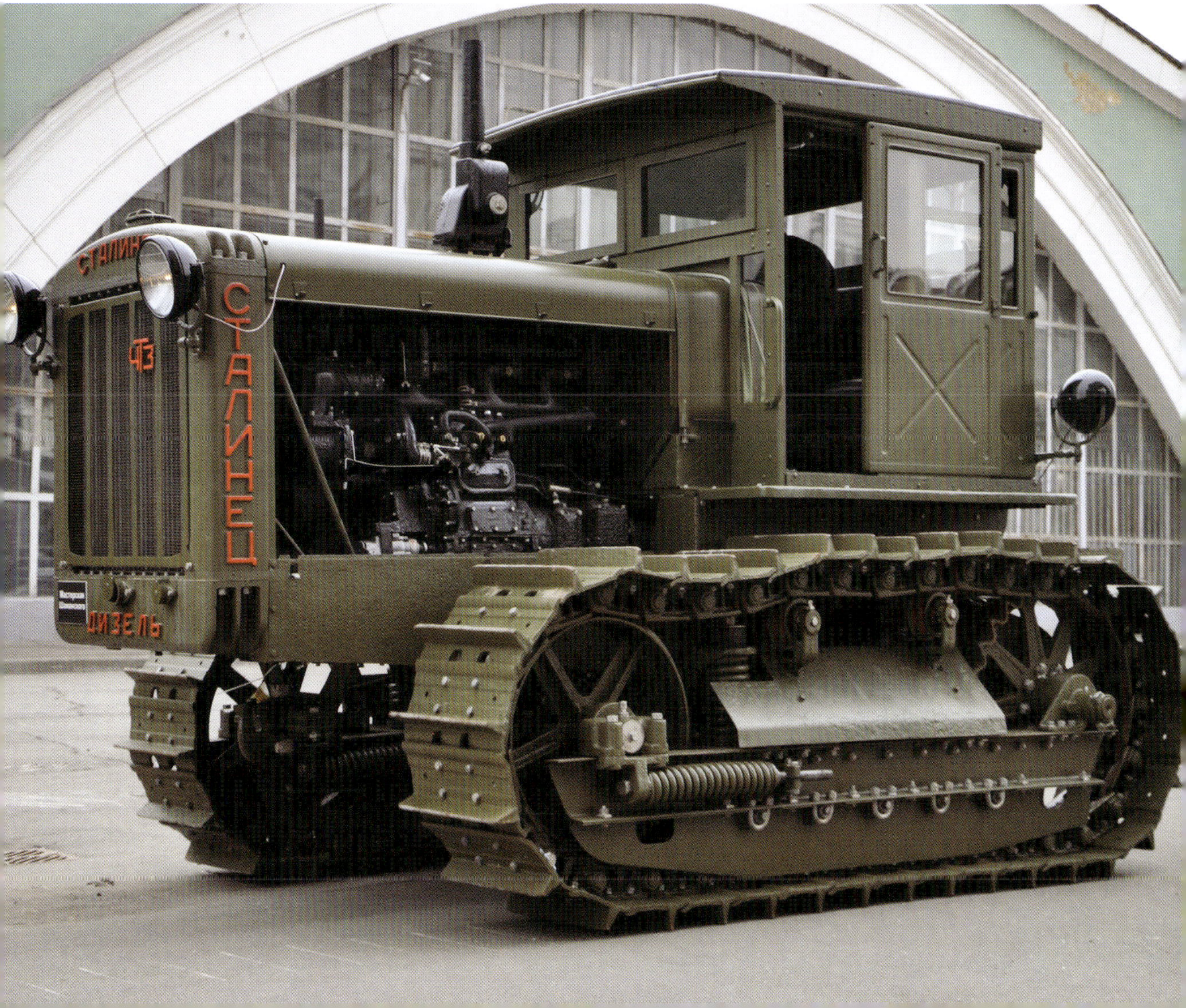

KOMINTERN TRANSPORT TRACTOR

Komintern of the Shamansky Collection on display at the Motors of War Museum, Moscow.

T-20 KOMSOMOLETS ARMOURED ARTILLERY TRACTOR

T-20 Komsomolets tractors located at the Museum of Russian Military History, Padikovo, and the Shamansky Collection at the Motors of War Museum, Moscow.

ВОЙНЫ
Мастерская

Мастерская

STZ-5 TRANSPORT TRACTOR

STZ-5 of the Shamansky Collection on display at the Motors of War Museum, Moscow.

As noted earlier this book, both 'civil' and 'military' variants of tractors such as the S-65 and SKhTZ-NATI 1TA (STZ-3/KhTZ-3) were used by the Red Army pre-1941, with large numbers drafted into service thereafter. They are distinguishable by details such as cab and towing hook arrangements, but performed the same artillery tractor role.

APPENDICES

Appendix 1: Gas Generator (Solid Fuel) Tractors

A specific of the Soviet Union, featuring wide expanses of forest with no shortage of wood as fuel, was the development of 'gazogeneratorny' (gas generator) versions of standard tractors and trucks. These vehicles were fitted with solid fuel burning gas generators, capable of running on coal, wood, peat and other flammable solid materials. Soviet development of gas generators for wheeled and tracked vehicles began in the early 1920s under the direction of S.I. Dekalenkov, later resulting in the Dekalenkov D-8 and D-12 gas generator systems. In 1932, the Moscow based NATI design institute took up the mantle and developed and built a variant of the Stalinets-60 (ChTZ-60) tractor fitted with the NATI G-13 gas generator, the Stalinets-65 based SG-65 fitted with the G-25 gas generator and the KhTZ-T2G variant of the SKhTZ-1TA fitted with the NATI G-19 gas generator.

BELOW The NATI-T2G (KhTZ-T2G) gas generator version of the STZ-NATI 1TA.

BELOW RIGHT Soviet drawing of the NATI-T2G (KhTZ-T2G).

SG-60

In May 1936, an experimental KB was established at ChTZ under the direction of Ya.B. Mamin, which developed to production stage the aforementioned D-8 and D-12 gas generators for the current S-60 and future tracked tractors. ChTZ built 264 SG-60 tractors fitted with the D-8 gas generator system developing 60–65hp at 870rpm for use in areas with abundant available wood resources, with the tractor having a similar sedate speed to the ligroin powered version. Some of these tractors were used by the Red Army in the 1939–40 Soviet–Finnish Winter War and the initial stages of the 1941–45 'Great Patriotic War'.

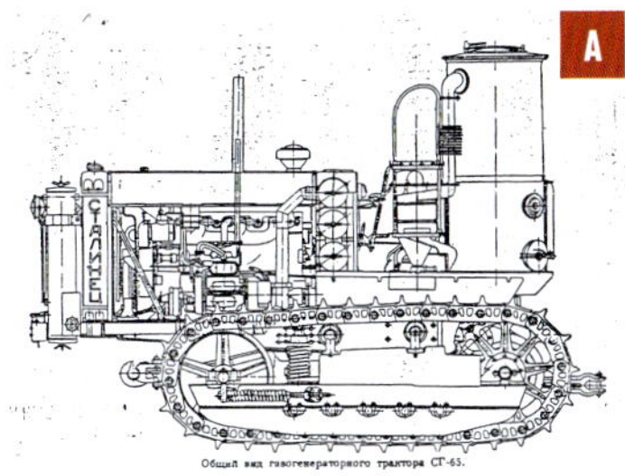

(A) An SG-65 side elevation drawing from a Soviet manual.
(B) An SG-65 tractor abandoned in Finland. (SA-Kuva)
(C) SG-65 tractors destroyed in combat in the summer of 1941.
(D) An SG-65 tractor abandoned in 1941.
(E) An SG-65 tractor in Finnish Army service under registration SA-24951, 25th Oktyabr Square, Äänislinna (Petrozavodsk), spring 1943. (Esa Muikku)

SG-65

The Stalinets SG-65, fitted with the MG-17 engine and NATI-25 (G-25) gas generator, entered series production in late 1937 at ChTZ, based on experience gained with the earlier SG-60 gas generator version of the S-60 tractor. Formal acceptance for series production was dated 28 January 1938. The SG-65, which had a combat weight of 11,200kg and the same power output as the earlier ligroin powered S-60 (60–65hp at 870rpm) and the same maximum road speed of 7km/h, was easily distinguished by its vertical gas generator system boiler, which consumed 100kg of wood or coal every one and half to two hours. ChTZ built a total of 7,365 SG-65 tractors which, like the SG-60, were used in the Soviet–Finnish Winter War and the months following Operation *Barbarossa* in June 1941.

KhTZ-T2G

The KhTZ-T2G solid fuel powered gas generator tractor was developed at NATI in accordance with Resolution SNK SSSR dated 28 February 1938 *About Development of Transport Gas-Generators* which required the tractor to be developed for series production at KhTZ in Kharkov and also envisaged for production at ChTZ in Chelyabinsk. The prototype, based on the SKhTZ-NATI 1TA agricultural tractor fitted with a NATI designed G-19 gas generator and developed by N.G. Yadushkin, G.G. Terzibashyan, M.S. Koronev and others, was completed on 1 May 1938 and tested for service in the summer of 1938. Around 12,000 of the KhTZ-T2G series production model, which developed 45–47hp at 1,250rpm providing a maximum towing speed of 5km/h, were built at KhTZ before the manufacturing plant in Kharkov was evacuated in the late summer of 1941. The gas generator is referred to as the T2G and sometimes D-2G in original manual sources.

The KhTZ-T2G, SG-60 and SG-65 gas generator tractors were all used in the Soviet–Finnish Winter War of 1939–40 and again in 1941, when significant numbers of gas generator tractors were drafted into Red Army service to replace the huge losses of artillery tractors of all types lost in combat in the initial months of the war. All were distinguished by their distinctive vertical boiler vessels.

Appendix 2: Barrel Carriage and Engineering Attachments

Red Army artillery tractors generally towed light and medium artillery pieces together with their limbers, though linked artillery pieces and limbers were also moved as road trains on long hauls. Small tractors such as the Komsomolets were limited by engine power output to towing a single 45mm anti-tank gun and limber, while more powerful tractors such as the S-65 and Voroshilovets could tow up to three 76mm guns and limbers as a road train. For heavier artillery pieces, in particular the 152mm, 203mm and 280mm 'tracked triplex' artillery systems, special gun barrel carriages (stvolnaya povozka/orudinnaya povozka) or 'povozki' were used to transport, position and facilitate disassembly and re-assembly of the barrel onto the tracked gun carriage of these extremely heavy artillery pieces, which were broken into carriage and barrel loads for road transport.

A

B

C

D

(A) The B-29 povozka was used with S-60, S-65 and some Lend-Lease tractors to transport the barrels of tracked heavy artillery pieces when broken into two loads for transport marches.
(B) Two S-65 tractors towing a 203mm B-4 tracked artillery broken into two loads, with the barrel located on a B-29 tracked povozka. The B-29 povozka was based on the T-26 light tank chassis.
(C) The Br-10 wheeled povozka was designed to transport heavy artillery barrels with less inertia, better road speed and less vibration.
(D) Horse-mounted Wehrmacht soldiers pass an abandoned STZ-5 and Br-10 povozka in the summer of 1941.
(E) (F) A Br-10 povozka at the Malaya Zemlya Memorial Complex, Novorossisk. (Alexander Morzhitsky)
(G) (H) KTs-6 fuel cisterns abandoned in Finland during the 1939–40 Soviet–Finnish Winter War. An S-65 could tow two cisterns in tandem. (SA-Kuva)

B-29 POVOZKA

Due to their tracked chassis and not insignificant travel order weight, the immensely powerful and destructive tracked 152mm Br-2 gun-howitzer, 203mm B-4 howitzer and 280mm Br-5 heavy mortar were broken down into gun carriage and barrel loads for long distance road marches. The barrels were removed from their gun carriages and transported on specialized tracked and wheeled 'povozki' gun barrel transport carriages. The B-29 (Б-29) tracked barrel povozka* was designed and produced at the Bolshevik plant in Leningrad based on the chassis and running gear of the T-26 light tank. The carriage with its barrel load was usually towed by a single S-60 or S-65 tractor. It could also be towed by the later Komintern tractor, but in icy winter conditions two such tractors were required in tandem, as a single tractor could not maintain traction due to track slip.

Br-10 POVOZKA

The Br-10 wheeled povozka was developed by the Barrikady plant in Leningrad. It provided smoother and faster road transit compared with the tracked B-29 carriage, and also required less tractive effort (only 20 per cent of the B-29) to

* Povozka – from the old Russian word for a (originally horse-towed) cart or wagon. The carriage designations are usually written 'Br' but also simply as 'B'.

get it moving, a significant factor in soft ground and icy conditions. The three 'axle' carriage was provided with large diameter road wheels, leaf suspension, reverse gearing and braking. Maximum towed road speed was 25km/h with the barrel mounted. In comparison with the tracked B-29, the Br-10 carriage could be towed by a single Komintern tractor in difficult conditions, but the B-29 tracked carriage retained better manoeuvrability in soft ground and snow.

Br-15 POVOZKA

In 1939, the Barrikady plant developed the modernized Br-15 povozka with wider rear wheels, and the front wheel diameter increased from 900mm on the Br-10 to 1,250mm, with ground clearance correspondingly increased from 310mm to 410mm, and improved brake band assemblies and an unladen weight of 5,650kg. The Br-15 underwent factory testing from 28 April to 7 May 1940 followed by service trials which showed better all-terrain capability than the Br-10. The Br-15 was recommended for service subject to redesign of the brakes. It was not however adopted for service, as the improved barrel carriage towing speed was irrelevant if the gun carriage assembly of tracked artillery such as the B-4 was in any event towed at a slower speed due to its tracked chassis. The standard S-65 tractor moved at a sedate 7km/h road speed and the faster Komintern and later Voroshilovets heavy tractors were in very limited supply relative to the number of artillery pieces to be towed. Improving the towing speed would necessitate a new wheeled carriage for the entire artillery piece, which was undertaken post-war with the introduction of the 203mm B-4M howitzer, mounted on a wheeled chassis.

Somewhat less complex to manoeuvre, the standard gun limber used with the 76.2mm M-1927 infantry gun, 76.2mm F-22 (USV) divisional gun and 76.2mm ZiS-3 dual-purpose gun was the 52-P-353M, originally developed for the 76.2mm M-1927 infantry gun (GAU Index 52-P-353) but used for all systems noted.

P SERIES POVOZKI

In the 1920s twin-axle trailers (povozki) were developed in accordance with an RVS resolution and under GAU direction for mechanized towing, singularly or as road trains, by tracked tractors for the transport of ammunition and general cargo. The P-12 and P-15 trailers had a 1,750kg payload capacity, while the larger P-13 had a 3,000kg payload capacity. In the 1930s the modernized 1,750kg capacity P-18/18A and P-28/28A, and the 3,000kg capacity P-26/P-26A were also introduced into service with the Red Army. As of 15 March 1938, the Moscow Military District had 131 P18, 22 P-26 and 62 P-26A trailers in service.

KTs-6 FUEL CISTERN

Artillery tractors such as the S-65 were also used by the Red Army in their original 'civil' role to tow civil engineering attachments such as rollers and graders. An interesting specifically military attachment as used in the campaigns in Finland was the KTs-6 (КЦ-6) container-cistern as described in Russian, which contained 5,500 litres of fuel and could be towed at road speeds of up to 13km/h to a range of up to 50km, the mobile fuel tank drum being sufficient to refuel a significant number of tanks or other transport vehicles. A single S-65 could tow two such container-cisterns coupled in tandem.

Red Army heavy tracked artillery system travel order weights	
152mm Br-2 (M-1935)	18,300kg
203mm B-4 (M-1931)	19,000kg
280mm Br-5 (M-1939)	19,000kg
210mm Br-17 (M-1940)	21,000kg
305mm Br-18 (M-1940)	21,000kg

Appendix 3: Official Colour Schemes

Official three-colour summer and two-colour winter camouflage schemes current at the time of the outbreak of war were similar to that applicable to Red Army tanks. Few artillery tractors were in practice actually painted in these schemes, usually being painted in single-colour 4BO green for summer and sometimes covered with whitewash in winter. Unit markings were generally confined to the cab rear. A variety of ad hoc camouflage schemes were applied to these tractors as shown in surviving photographs, but the vast majority of artillery tractors did not have specialized colour applications, perhaps reflecting their secondary service rather than front line role. The exception was the Komsomolets armoured artillery tractor, which was more frequently camouflage painted, as was the ZiS-30 SAU.

FAR LEFT STZ-5 official summer camouflage scheme.

LEFT STZ-5 official winter camouflage scheme.

RIGHT S-65 official summer camouflage scheme.

FAR RIGHT S-65 official winter camouflage scheme.

BELOW Voroshilovets official summer camouflage scheme.

BOTTOM Voroshilovets official winter camouflage scheme.

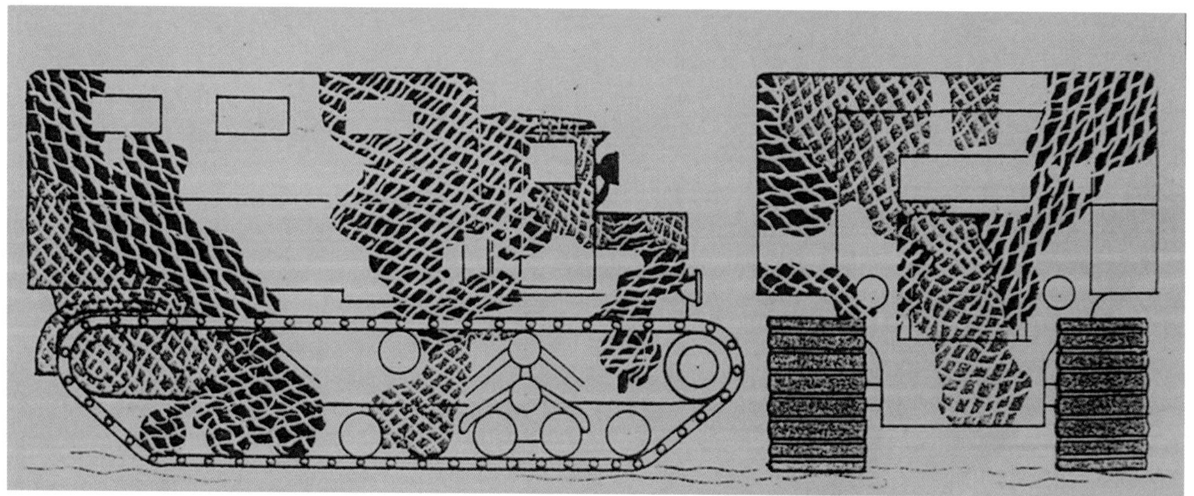

The attached official colour schemes for the STZ-5 and S-65 are also applicable to the S-2, S-60 and STZ-3/KhTZ-3. The colour scheme for the Voroshilovets is also applicable to the Komsomolets.

Appendix 4: Artillery Dispositions in 1941

Disposition of Red Army Artillery requiring mechanized transport as of 1 January 1941	
45mm anti-tank gun	14,088
76mm regimental gun	4,473
76mm divisional gun (new type)	3,977
76mm divisional gun (old type)	4,270
152mm howitzer	3,494
203mm howitzer	776
280mm mortar	66
305mm mortar	36
37mm anti-aircraft gun	1,090
76mm anti-aircraft gun	4,462
120mm mortar	2,560

Disposition of Red Army Artillery requiring mechanized transport by Military District (OVO) as of 1 June 1941					
	Leningrad OVO	Baltic OVO	Western OVO	Kiev OVO	Odessa OVO
45mm anti-tank gun	1,068	1,059	2,154	1,912	963
76mm guns (all types)	732	1,029	1,689	2,142	723
152mm howitzer (M-30)	284	261	578	546	200
152mm gun-howitzer (ML-20)	179	332	494	566	213
203mm howitzer	61	59	119	192	86
280mm mortar	3	n/a	6	24	12
37mm anti-aircraft gun	127	116	212	240	70
120mm mortar	280	218	613	264	171

RED ARMY ARTILLERY – GROSS WEIGHTS IN TRAVEL ORDER

The heavy artillery pieces noted below were broken down into two loads for transport by two tracked tractors on road marches, with the barrels mounted on special wheeled or tracked povozki.

152mm Br-2	17,200kg
203mm B-4	17,700kg
210mm Br-17	44,000kg
280mm Br-5	17,600kg
305mm Br-18	45,700kg

On 22 June 1941, the Red Army had 6,561 122mm M-1938 (M-30) howitzers in service, of which 2,482 were lost in the months to 1 January 1942, artillery and artillery tractor losses being statistically similar in the first months of the war.

Appendix 5: Lend-Lease Tractors

As related previously, a wide range of foreign wheeled and tracked tractor designs were imported to the Soviet Union in the years following the Russian Revolution, with such imports leading over the next decade to the development of Soviet indigenous designs based on the adoption of the best design features and engineering practices of these imported machines. By the late 1930s Soviet mass production tracked tractor output was a mix of designs based on imported technology with Soviet adaptation (such as the S-60 and S-65) and indigenous designs such as the STZ-NATI 1TA (SKhTZ-3) and STZ-5 based on Soviet designs honed as a result of many years of testing foreign equipment. This Soviet specific of always being open to testing for local adoption or redesign where appropriate would continue until the outbreak of war in 1941. Even as the Komsomolets armoured artillery tractor was entering series production in 1937, an (unarmoured) FIAT OCI 708 CM tracked artillery tractor developed in Italy from 1934 and purloined during the Spanish Civil War was evaluated by the Red Army from June to August 1937 at the NIABT test polygon at Kubinka, towing the 45mm M-1932 anti-tank gun and limber. The adoption of foreign (primarily US-built) Lend-Lease tractors was the continuation of long-standing collaboration, but now with the direct import of foreign-built tractors rather than local production of designs in some cases developed abroad.

(A) A Caterpillar D-7 in Red Army service. (Sergei Popsuevich)
(B) An Allis-Chalmers HD-10W towing a Br-10 povozka, Karelian Isthmus near Vyborg.
(C) An International (Allis-Chalmers HD-10W) tractor with Br-10 povozka near Minsk, 1944.

The Allied Lend-Lease programme has always been acknowledged by the Soviet Union and its successor states as of significant support to the country during the war. The first Lend-Lease vehicles were delivered from Great Britain in November–December 1941, with American and Canadian vehicles following in later months. Lend-Lease delivery of tracked artillery tractors, particularly from the United States, was gratefully received by the Soviet Union, which by late 1941 had lost production output in Kharkov and Chelyabinsk, the former to Axis attack and the latter due to the change in production from tracked tractors to KV heavy tanks, with the STZ plant in Stalingrad being overrun the following year.

The Soviet Union received some 7,570 track-laying tractors through Lend-Lease during World War II, the three main foreign suppliers being Caterpillar, International and Allis-Chalmers. The majority of tractors were light and medium types, with over 1,000 being heavy tractors. Among the latter were 243 D-7 tractors produced by Caterpillar during 1942 and 1943, the balance being Allis-Chalmers HD-10W and IHC TD-18 types. Caterpillar also produced 453 Medium Tractor M1 tractors, the D-6, which were very similar in appearance to the D-7 and best recognizable by the different position of exhaust pipe and air cleaner. The Red Army deployed both types to their heavy artillery units where they excelled mainly as prime movers, e.g. during the fierce Carpathian mountain fighting of 1944.

(D) An International TD-14 tractor with Br-10 povozka, 1943.

(E) A Studebaker US6 towing a ZiS-3 missing the gun shield. (Sergei Popsuevich)

(F) Lend-Lease Studebaker US6 trucks with 76.2mm ZiS-3 dual-purpose guns. (Sergei Popsuevich)

(G) A Studebaker US6 towing a 76.2mm M-1939 USV (F-22 USV/GRAU Index 52-P-254F) divisional gun. (Sergei Popsuevich)

(H) As with all armies, the Red Army tested and often adopted captured equipment. (Sergei Popsuevich).

(I) A Lend-Lease Jeep in Red Army service towing a 45mm anti-tank gun (Sergei Popsuevich)

From the beginning of deliveries in early 1942 until September 1945 (the entire war in Europe and Asia), the United States delivered 7,570 tracked tractors. A total of 8,071 tractors were actually shipped, the missing balance of 501 tractors having been lost to enemy action in transit to the Soviet Union.

(J) Captured Maultier 3 (Sd.Kfz.3) half-tracks towing 122mm M-30 howitzers, 1st Ukrainian Front, Lvov, July–August 1944. Photographer: Arkady Shaikhet.
(K) Allis-Chalmers HD-7W tractors towing 152mm ML-20 howitzers at the Victory Parade in Harbin, September 1945.
(L) Dodge WC51 trucks towing 57mm ZiS-2 anti-tank guns at a Victory Parade in Kiev, 1945 or 1946. (Sergei Popsuevich)
(M) Lend-Lease D-6/D-7 tractors towing 152mm ML-20 howitzers at the Victory Parade in Kiev, 1945.
(N) Allis-Chalmers HD-10W tractors on parade in Red Square, 1 May 1949.
(O) Allis-Chalmers HD-10W tractors on parade in Red Square, 1 May 1948.

In addition to 'civil engineering' tractors used in militray service, the Soviet Union also received quantities of the specialized M5 medium/high speed tractor. The M5 was produced by the International Harvester Corporation (IHC) from 1942, being purpose designed as a fast prime mover for heavy artillery. The M5 used the running gear, wheels and tracks of the M3 Light Tank but with a modified suspension. The M5 was powered by a Continental petrol engine providing a maximum speed of 56km/h while towing a Soviet 152mm howitzer. The vehicle was equipped with a front mounted winch. A total of 172 M5 tractors were delivered to the Soviet Union in 1944.

As well as using indigenous and Lend-Lease artillery tractors, the Red Army as with all armies also made use of captured enemy tractors, particularly in the later years of the war as the number of captured examples increased exponentially.

The following tracked tractors were delivered to the Soviet Union by Lend-Lease:

Caterpillar D-6	296 (1942–44)
Caterpillar D-7	243 (1942–44)
International IHC TD-14	246 (1942–44)
International IHC TD-18	404 (1942 44)
Allis-Chalmers HD-7W	2,106 (1942–44)
Allis-Chalmers HD-10W	413 (1942–44)
M5 HST	172 (1943–45)

The Red Army also made extensive use of the Lend-Lease Studebaker US6, and also M3A1 White scout cars and M2/M3 half-tracks as tractors for artillery such as the 76.2mm ZiS-3 dual-purpose gun and the 122mm M-30 howitzer. Per Soviet sources, the Soviet Union received 114,500 GMC CCKW-353 and Studebaker US6 trucks and 3,340 M-3A1 White vehicles between 1942 and 1945, both of which were frequently used as artillery tractors. The United States also provided the Soviet Union with 2,278 half-tracks, which were usually used as command vehicles but also occasionally used to tow anti-tank weapons.

Appendix 6: Foreign Service

In 1930, the Kommunar participated in trials in Turkey against Caterpillar and Hanomag designs including for consideration as an artillery tractor. A small number of Stalinets artillery tractors were exported during the 1930s, the first batch of S-65 tractors having in fact been manufactured for export.

The Red Army lost a significant number of STZ-3/KhTZ-3, STZ-5, Stalinets-60, Stalinets-65 and Komsomolets artillery tractors during the Soviet–Finnish Winter War of 1939–40. Finland captured a number of Komsomolets tractors during the war, of which 62 were repairable and adopted for service with the Finnish Army; six were subsequently lost back to the Red Army. Additional artillery tractors were captured and taken into Finnish service during the later Continuation War, with as many as 200 Komsomolets tractors being at one

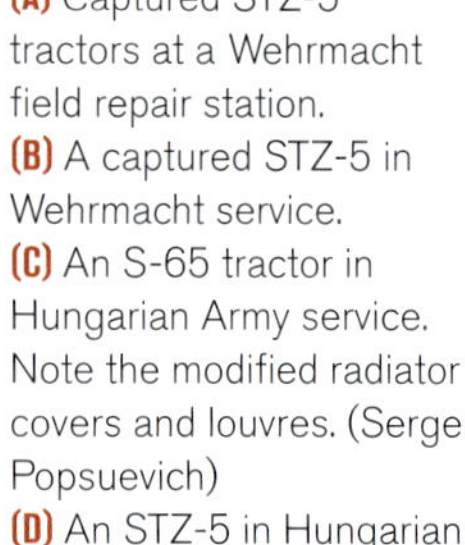

(A) Captured STZ-5 tractors at a Wehrmacht field repair station.
(B) A captured STZ-5 in Wehrmacht service.
(C) An S-65 tractor in Hungarian Army service. Note the modified radiator covers and louvres. (Sergei Popsuevich)
(D) An STZ-5 in Hungarian Army service. (Sergei Popsuevich)
(E) A front view of an S-65 tractor in Hungarian Army service. (Sergei Popsuevich)
(F) An STZ-5 towing a 7.5cm Pak-40 gun
(G) An S-65 also in Hungarian Army service. (Sergei Popsuevich)

point in service with the Finnish Army. A total of 62 tractors were lost during the fighting in the summer of 1944, mostly abandoned due to their fire positions being overrun, or due to mechanical failure. As of 20 June 1944, Finland had in inventory 242 STZ-NATI, 123 'Stalinets' (S-60 and S-65), 68 'HTZ' (KhTZ-3/STZ-NATI-1TA) and 38 STZ-5 artillery tractors. In accordance with the Moscow Armistice between the countries, all repairable unarmoured tractors were returned to the Soviet Union in early 1945 (tanks and armoured vehicles including the Komsomolets were not requested to be returned). The last batch of ten Komsomolets tractors was decommissioned by the Finnish Army as late as 1961.

The losses endured by the Red Army during the first weeks of Operation *Barbarossa* also resulted in all manner of captured tractors being used by the Wehrmacht and other Axis forces, particularly Hungary and Romania. Soviet tractors deemed useful as artillery tractors or general towing vehicles in Wehrmacht service were officially adopted and given formal foreign vehicle designations. The Komintern was designated Artillerieschlepper Kom-604(r); the Komsomolets was designated Gepanzerter Artillerieschlepper 630(r); the Stalinets-65 was known as the Raupenschlepper St(r) Typ. 'Stalinets 65'; the STZ-5 was designated Artillerieschlepper STZ-601(r) and the Voroshilovets was known as the Artillerieschlepper Stalin-607(r) – and colloquially referred to as the 'Stalin' tractor though it was the most unrelated of all the tractors to the name. Other tractors such as the ostensibly civil tracked STZ-3/KhTZ-3 and wheeled STZ-1/KhTZ-1 were used by Wehrmacht and Axis forces on an ad hoc basis, though not officially adopted.

By far the largest foreign user of Komsomolets armoured tractors was the Wehrmacht. Several dozen tractors were also captured by Romanian forces, mainly in the Odessa area in late 1941. In the Romanian army, they were used primarily for towing 50mm PaK-38 anti-tank guns. As of 1944, there were twelve vehicles each in the 5th and 14th Infantry Divisions, four in the 5th Cavalry Division and six more in the 2nd Tank Regiment. Most of them were lost during the Yassko-Kishinyevskaya operation in August 1944. Tractors captured by Axis forces were used by these countries for as long as they remained serviceable. The US TM-30-340 *Handbook on USSR Military Forces* manual published in 1945 noted the S-65 as in service with the USSR, but 'probably' also used by Romania. Ya-12 tractors were used by Poland and Czechoslovakia in the immediate post-war era. Hungary and Romania used a number of captured Red Army tractors including the S-65 and STZ-5.

The Moscow Armistice signed between the Soviet Union and Finland at the end of the Continuation War in September 1944 included clauses requiring Finland to return all Soviet origin tractors, trucks and light vehicles to the Soviet Union, in repaired serviceable condition where possible. The Finnish inventory of tractors held as of 14 February 1945 and returned to the Soviet Union in the first half of 1945 is as follows:

	Operational condition	For repair	Scrap condition	Returned to USSR
KhTZ-3/STZ-3 (NATI)	4	79	101	167
Stalinets-60	0	1	48	2
Stalinets-65	5	35	43	73
STZ-5	1	8	17	0
(Data courtesy of Esa Muikku)				

Appendix 7: The Horse

The Red Army and Axis forces made extensive use of mechanized artillery transport during World War II, or the Great Patriotic War as known in the Soviet Union. The horse however remained a staple means of anti-tank gun and light artillery transport, particularly during the early stages of the war. There are no known statistics on losses of horses during the war, but the numbers were extremely high, especially when used in anti-tank units with their close proximity to enemy small arms and artillery fire. The suffering of these intelligent and noble animals in military service is but one of many human failings.

A

B

(A) Horse-drawn Red Army artillery during the Battle for Moscow, December 1941. Photographer: Viktor Termin.
(B) A horse-drawn Red Army 76.2mm M-1936 (USV) in the early war years.
(C) A 76.2mm ZiS-3 dual-purpose gun being towed by a four-horse team.
(D) A soldier with a humorous take on how best to transport 45mm anti-tank guns.
(E) A Red Army horse-drawn 76.2mm ZiS-3 gun in the outskirts of Vienna, 3rd Ukrainian Front, March–April 1945.
(F) Red Army 45mm M-1942 anti-tank guns being paraded with two-horse teams, Berlin, 4 May 1945.
(G) A 45mm M-1942 anti-tank gun being towed by a two-horse team in the later war years.

Appendix 8: Drawings

The drawings below are from taken from original Soviet Operator's manuals.

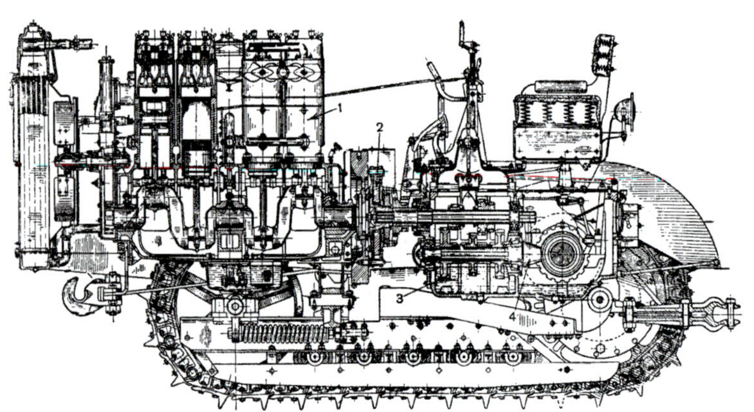

S-60 sectioned side elevation.

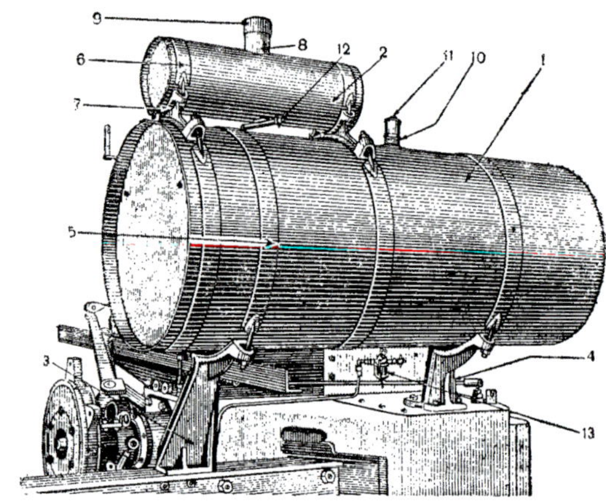

The distinctive S-60 horizontal fuel tank.

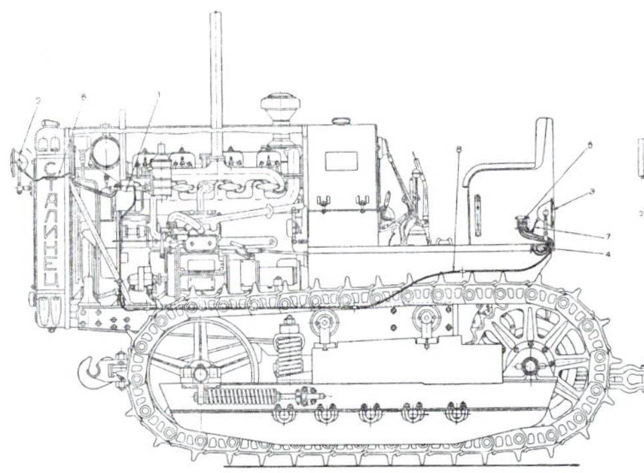

S-65 external side elevation with engine cover removed.

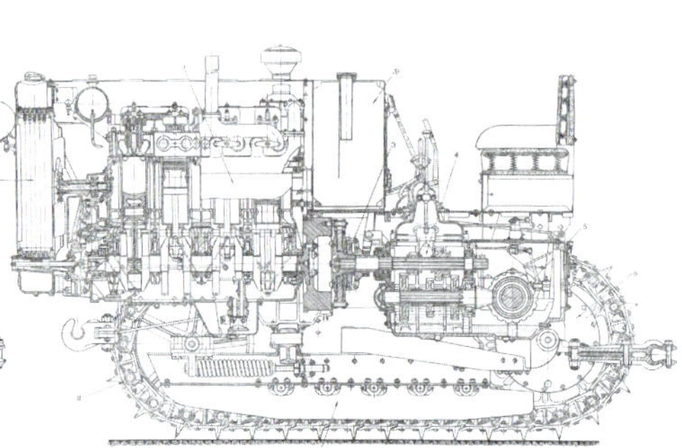

S-65 sectioned side elevation.

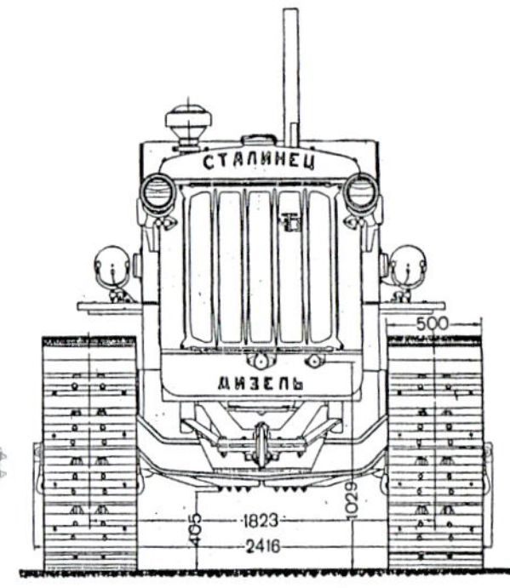

S-65 front elevation with dimensions.

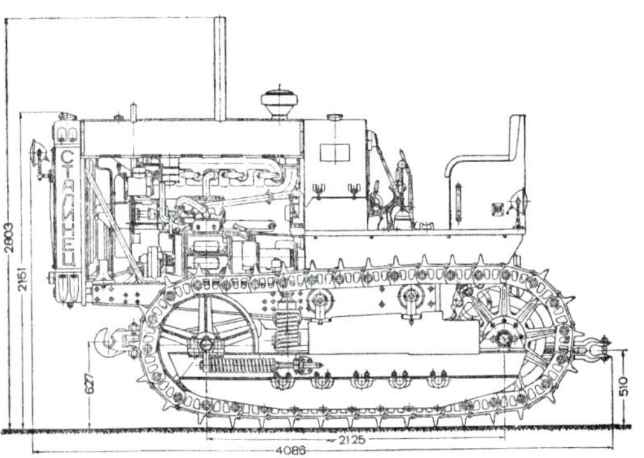

S-65 side elevation with dimensions.

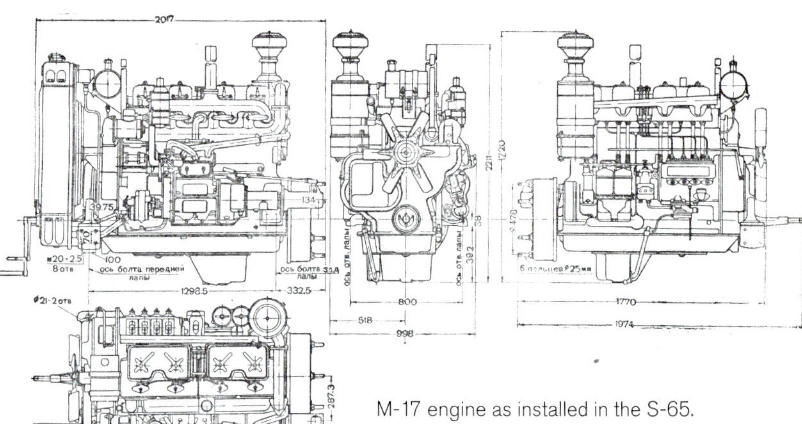

M-17 engine as installed in the S-65.

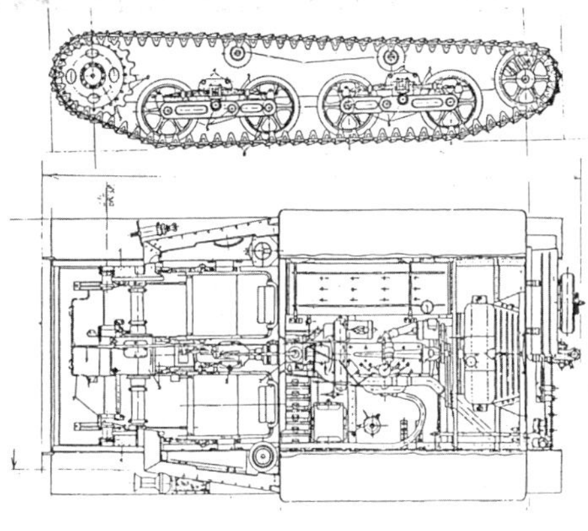

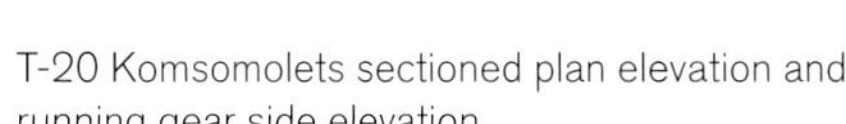

T-20 Komsomolets sectioned plan elevation and running gear side elevation.

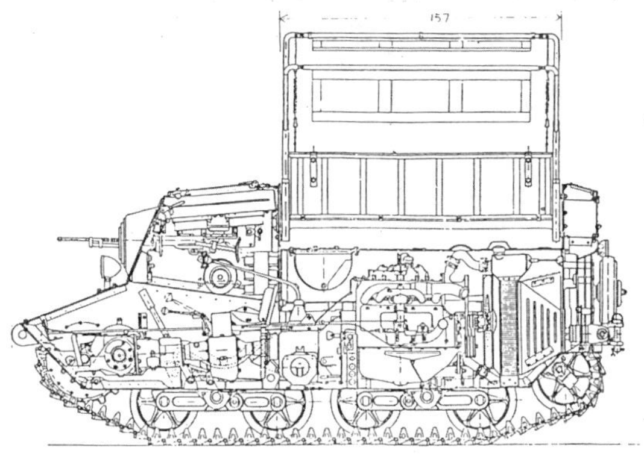

T-20 Komsomolets sectioned side elevation.

KhTZ-T2G gas-generator general view.

STZ-NATI 1TA (STZ-3 Stalingrad production version) general view.

M-17 engine.

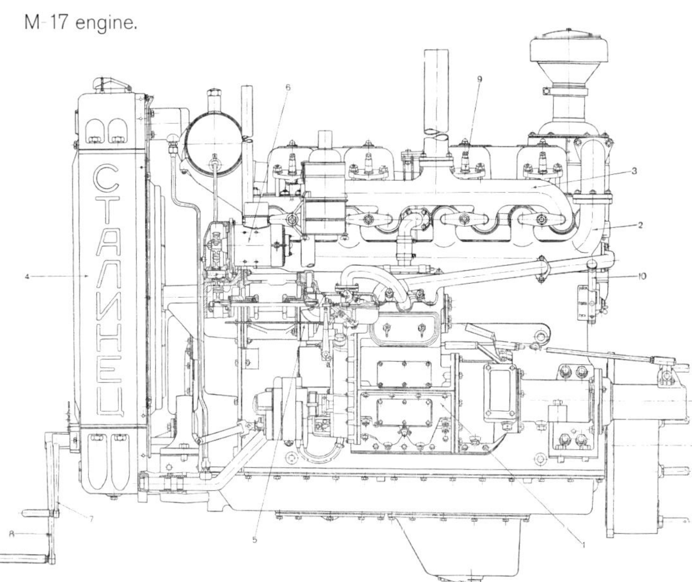

DATA TABLES

Soviet Artillery Tractors - 1930-1945									
Vehicle	**Bolshevik**	**Kommunar**	**SKhTZ-15/30**	**STZ-3**	**STZ-5**	**Stalinets-60**	**Stalinets-65**	**Stalinets-2**	**Komintern**
Alternative Designation(s)		(3-90)	KhTZ-1	KhTZ-3	NATI-2TV	S-60	S-65	S-2	
			STZ-1	SKhTZ-NATI					
Manufacturing Plant	Bolshevik	KhPZ	STZ/KhTZ	STZ/KhTZ	STZ	ChTZ	ChTZ	ChTZ	Plant No. 183
Dates Produced	1924–30	1924–31	1931–37	1937–52	1938–42	1933–37	1937–41	1939–42	1934–40
Total production	100–150	3,500–3,700		210,744	9,944	68,997	37,626	1,275	1,798
Vehicle Weight (kg)	4,600	8,500–9,000	3,000	5,100	6,090	9,500	11,200	11,787	10,500
Maximum Towed Load (road) (kg)	3,500	9,000		4,800	4,500	10,000		19,000	14,000
Maximum Towed Load (terrain) (kg)								19,000	14,000
Load Platform Capacity (kg)	n/a	n/a	n/a	n/a	1,500	n/a	n/a	1,500	2,000
Armament	n/a	n/a	n/a	n/a	n/a	n/a	n/a	n/a	n/a
Armour (mm)	n/a	n/a	n/a	n/a	n/a	n/a	n/a	n/a	n/a
Dimensions (m)									
Length (m)	3.40	4.35	3.49	3.70	4.15	4.09	4.09	4.67	5.70
Width (m)	1.65	2.06	1.69	1.86	1.91	2.40–2.42	2.42	2.44	2.21
Height (cab) (m)	1.80	2.46	2.45	2.21	2.37	2.77	2.80	2.76	2.54
Height (tilt) (m)				n/a		n/a	n/a	3.01	2.98
Load Platform (LxWxH) (m)	n/a	n/a	n/a	n/a		n/a	n/a		2.00/2.10/0.60
Ground Clearance (m)	0.24	0.43		0.34	0.31	0.40	0.41	0.46	0.40
Track width (mm)	278	400		390	310	500	500	420	360-400
Crew	1	1	1	1	2+8	1	1	2+8	2+12
Engine									
Type				1MA	1MA	S-60	M-17	MT-17	KIN
Fuel		Petrol	L/K	L/K (MF)	L/K (MF)	L/K (MF)	Diesel	Diesel (MF)	Petrol (MF)
Cylinders	4	4		4	4	4	4	4	4
Engine Capacity (cm³)	6,600	3,180	6,400	7,460	7,460	18,450	46,540	46,540	15,095
Power Output (hp/revs)	40/1,050	90/1250	30/1,050	52/1,250	52/1,250	60/650	65/850	115/1,350	131/1,280
Fuel Tank Capacity (litres)	190	380	70	170	148+14	390	300	222	297+81
Fuel Consumption (l/100km)		180–300	n/a	260–450	150–250	300–500	286–300	100	400–600
Gearbox									
Forward/Reverse Gears	3/1	3/1	3/1	4/1	5/1	3/1	3/1	4/1	5/1
Performance									
Maximum Road Speed (km/h)	11	14	7.4	8–10	25–32	6.5–8.5	6.9–7.5	26	29–31
Dirt Road Speed (towing) (km/h)	7	8	4–5	8	14–22	4	6.8	15	12–16
All Terrain Speed (towing) (km/h)	2	5	4	4	11	4	4	10	4.7
Maximum Road Range (km)		150	n/a	65	140	75–95	75–100	183	170–220
Maximum Terrain Range (km)		70–80	n/a	40	70–90	50–60	70–80	150	70
Trench (m)		0.7	n/a	0.6	1.00	0.7	0.7	0.77	1.30
Fording (m)		0.7	n/a	0.8	0.80	0.6	0.6	0.6	0.8
Ground Pressure (kg/cm²)		0.52	n/a	0.36	0.54–0.57	0.47	0.52	0.77	0.45–0.49

Note: Where specifications such as speed seem rather precise such as '3.64km/h all terrain speed' the numbers are those specifically as noted in Soviet test reports.
Where data is conflated, State test results where available have been used.
MF – Multi-fuel, L/K – Ligroine/Kerosene

*The first noted Pioner dimensions are taken from the prototype test report.

	Voroshilovets	Ya-12	GAZ-60	ZiS-42	ZiS-42M	Pioner	Komsomolets	T-26T	T-26T2	AT-42	AT-45	GAZ-61-416
							T-20					
	Plant No. 183	YaAZ	GAZ	ZiS	ZiS	Plant No. 37	Plant No. 37	Plant No. 174	Plant No. 174	Plant No. 183	Plant No. 183	GAZ
	1939–41	1943–45	1939–40	1942–43	1942–46	1936–37	1937–41	1934–36	1934–36	1940	1944	1941
	1,123	1,666	1,134 (est.)	2,426	3,505	50	7,780	211	173+28	2	6	36
	15,700	6,550	3,375	5,268	5,495	2,300	3,460	8,000	7,700	15,000	19,000	
	22,000	8,700	1,300	4,380	4,380	1,500	1,500–2,000	5,000	5,000		22,000	750–1,650
	22,000	5,350		1,750	1,750	520	1,500	5,000	5,000			250
	3,000	2,000	1,200–1,300	2,250	2,250	400	500	n/a	n/a	3,000	6,000	400
	n/a	n/a	n/a	n/a	n/a	n/a	7.62mm DT	n/a	n/a	7.62mm DT	n/a	n/a
	n/a	n/a	n/a	n/a	n/a	n/a	4–9	6–15	6–15	15–50	n/a	n/a
	6.28/5.99	4.89 (late)	5.30	6.10	6.10	2.34/3.23*	3.46	4.62	4.62	5.95		4.80
	2.85/2.29	2.44	2.40	2.36	2.36	1.60/1.66*	1.86	2.44	2.44	3.00		1.70/1.77
	2.61/2.73	2.21	2.09	2.17	2.16	1.48/1.53*	1.58	1.84	1.01			1.60
	3.10	2.20		2.94	2.90	2.23	2.23		1.96			
	2.76/2.09/0.60	2.06/1.64/0.60			3.09/2.09/0.60			n/a	n/a	n/a		n/a
	0.40	0.31		0.32	0.32	0.28	0.30	0.38	0.38	0.37	0.40	0.21
	428			415	415	200	200	260	260			Wheeled
	3+16	2+8		2+9	2+9	1+6	1+6	1+5	1+4	2		2+6
	V-2V	GMC-4-71	GAZ-M	ZiS-5	ZiS-5M	GAZ-A	GAZ-MM-6002	T-26	T-26	V-2-34	V-2V	GAZ-11
	Diesel	Diesel	Petrol	Petrol	Petrol	Petrol	Petrol	Petrol	Petrol	Diesel	Diesel	Petrol
	12	4	4	6	6	4	4	4	4	12	12	6
	38,880	4,650	3,285	5,555	5,555		3,285	6,600	6,600	38,880	38,880	3,480
	375/1,500	110/2,000	50/2,800	73/2,300	76/2,400	40/2,200	50/2,800	80/2,100	80/2,100	500	375	85/3,600
	564 (540)	124+176	100	180/300	300	121	115 (121)	182	182	455		60
	170–230	92–120	46–66	55–150	73–165			95–120	95–120			17–22
	4/1	4/1	4/1	4/1	4/1	4/1	4/1	5/1	5/1	4/1	4/1	4/1
	36–42	38	35	36	42	40–50*	48–50	28	28	34	42	98–107
	15–18	13–18	15–20	24–30	24–30	15–20	15–20	11	11		28	
	11–13	13	10–15	16–20	16–20	8–11	8–11					
	270–350	290	500	300–390	425–500	140–150	152–250	120	120			350–375
	150–200	140	280	175	197		150					
	1.5	1.80				0.90	1.40	0.8	0.8	2.50	2.50	
	1.30	0.60	0.50	0.60	0.60	0.50	0.60	0.8	0.8	1.30		0.70
	0.52	0.53		0.3	0.3	0.34–0.48	0.32–0.54	0.50–0.76	0.47–0.76			

For mobilization preparation purposes, all users of tractors, civil and military, were required to account for vehicle inventory twice a year, in January and July, hence now that archive material is accessible, and the exact number of tractors in service in any given year is accurately known.

Tracked Artillery Tractors in Red Army Service – 1 January 1941					
	Manufacturing Plant	**Statute**	**Serving with Artillery Units**	**Undergoing Medium Repair**	**Undergoing Capital Repair**
Tractors					
Kommunar	KhPZ	94	504	71	198
SKhTZ-NATI (1TA)	STZ/KhTZ	384	3,658	504	348
S-60	ChTZ	44	1,631 (5,559)	206	343
S-65	ChTZ	3,068	7,170	677	320
Transport Tractor Tyagachi					
STZ-5	STZ	5,478	2,839	251	55
Komintern	KhPZ (Plant No. 183)	6,891	1,017 (1,581)	164	87
Voroshilovets	KhPZ (Plant No. 183)	733	228 (470)	23	15
S-2	ChTZ	951	0 (4)		
Armoured Tyagachi					
T-20 Komsomolets	Plant No. 37	2,810	4,401	506	337
T-26T	Plant No. 174				
T-26T2	Plant No. 174				
GAZ-60	GAZ		1,416		
ZiS-42	ZiS/UralZiS		1,229		

Soviet Tractor, Artillery Tractor and Half-Track Production – 1933–1945														
Production Totals	**1933**	**1934**	**1935**	**1936**	**1937**	**1938**	**1939**	**1940**	**1941**	**1942**	**1943**	**1944**	**1945**	**TOTAL**
Kommunar*	325	473	317	0	0	0	0	0	0	0	0	0	0	3,499
S-60	1,650	10,000												68,997
S-65														37,626
S-2							12	23	1,168	5				1,173+
SKhTZ-3 (STZ-3/ KhTZ-3)				25+										191,000
STZ-5			135		173	309**	1,256	1,274	3,146–4,730	3,359				9,944
Komintern		5	50	401	368	495	467	12	0					1,798
Voroshilovets					2	0	67	526	706					1,123/1,128
T-20 Komsomolets														7,780
Ya-12 (includes Ya-13, Ya-13F)											285	965	416	2,296
ZiS-42/ZiS-42M										752	2,115	2,334	1,102	5,931
GAZ-60						238	691 (plan)	205						2,015+
T-26T														
T-26T2														
Ya-12											218+	965	1,666	2,296

*Kommunar production began in 1924, with 12 built that year, and 26 in 1925, rising to 103 in 1927 as full series production commenced. Peak production was in 1930 (714 3-90 tractors).

** STZ-5 production for 1938 includes all batch production to that date.

Where '+' is indicated the number is for part-year only, hence the overall figure will be higher.

In some cases, total production does not coincide with annual production numbers, due to missing or conflated data.

Tracked Artillery Tractors in Red Army Service – 1 January 1941		
	Total	Serving in Artillery Units
Kommunar	1,488	504
S-60	5,559	1,631
S-65	10,603	7,170
S-2	4	0
SKhTZ-3 (STZ-3/KhTZ-3)	9,073	3,658
STZ-5	2,839	2,839
Komintern	1,581	1,017
Voroshilovets	470	228
T-20 Komsomolets	4,401	4,401
ZiS-42	1,129	n/a
GAZ-60	1,461	n/a

Tracked Artillery Tractors in Red Army Service – 1 September 1942		
	Total	Serving in Artillery Units
Kommunar	254–257	n/a
S-60/S-65	9,464	n/a
S-65	10,415	n/a
S-2	892	n/a
STZ-3/KhTZ-3	9,704	n/a
STZ-5	4,678	n/a
Komintern	568–624	n/a
Voroshilovets	528	n/a
T-20 Komsomolets	1,662	n/a

Tracked Artillery Tractors in Red Army Service – 9 May 1945		
	Total	Serving in Artillery Units
S-60/S-65	16,132	n/a
S-65	9,631*	8,220
S-2	81	43
STZ-3/STZ-5	9,781	n/a
Komintern	568	n/a
Voroshilovets	336	251
T-20 Komsomolets	500+	n/a
Ya-12/Ya-13/Ya-13F	1,270	n/a
Lend Lease	3,058	n/a
ZiS-42/ZiS-42M	1,942	n/a
GAZ-60	n/a	n/a
*As at 1 May 1945.		

Preserved Red Army Artillery Tractors – 1930–1945

Country and Location	SKhTZ-15/30	Kommunar	STZ-3	STZ-5	S-60	S-65	S-2	Komintern	Ya-12
	(SKhTZ-1)								
Belarus									
Minsk, Great Patriotic War Memorial Museum	X								
Finland									
Hameenlinna, located near Military Museum (ex-Artillery Museum)									
Kuhmo, Winter War Museum									
Mikkeli, Infantry Museum									
Parola Armour Museum									
Parola Armour Museum (not on permanent display)									
Parola Armour Museum (not on permanent display)									
Suomenlinna Island, Helsinki (not on public display as of 2025)									
Russian Federation									
Bryansk, Partisanskaya Polyana						X			
Chelyabinsk, ChTZ plant (gate guardian)					X				
Kerch, Partisan Memorial					X				
Moscow, Motors of War Museum				X		X		X	
Moscow, Museum of Russian National Military History, Padikovo						X			
Moscow, Paklonnaya Gora (Victory Park)									
Moscow, Muzei Tekhniki Chernogolovka	X								
Moscow, Muzei Tekhniki Vadim Zadorozhny, Krasnogorsk						X			
Moscow, Shamansky Workshops, Mytischi	X	X	X		X	X	X		
Novomoskovsk, Local Museum (STZ-5 BM-13)				X					
St. Petersburg Arctic Museum Exhibition Centre (2019)		X			X				
Museum of Combat & Labour Glory, Saratov						X			
Toliatti, Park Complex (Muzei Tekhniki)						X			
Verkhnyaya Pyshma (Ekaterinburg), Urals Military Glory Museum			X	X	X	X			
Yaroslavl, YaMZ (former YaAZ/YaG) plant (gate guardian)									X
Ukraine									
Kyiv, Great Patriotic War Memorial Museum									
Odessa (Odesa), 411 Battery Museum									
Odessa (Odesa), Ordzhikidize Street (in a small park)									

	GAZ-V (GAZ-60)	ZiS-33	ZiS-42/42M	Komsomolets	GAZ-64-416	NI-1	KhT-16	ZiS-30
				X				
				X				
				X				
				X				
				X				
				X				
				X				
				X				
	X	X	X	X				
		X	X	X				
				X				
				X				
					X			
				X	X		X	X
							X	
						X		
						X		

ARTWORK

Pioner
Pioner tractors were painted in ZB-AU (ЗБ-АУ) dark green, which was common for Red Army armour and artillery in the mid-1930s. The star on the front of the engine cover was brass. (Artwork by Andrey Aksenov)

Komintern
A Komintern artillery tractor in typical 4BO (4БО) green. Komintern tractors generally had no unit markings. (Artwork by Andrey Aksenov)

T-27 Artillery Tractor
A T-27 tankette converted to a light artillery tractor. The original tow hook was replaced by a more complex device which allowed remote uncoupling of the gun by the tankette crew. Two seats for the gun crew were added on the rear corners of the hull. A third seat was sometimes bolted to the glacis plate but was precarious for the occupant. The frames on both sides of the hull were used for ammunition stowage. The last surviving T-27 artillery tractors were seen during the battle for Moscow in 1941. (Artwork by Andrey Aksenov)

T-20 Komsomolets (early production)
An early production '1st series' T-20 Komsomolets armoured artillery tractor with box gun mantlet. (Artwork by Andrey Aksenov)

T-20 Komsomolets (late production)
A late production '4th series' T-20 Komsomolets armoured artillery tractor with increased use of welding in assembly. Most Komsomolets tractors were unmarked in Soviet service. (Artwork by Andrey Aksenov)

KhTZ-3
A KhTZ-3 agricultural tractor in typical medium grey finish, unknown Red Army artillery regiment (originally photographed towing a 152 mm M-10 M-1938 howitzer), Ukraine, June 1941. The tractor was probably requisitioned for Red Army service before the outbreak of war as the tactical signs were already painted on the cab sides, there being no time for such detail in the chaos of the first days of war. (Artwork by Andrey Aksenov)

STZ-5 (1940)
A STZ-5 1938 –1940 production model from an unknown Red Army artillery unit, Karelian Front, summer 1941. Many pre-war STZ-5s had the serial number V (in Russian "B") No. XXXXX (i.e. B No. 61608 on this vehicle) stencilled on the cab left side door. (Artwork by Andrey Aksenov)

STZ-5 (1942)
An STZ-5 from the final production batches of summer 1942, 154th Guards Artillery Regiment,* 76th Guards Rifle Division, 114th Rifle Corps, 70th Army, Toruń, Northern Poland, 1944. This STZ-5 has typical wartime simplifications: the rounded windows on the cabin front corners were deleted due to shortage of transparent acrylic glass, with a single front headlight on the left side of the cab, all-steel cast wheels from the STZ-3 agricultural tractor, simplified cargo bed construction and the mechanical winch deleted. The camouflage is 4BO (4БO) dark green/6K (6K) dark brown. (Artwork by Andrey Aksenov)

Ya-12
A Ya-12 from an unknown Red Army Artillery unit, Germany, 1945. The unit sign was repeated on both sides and at the right rear of the cargo area. (Artwork by Andrey Aksenov)

AT-45
The small pre-series batch of AT-45 artillery tractors were painted 4BO green without markings of any description. The vehicles differed slightly from each other. (Artwork by Andrey Aksenov)

* Formed as the 422nd Howitzer Regiment of 157th Rifle Division in 1939, the unit took part in the defence of Odessa and Crimea after the outbreak of war before being sent to the Stalingrad Front where it received new STZ-5 artillery tractors in July 1942. The unit was awarded Guards status on 1 March 1943 after the Battle of Stalingrad and was renamed the 154th Guards Artillery Regiment, while the 157th Rifle Division became the 76th Guards Rifle Division. The Regiment later took part in the battles in the Kursk salient and the liberation of Ukraine, Belorussia and Poland. The last worn-out STZ-5 tractors were written off when the unit was near the Polish city of Toruń in February 1945, when they were far beyond their expected service life. The Regiment ended the war in Rostock, northern Germany. The Artillery Regiment exists to the present day.

GLOSSARY

ABTU RKKA Avtobronetankovoye Upravlenye – Auto-Armoured-Tank Command of the Red Army (1934–40)

ANIOP Artillerisky Nauchno-Issledovatelsky Opitny Polygon – Artillery Research Experimental Test Range

ArtKom GAU KA Artilleriisky Komitet Glavnogo Artilleriiskogo Upravlenya KA – Artillery Committee of the Main Artillery Directorate of the Red Army

ARV Armoured Recovery Vehicle

ATZ Altaisky Traktorny Zavod – Altai Tractor Plant

BPK Battalionaya Pushka Kurchevskogo – Kurchevsky Battalion Gun

BM Boevaya Mashina – Combat Machine (i.e. Katyusha MRS)

ChTZ Chelyabinsky Traktorny Zavod – Chelyabinsk Tractor Plant (1930–41)

ChKZ Chelyabinsky Kirovsky Zavod – Chelyabinsk Kirov Plant (1941–)

DOSAAF Dobrovolnoe Obshestvo Sodeistvya Armii, Aviatsii i Floty SSSR – Volunteer Society for Assistance to the Army, Air Force and Navy of the Soviet Union

DOT Concrete bunker

DZOT Earth bunker

GABTU KA Glavnoye AvtoBronetankovoye Upravlenye KA – Main Auto–Tank Command of the Red Army. On 7 December 1942 renamed to GBTU KA – Main Armoured Directorate of the Red Army

GBTU KA Glavnoye Bronetankovoye Upravlenye – Main Armoured Directorate of the Red Army

GAZ Gorky Avtomobilny Zavod – Gorky Automobile Plant

GAU KA Glavnoye Artilleriiskye Upravlenye KA – Main Artillery Directorate of the Red Army

GAU KA Glavnoye Avtomobilnoye Upravlenye KA – Main Automobile Directorate of the Red Army

GKO Gosudarstnenny Komitet Oborony – State Defence Committee

Gosplan The Soviet central planning organization in charge of state economy level planning and implementation

GUATP Glavnaya Upravlenya Avto-Traktorny Promishlennosty – Auto-Tractor Industry Directorate

GUVP	Glavnoe Upravlenye Voennoi Promishlennosti SSSR – Main Directorate of War Industry of the USSR
GVS	Glavny Voenny Sovet RKKA – Main Military Council of the Red Army
GVTU KA	Glavnoye Voenno–Tekhnicheskoye Upravlennye – Main Military–Technical Directorate of the Red Army
KA	Krasnaya Armya – Red Army (also known as RKKA)
KB	Konstruktorskoye Buro – Design Bureau
KEhO	Konstruktorsky Experimentalny Otdel – Experimental Design Department
KhTZ	Kharkovsky Traktorny Zavod – Kharkov Tractor Plant
KO	Komitet Oborony – Defence Committee
KhPZ	Kharkov Steam Locomotive Plant (the Komintern Plant, renamed Plant No. 183 from 1936)
KhTZ	Kharkovsky Traktorny Zavod – Kharkov Tractor Plant
KMZ	Kolomesnsky Machine Building Plant – Plant No. 183 at Nizhny Tagil
KPD	Katerpillar Podolsk Diesel
MRS	Multiple Rocket (Launcher) System
NAMI	Nauchny Avtomibilny Institut – Scientific Automobile Institute (1920–31) (NATI 1931–46)
NATI	Nauchny Avtotraktorny Institut – Scientific Auto Tractor Institute (1931–46)
NIABP	(22 NIABP) Nauchno-Ispitatelny Avtobronetankovy Polygon – Scientific Experimental Auto (armoured) and Tank Test Range (Kubinka) (1931–72, later NIII-38); also known as NIBT
NIABP UMM	Nauchno-Ispitatelny Avtobronetankovy Polygon Upravlenye Mekhanizatsy i Motorizatsy – Scientific Experimental Auto and Tank Test Range of the Mechanization and Motorization Command
PTO	Protivo-Tankovoye Oruzhye – Anti-Tank Weapon
PU	Puskovaya Ustanovka (launch system/unit)
RBVZ	Russko-Baltiysky Vagonny Zavod – Russo-Balt Wagon Plant (РБВЗ)
RKKA	Raboche-Krestyanskaya Krasnaya Armya – Workers and Peasants Red Army (the Red Army)
RVK	Reserv Glavnogo Komandovanya – Main Command Reserve
RVGK	Reserv Verkhovnogo Glavnogo Komandovanya – Reserve of the Supreme Command

RVS	RevVoenSovet – Revolutionary Military Council of the USSR
SAU	Samokhodnaya Ustanovka – Self Propelled Gun
SKB	Spetsialnoye Konstruktorskoye Buro – Special Design Bureau
SM SSSR	Sovet Ministrov SSSR – Council of Ministers of the USSR
SNK SSSR	Sovet Narodnykh Kommissarov – Council of People's Commissars of the Soviet Union
SSR	Sovietskikh Sotsialisticheskikh Respublik – Soviet Socialist Republic
SSSR	Soyuz Sovietskikh Sotsialisticheskikh Respublik – Union of Soviet Socialist Republics (i.e. the USSR or Soviet Union)
STZ	Stalingradsky Traktorny Zavod – Stalingrad Tractor Plant
TAON	Tyazhelaya Artillerya Osobogo Naznachenya – Special Purpose Heavy Artillery
TsK KPSS	Tsentralny Komitet Kommunisticheskoy Partii SSSR – Central Committee of the Communist Party of the USSR (CPSU)
TsK VKP(b)	Tsentralny Komitet Vsesoyuznoy Kommunisticheskoy Partii (Bolshevik) (of the SSSR) – Central Committee of the All-Union Communist Party (Bolshevik) (of the USSR)
TsK VKP(b) i SM SSSR	Tsentralny Komitet Vsesoyuznoy Kommunisticheskoy Partii (Bolshevik) i Sovet Ministrov SSSR – Central Committee of the All-Union Communist Party (Bolshevik) and Council of Ministers of the USSR
TBr	Tankovaya Brigada – Tank Brigade
TK	Tankovy Korpus – Tank Corps
TT	Transportny Tyagach – Transport Tractor
TTT	Taktiko Tekhnicheskye Trebovaniya – Tactical Technical Requirements
TU	Tank Upravlenya – Control Tank (on remote-controlled 'teletank' systems)
UMM RKKA	Upravlenye Mekhanizatsii i Motorizatsii RKKA – Mechanization and Motorization Command of the Red Army (renamed ABTU RKKA from 22 November 1934)
UZTM	Uralsky Zavod Tyazhelogo Mashinostroenya – Urals Heavy Machine Building Plant
VMU	Voenno-Mobilizatzionnoye Upravlenye – Military Mobilization Command
VgTZ	Volgograd Tractor Plant
VSNKh	Supreme Council of the National Economy

YagAZ	Yaroslavlsky Gosudarstveny Avtomobilny Zavod – Yaroslavl Automobile Plant (to 1943)
YaAZ (YAZ)	Yaroslavlsky Avtomobilny Zavod – Yaroslavl Automobile Plant (from 1943)
YaMZ	Yaroslavlsky Motorny Zavod – Yaroslavl Motor Plant

SOVIET MINISTRIES

Soviet ministries were abbreviated to NK (Narodny Kommissariat – People's Commissariat) followed by the responsibility, e.g. NKV (Vooruzhenye – armaments), NKSM (Srednee Mashinostroenye – medium machine building) (responsible for tank production) etc. The minister was known as the Narkom (Kommissar). Commissariat can be interpreted as Ministry, and Commissar as Minister.

NKAP	People's Commissariat of Aviation Production
NKGK	People's Commissariat of State Control
NKO	People's Commissariat of Defence (State Defence Committee)
NKS	People's Commissariat of Machine Tool Building
NKSM	People's Commissariat of Medium (i.e. tank) Machine Building (Narkomsredmash)
NKSP	People's Commissariat of Ship Building
NKTM	People's Commissariat of Heavy Engineering
NKTP	People's Commissariat of Heavy (i.e. tank) Production
NKV	People's Commissariat of Armaments
NKVD	People's Commissariat of Internal Affairs
NKVMF	People's Commissariat of Military Naval Forces

Narkomat (Ministry) and Narodny (People's) are from the same word root, and effectively interchangeable.

BIBLIOGRAPHY

Several recent books in Russian have revealed a wealth of new information on Red Army artillery tractors of the World War II era, with the book series by Aleksandr Kirindas being of particular note. The articles by the Soviet engineer A. Prochko published in Soviet and Russian magazines over a period of years remain for the most part as accurate today as when they were published decades ago. The opening of Russian state archives in recent years has greatly widened the original archive record available to researchers.

The default book in English (and German) on Red Army artillery tractors of World War II remains *Tyagatshi* by Jochen Vollert, published by Tankograd Publishing, with photographs mainly taken by Wehrmacht forces. The self-published French language books by Alain Dupouy are a treasure trove of information researched from original records in the Polytechnical Museum in Moscow and other official Soviet archives.

Books

Belyaevsky, K.V. and Kotylov, B.I., *Mekhanicheskaya Tyaga Artillerii*, Voennaya Artilleriiskaya Komandnaya Akademiya, Leningrad (1960).

Busheyev, A.V. (ed.), *Legkovie Avtomobili GAZ-M1 i Modifikatsii*, GAZ, Nizhny Novgorod (date unknown).

Chubachin, Aleksandr, *Tanketta T-27*, Voennaya Letopis, BTV-MN, Moscow (2005).

Dashko, Dmitry (ed.), *Transport Krasnoy Armii v Veliky Otechestvennoy Voine*, Avtomibilnogo Arkhivnogo Fonda, Moscow (2015).

Degtyarev, P.A. and Ionov, P.P., *'Katyushi' Na Polye Boya*, Voennoe Izdatelstvo, Moscow (1991).

Dupouy, Alain, *Les Dossiers des Vehicules Sovietiques. No.10. Les Vehicules Militaires*, Grenoble (1994).

Dupouy, Alain, *Les Tracteurs et Engins Speciaux Chenilles Sovietiques. Tome I. Les Tracteurs Agricoles et Industriels*, Grenoble (1986).

Dupouy, Alain, *Les Tracteurs et Engins Speciaux Chenilles Sovietiques. Tome II. Les Remorqueurs et Transports Chenilles*, Grenoble (1986).

Gogolev, L.D., *Avtomobili-Soldati*, Patriot, Moscow (1990).

Irinarkhov, Ruslan, *Krasnaya Armya v 1941 gody*, Eksmo/Yauza, Moscow (2009).

Karasev, A.V., *Khronika Avtomotornogo Instituta 1918–46 (NATI/NAMI)*, Svitok, Smolensk (2010).

Kasheev, L.B. and Reminsky, V.A., *Avtomobili ZiS v Krasnoy Armii*, Tom 2, *Voennye Mashini* No. 48., Kirovskim Obshestvom Lubitelei Voennoi Tekhniki i Modelizma, Kirov (2000).

Kirindas, Aleksandr, *Artilliisky Tyagach SKhTZ-NATI (STZ-3)*, Yauza, Moscow (2022).

Kirindas, Aleksandr, *Artilleriisky Traktor 'Stalinets'*, Yauza/Eksmo, Moscow (2019).

Kirindas, Aleksandr, *Artilleriisky Traktor 'Komintern' Na Sluzhbe u Boga Voini*, Yauza/Eksmo, Moscow (2017).

Kochnev, Evgenny, *Avtomobili Velikoy Otechestvennoy*, Yauza/Eksmo, Moscow (2010).

Kochnev, Evgenny, *Avtomobili Krasnoy Armii 1918–1945*, Yauza/Eksmo, Moscow (2009).

Kochnev, E.D., *Entsyklopedya Voennykh Avtomobiley 1769–2006*, Za Roulem, Moscow (2006).

Melnikov, Nikita, *Tankovaya Promishlennost SSSR v Gody Velikoy Otechestvennoy Voiny*, Yauza-Katalog, Moscow (2019).

Mernikov, A.G., *Vooruzhenye Sili SSSR i Germanii 1939–1945*, Harvest, Minsk (2010).

Mernikov, A.G., *Armya Pobedy Protiv Vermakhta*, Harvest, Minsk, AST, Moscow (2005).

Paderin, Ivan and Dobrovolsky, Nikolai, *Shestitsilindrovye Ehmki*, Gorky Classic, Moscow (2012).

Paderin, Ivan, *GAZ 1932–1982. Russkye Mashini*, Gorky Classic, Krasnodar (2011).

Pasholok, Yuri and Pavel, Ivanov, *Pervie Sovietsky Voenny Vnedoroozhik*, Art-Lait, Samara (2021).

Pervov, Mikhail, *Rodilas v Moskve 'Katyusha'*, Izdatel Dom Stolichnaya Entsiklopedya, Moscow (2010).

Prochko, E., *Artilleriiskye Tyagachi Krasnoy Armii*, *Bronekollekytsya* No. 2 (59), 2005, Modelist Konstruktor, Moscow (2005).

Sergeev, P.N., *Gusenichnye Tyagachi Krasnoy Armii*, Part 1, *Voenny Mashini* No. 74, Kirovskoye Obshestvo Lubitely Voennoy Tekhniki i Modelizma, Kirov (2004).

Sergeev, P.N., *Gusenichnye Tyagachi Krasnoy Armii*, Part 2, *Voenny Mashini* No. 75, Kirovskoye Obshestvo Lubitely Voennoy Tekhniki i Modelizma, Kirov (2004).

Sergeev, P.N., *Gusenichnye Tyagachi Krasny Armii*, Part 3, *Voennye Mashini* No. 76. Kirovskoye Obshestvo Lubitely Voennoy Tekhniki i Modelizma, Kirov (2004).

Sergeev, P.N., *BM-13 Katyusha,* Kirovskoye Obshestvo Lubitelely Voenny Tekhniki i Modelizma, Kirov (2000).

Shugurov, L.M., *Avtomobili Rossii i SSSR*, Part 1, Ilbi/Prostryeks, Moscow (1993).

Sokolov, Mikhail, *Vezdekhodi SSSR 1918–1945*, Yauza/Eksmo, Moscow (2012).

Soviet Ministry, *Tekhnichesky Kharakteristiki Sovietskikh i Importnikh Avtomobiley*, Voenny Izdatelstvo Ministerstva Voorushennykh Sil USSR (1946).

Solyankin, A.G., Pavlov, M.V., Pavlov I.V. and Zheltov I.G., *Otechestvenny Bronirovanny Mashini XX Vek, Volume 1. 1905–1941*, Eksprint, Moscow (2002).

Svirin, Mikhail. *Bronetekhnika Stalina, Tanki i Samokhodki SSSR*, Yauza/Eksmo, Moscow (2014).

Svirin, Mikhail and Kolomiets, Maksim, *Legkiy Tank T-26*, Part 1, Armada No. 20, Eksprint, Moscow (2000).

Svirin, Mikhail and Berskurnikov, A., *Pervy Sovietsky Tanki*, Armada, Moscow (1995).

Svirin, Mikhail, *Samokhodki Stalina. Istoriya Sovietskoy SAU 1919–1945*, Yauza/Eksmo, Moscow (2008).

USSR MoD, *Kratky Spravochnik po Otechestvennym Avtomobilyam, Tyagacham, Traktoram i Spetsialnim Mashinam*, Ministry of Defence of the USSR, Moscow (1953).

Vollert, Jochen, *Tyagatschi – Soviet Full-Track Artillery Tractors of World War Two in Red Army and Wehrmacht Service*, Tankograd Publishing, Erlangen, Germany (2006).

Vooruzheny Sili SSSR 1941–1945 (authors unstated), Harvest, Minsk (2011).

Articles

Astrov, Nikolai Aleksandrovich and Bakh, I.V., 'Boevy Mashini', *Tekhnika i Vooruzhenye* No. 9, 2014, pp.27–32.

Dmitriev, Valery, 'Artilleriisky Bystrokhodny Tyagach Ya-12', *M-Hobby* No. 4 (60), 2005, pp.6–21.

Kinnear, James, 'From Fields to War', *Classic Military Vehicle* No. 2 (189), 2017, pp.32–37.

Kinnear, James, 'Caterpillar Copy', *Classic Military Vehicle* No. 8 (183), 2016, pp.36–38.

Kirindas, Aleksandr, 'Konkurs Bez Konkursantov', *Tekhnika i Vooruzhenye* No. 4, 2013, pp.21–23.

Kirindas, Aleksandr, 'Dostich Nevozmosnogo', *M-Hobby* No. 3 (43), 2003, pp.30–35.

Kolomiets, M. Mikhail, 'Bronetraktori', Part 3, *M-Hobby* No. 3, 1997, pp.29–31.

Nikolai, Polikarpov, 'ZiS-42', *M-Hobby* No. 2, 1999, pp.28–31.

Pasholok, Yuri and Ivanov, Pavel, 'Polniy Privod dlya Krasnoi Armii', *Rolling Wheels* No. 3, May–June 2012, pp.114–125.

Pavlov, I. and Pavlov, M., 'Gost s Gor', *Tekhnika i Vooruzhenye* No. 9, 2015, pp.47–51.

Pavlov, M.V. and Pavlov, I.V. , 'Nasledniki "Voroshilovetsa"', *Tekhnika i Vooruzhenye* No. 4, 2015, pp.30–39.

Prochko, E., 'Ravnikh Sebye Ne Imel', *Modelist Konstruktor* No. 5, 1995, pp.16–17.

Prochko, E., 'Tyagach – v Brone i s Pulemetom', *Modelist Konstruktor* No. 7, 1994, pp.25–27.

Prochko, Evgenny, 'AT-P', *Tekhnika-Molodozhi* No. 12, 1993, p.17.

Prochko, Evgenny, 'Komsomolets', *Tekhnika i Molodozhi* No. 1, 1993, pp.16–17.

Prochko, Evgenny, 'STZ Transportny', *Tekhnika Molodozhi*, issue and date unknown, pp.21–22.

Protasov, A., 'Artilleriisky Tyagach Voroshilovets', *Tekhnika i Vooruzhenye* No. 12, 1991, p.28.

Ryabkov, Andrey, 'Moguchy Kharkovchanin', *M-Hobby* No. 3 (March), 2011, pp.22–23.

Shpakovski, Slava, 'The Frightener. The Russian Home-Made Tank', *Tankette Magazine*, date unknown.

Shugurov, L. 'Mashini Voennikh Let', *Nauka i Zhizn*, issue unknown, pp.132–133.

Shugurov, L. 'Tak Mi Rabotali v Tridtsatye', *Za Roulem* No. 5, 1994, pp.26–27.

Sorokin, Anatoly, '122mm Gaubitsa M-30 v Istorichesky Retrospektive', *Tekhnika i Vooruzhenye* No. 10, 2013, pp.1–29.

Vollert, Jochen, 'ChTZ-16', *Tankograd-Militarfahrzeug* No. 4, 2012. pp.12–15.

Zaloga, Steven, 'The Factory Tanks of Odessa', *AFV News* Vol. 14, No. 4, pp.9–10.

Journals and magazines

Avtomobilist, Gruzovik Press, Nauka i Zhizn, M-Hobby, Modelist Konstruktor, Polygon, Popularnaya Mekhanika, Rolling Wheels, Soviet Military Review, Nashi Tanki, Tekhnika Molodozhi, Tekhnika i Vooruzhenye, Traktori, Za Roulem.

Operator manuals

Karnaukhov, I.F., *Traktor 'Stalinets-60'*, Gosudarstvenny Izdatelstvo Selskokhozaystvenny Literatury, Moscow (1947).

Mamin, V.Ya., Nikiforov A.A. and Sherbin V.I., *Gazogeneratorny Traktor ChTZ SG-65*, OGIZ Chelyabiz, Chelyabinsk (1941).

Rozanov, V.G., *Traktor SKhATZ-NATI*, Eesti Riiklik Kirjastus, Tallinn, Estonia (1951).

Soviet Ministerial Publication, *Gazogeneratornye Traktori. Teoriya, Konstruktsya i Raschet*, Gosudarstvenny Nauchno-Tekhnichesky Izdatelstvo Mashinostroitelnoi Literatura, Moscow (1955).

INDEX

Page numbers in **bold** refer to illustration and their captions